Cultural Economics & the Creative Economy

This series aims to provide original and societally relevant perspectives on the modern creative economy from the perspective of cultural economics broadly understood. In the past decades it is increasingly realized that value in the economy is realized in the creative industries and the more traditional cultural sectors. This series will aim to shed light on how value is created and realized and how the creative economy shapes the broader economy. We believe that trends in the creative economy are often a sign of things to come in the broader economy, this is true for the way in which work is organized, how innovation happens, how entrepreneurs act and the relevance of cities in the modern economy.

The series will provide a collection of works of leading cultural economists on theoretical and empirical topics. It will cover the field in its most broad sense and focus on the current open problems and topics in cultural economics, covering micro, macro end methodological aspects.

More information about this series at
http://www.palgrave.com/gp/series/16422

Jimmyn Parc · Patrick A. Messerlin

The Untold Story of the Korean Film Industry

A Global Business and Economic Perspective

palgrave
macmillan

Jimmyn Parc
Sciences Po
Paris
France

Patrick A. Messerlin
Sciences Po
Paris
France

ISSN 2662-4478 ISSN 2662-4486 (electronic)
Cultural Economics & the Creative Economy
ISBN 978-3-030-80341-4 ISBN 978-3-030-80342-1 (eBook)
https://doi.org/10.1007/978-3-030-80342-1

This Palgrave Macmillan imprint is published by the registered company Springer Nature Switzerland AG
The registered company address is: Gewerbestrasse 11, 6330 Cham, Switzerland

Prologue: Why the Korean Film Industry?

Since the birth of film in the late nineteenth century, this revolutionary medium has drawn in a great deal of attention from a wide range of people who seek to understand more about the workings of its industry. When it comes to films, a large number of moviegoers have enjoyed watching Hollywood blockbusters while French and Italian films still benefit from their reputation for being artistic and cultural works. Therefore, numerous academic articles and books have been devoted to covering Hollywood or European films as well as their related film industries. To a lesser extent, films from Japan and Hong Kong have also been at the center of interest in more recent decades.

Among the film industries around the world that have received little attention, the Korean film industry has slipped by under the radar among many observers despite its consistent progress. Yet as it marks its one hundredth anniversary in 2019, its achievements are coming to be recognized. Notably, several films have received prestigious international film awards. The most prominent example in this regard is the recent hit film *Parasite*, which not only won the 2019 *Palme d'Or* at the Cannes Film Festival but also went on to receive four Oscars in 2020 including the prestigious Best Picture. As a result, several Korean directors such as Bong Joon-ho and Kim Ki-duk as well as a number of Korean actors and actresses like Jeon Do-yeon, Lee Byung-hun, Song Kang-ho, and Youn Yuh-jung, have been known among film lovers.

In fact, it is not only moviegoers or audiences who are interested in Korean films, but also a number of countries, international organizations, and film companies have begun to pay close attention to the Korean film industry and its market. For example, as Hollywood studios were the first to realize the promising potential of the Korean film market in the 1980s, they pushed the US government to open up the market for further opportunities. More recently, a number of foreign companies have been interested in both distributing Korean films and investing in the industry. Even the United Nations Educational, Scientific and Cultural Organization (UNESCO) has witnessed the Korean film industry's influence grow in its multilateral forum since that country opened up its market to foreign companies.

The history of the Korean film industry is nothing short of profound since the release of its first Korean film *The Righteous Revenge* in 1919. During the Japanese occupation period (1910–1945), films were censored and the Korean film industry was under the influence of the Japanese authorities. Following the country's liberation in 1945, the Korean film industry began to make tentative steps on its own, but the Korean War (1950–1953) interrupted these efforts. While the film industry managed to emerge from the ashes of the Korean War and endure decades of military rule, it would come to face a greater challenge. By the 1970s, the industry was in a steep decline as few Koreans went to see domestic films let alone even foreign titles. Having hit rock bottom by the 1990s, Korea's film companies then underwent a decade of painful and uncertain industrial restructuring before experiencing an impressive revival around the new millennium. After a brief plunge between 2007 and 2008, the film industry bounced back and has since consolidated its success. Today, Korean films enjoy a strong share of the domestic market while the overall film market that includes foreign films is very healthy.

What has been behind such ups and downs? A number of existing studies often raise the issue of censorship by the Korean government or even the lack of cultural creativity and diversity. However, they cannot fully answer the question by relying exclusively upon an analysis of the industry's cultural characteristics. Rather it becomes evident when examining the history of the Korean film industry that it has been shaped by economic and business decisions—both foreign and domestic—which suggest the need for an analysis centered upon these issues, including those raised by film policies.

This book constitutes a search for the main contours of an effective film policy, one that is both friendly to culture and economically sound. In this respect, Korea is the central character: by ensuring a better and stable economic and regulatory environment, it has provided its film companies with the opportunity to take the lead in the successful reshaping of the domestic film industry. Korea's film policy therefore appears as an attractive benchmark for other countries as they seek to develop their own film industry. This result is important since, in almost every decisive aspect, it challenges the approaches generally suggested when faced with the growing dominance of Hollywood, such as using quotas and subsidies for developing and advancing the domestic film industry.

Highlighting the uniqueness of the Korean film industry and its policies is a meaningful task, but it may place the reader in a narrow box. In addition, while many studies have focused on Korean cinema, very few have taken on a broader and comparative assessment of its film industry. Such a gap in the literature has missed the important example that the Korean film industry holds for others that wish to achieve a similar level of success as well as enrich their cultural industries. To pursue this goal with more rigorous and insightful research, we compare the Korean film industry and its policies with its counterparts in the global film industry. By doing so, it shows the status of the Korean film industry in an international setting in terms of production, consumption, and market. Such an expanded comparison reveals the sharp differences in their film policies and helps to understand why certain policies have been effective while others have not. Given that the Korean film industry emerged from almost zero to one of the important global players today, it is meaningful to examine how Korea has overcome such challenges while others have not.

This book has thus been developed entirely within an international framework. It compares Korea with the five most important markets in the world, specifically China, France, Japan, the United Kingdom (UK), and the United States (US).[1] Furthermore, this study provides a comparative analysis of the effects regarding the whole range of policy instruments

[1] Together these six markets account for more than sixty percent of today's international box office revenues. The only large film industry not included in this study is India due to lack of reliable data for this market. However, this absence is not a significant problem for the period covered by this book: in 2018, the Indian film market is still smaller than Korea or France in terms of box office revenues and is much less integrated into the global film markets than the six countries covered in this study.

used by these countries toward their film industries: import and screen quotas, subsidies and tax reliefs, as well as regulatory measures and institutions. By comparing these six film markets over the past four decades, this book offers a comprehensive view of the Korean film industry's impressive growth. Today, this industry is a powerhouse which has "outperformed" all of the major film industries around the world in almost every conceivable economic criterion—a point not fully realized even in Korea. More crucially from a cultural perspective, Korea's "quantitative" successes have not been achieved to the detriment in the "quality" of its films. This study presents evidence showing that the average quality of Korean films over the last decade fares better than that of French, UK, or even US movies.

This book relies on a vast data set compiled specifically for this publication. In particular, it makes use of data on the amount of subsidies and tax relief schemes granted to film industries, on the laws and implementing measures that regulate these industries, on the institutions in charge of film policies, and on film quality in the key countries covered. Gathering these data has required the recourse to primary sources since these measures have almost never been explored in a comprehensive manner within the existing literature. Data have been collected over long periods of time, from twenty to seventy years, depending on the topic and availability. Such a long time frame ensures more robust results—too many studies of the film industry rely upon short time periods, which fail to identify major changes that may happen down the line given the high volatility of the film industry. Long periods also possess the significant advantage of revealing changes that are not perceptible if the time period is too short.

In completing this book, we would like to thank our research assistants, Dr. Yeon W. Lee and Dr. Wenyan Yin. We would also wish to extend our gratitude to Dr. Kyuchan Kim for his support, critique, and insights. Furthermore, we want to express our appreciation to Korean Film Council (KOFIC) and *Centre national du cinéma et de l'image animée* (CNC) for sharing their knowledge and data with us. Special thanks goes to Stephen Ranger for his editing and comments for this book. Finally, we are grateful to Springer Nature for their early reviews of parts of the manuscript and helpful comments, and in particular to Ruth Jenner who recognized the value of this book.

Finally, we would like to thank all the scholars who conducted research on the Korean film industry. Without their previous works, which have been the base of this book, we would not have been able to produce this work.

This work was supported by the Laboratory Program for Korean Studies through the Ministry of Education of the Republic of Korea and the Korean Studies Promotion Service of the Academy of Korean Studies (AKS-2015-LAB-2250003).

Jimmyn Parc and Patrick A. Messerlin
Sciences Po Paris

Contents

List of Figures

Chapter 1

Chapter 2

Chapter 3

Chapter 4

Chapter 6

List of Tables

Chapter 1

Chapter 3

Chapter 4

Chapter 5

Chapter 6

Chapter 7

List of Boxes

CHAPTER 1

The Korean Film Industry: From Domestic "Straggler" to Global "Outperformer"

In recent years, a number of Korean films have been recognized at prestigious international film festivals and have received a number of awards. As the Korean film industry is relatively not well known, these achievements appear to be one-time events that happen out of blue. For instance, it is telling that the richly-documented international panorama on the world's film industries in the *Bilans* or annual reports produced by the French state film body *Centre national du cinéma et de l'image animée* (CNC) deals with the Korean industry in only a few lines.[1] By contrast, it devotes a much larger space to other film industries around the world, which are comparatively smaller or under-performing or both. However, the reality is that Korea has not only been able to produce a large number of films, but it has the world's fourth largest film market according to the Motion Picture Association of America (MPA) (2020). This is a significant achievement. Moreover, if one compares Korea with other countries

[1] CNC is the public body founded in 1946 with the task to manage all the issues concerning the French film industry and policy. As analyzed in following chapters (especially Chapter 5), it has extensive powers.

This chapter is based on Parc (2017, 2020) but has been further updated and expanded.

J. Parc and P. A. Messerlin, *The Untold Story of the Korean Film Industry*, Cultural Economics & the Creative Economy,
https://doi.org/10.1007/978-3-030-80342-1_1

that are regarded as important, this industry tells a very interesting story in terms of its history and policies.

Before undertaking an in-depth analysis on the various aspects of this evolution in the following chapters, this chapter seeks to present the performance of the Korean film industry by comparing it with a select group of countries that represent the most important and largest film industries in the world. These include China, France, Japan, the United Kingdom (UK), and the United States (US). The main conclusion of this chapter is that the Korean film industry has "outperformed" most of its counterparts across a range of key dimensions (number of films produced, box office revenues, etc.), a position it has achieved within three decades. Even more importantly, this has come about with much lower level of subsidies than the other countries and—above all from a cultural perspective—with a higher degree of quality on average for its films when compared to its main competitors.

While this outperformance is important on its own, this success has very important implications for other countries. The key lesson here is that it is possible to develop a film industry from a very low level or even from an almost zero starting point. In this regard, it is critical to understand how to design effective film policies and how these policies work in the real world; in particular, given the context of the long dominance of Hollywood films around the world. In respect of this challenge, most countries believe that protectionism led by trade barriers or public financial support is the most effective policy to boost their domestic film industry for which the French film industry and its film policies are a prime example. As France has enjoyed its legacy image of being at the forefront of the film industry, this "tradition" has been widely accepted in many countries without question. Surprisingly, the Korean film industry offers a living proof example that competing against Hollywood's dominance does not require huge barriers on imported films nor the provision of massive subsidies to domestic films. In short, Korea is a "game changer" in terms of a film policy that every analyst of the film industry and its related policies should carefully study.

The chapter is organized as follows. Section 1 provides an overview by presenting basic information on the performance of the Korean film industry in the world. Section 2 offers a snapshot of the Korean film industry's performance throughout 2018 in comparison with the aforementioned five other countries. Sections 3 and 4 describe the growth paths that have led to the 2018 situation. Section 3 focuses on the dynamics of the "overall" demand (for both domestic and foreign films) showing how lively the selected film markets have been. Section 4 goes further by examining separately the evolutions of the demand for both foreign and domestic films in each selected country. The dynamic perspective of Sects. 3 and 4 underlines the extent to which Korea's growth is sustainable.

How can the clear growth pattern demonstrated by the Korean film industry be explained? More precisely, to what extent are these inflexion points related to changes in the Korean film policy or/and to changes in the strategies of the film companies? These questions are explored in the following chapters based upon the preliminary knowledge in this chapter.

1 Korea and the Korean Film Industry in the World

Despite the achievement of films like *Parasite* (2020), a number of observers still see Korea at the margin of the global film industry. To challenge such perceptions, it is meaningful to offer a brief and broad picture on the Korean film industry in the world. Table 1 presents Korea and its five most relevant counterparts. Indeed, these countries are used

Table 1 The global film industry and background information

	No. of films produced (2017)[a]	*Box office revenues (2018, billion USD)*[b]	*Population (2019, million)*[c]	*GDP nominal (2019, current USD billion)*[c]	*GDP (PPP) per capita (2019, USD)*[c]
Korea	494	1.6	51.7	1,642	43,143
Japan	594	2.4	126.3	5,081	43,236
France	300	1.6	67.1	2,715	49,435
UK	285	1.6	66.8	2,827	48,693
US	660	11.4	328.2	21,427	65,298
China	874	9.2	1,397.7	14,313	16,830

Note Data on US films include Canada
Sources [a]UNESCO Institute for Statistics; [b]Motion Picture Association (MPA); [c]The World Bank

throughout the whole book as "references" to measure Korea's performances in the film industry and the extent to which it can be considered as a game changer in terms of film policy.

In contrast with many people's expectations, Korea has produced a large number of films (see Table 1). According to the UNESCO Institute for Statistics (UIS), Korea currently produces a greater number of films than either France or the UK. The MPA data on the Korean, French, and UK box office revenues are very similar but its report underlines that in fact Korea surpassed the UK in 2019 (it overtook France a few years before), acceding to the rank of the fourth largest film market in the world.

All these results are even stronger by considering the other data of Table 1 and its implications. In terms of population, Korea is the smallest country compared to its five counterparts. This is an important point to take into consideration when one makes comparisons: the rest of the book often uses a per capita basis in order to have a less distorted view of the international landscape. The nominal GDP in current USD is the first step to realize how Korea's handicap of "smallness" in demographic terms has been compensated by strong economic power. The GDP (PPP) per capita makes this catch-up process even more visible: the average Korean enjoys a level of income close to the one existing in Japan or Europe.

2 Korea's Outperformance: A Snapshot in 2018

A comparison of the Korean film industry with the other five film industries in 2018 provides the often-lacking viewpoint regarding the position of the Korean film industry in the world. Moreover this selection mirrors a wide set of considerations: the US is still the dominant film industry for which every country should measure up to; China is a massive market that is rapidly expanding and is of huge importance for Korea as a potential outlet and competitor; Japan has long been a major film producer and market in East Asia; France has advocated for decades the need for massive state support in order to build a domestic industry capable of competing with Hollywood's dominance; the UK is another illustration of an industry that has enjoyed strong state support, though with a markedly different approach from the French one (see Chapter 4 for further details).

2.1 *The Demand for Films*

As the film industry has been considered to be related to national identity and culture, the nationality of films is very important. There are then two main components related to demand: domestic and foreign films, which can be both measured by the number of admissions and/or the box office revenues. In this section, the analysis relies on admissions, leaving the box office revenues for the following more detailed sections.

The number of admissions for overall demand reflects the "attractiveness" of films, and the global vigor of the national film market. It is important to stress that this study makes a distinction between the attractiveness and quality of a film. Attractiveness merely captures the fact that a film has been watched by moviegoers who have made their choice on the basis of advertisements, appearance of favorite actors, involvement of favorite directors, and reviews by film critics. By contrast, quality refers to the evaluation of films expressed by audiences, film critics, and juries of film festivals, among others, once they have watched the films. Further explanation about this distinction can be found in Chapter 6.

That said, it is important to mention that the absolute number of admissions is a biased indicator since it depends on the size of the population—for instance, China's population is 27 times larger than that of Korea. This problem is resolved by calculating the number of total admissions per capita (or inhabitant), hereafter the "frequentation index." Table 2 shows that Korea has by far the highest frequentation index among the countries selected. The difference is particularly striking with three countries: it is substantially higher than in the US, three times larger than in Japan, and 1.5 times larger than in France, which has the largest audience in Europe.

Turning to the demand for domestic films, one should use the frequentation index associated to this demand, rather than the absolute number of admissions. Table 2 shows again that Korea has outperformed all the other countries—except the US. It is noteworthy to point out that the US is one of the largest film-producing countries in the world and that its moviegoers predominantly watch domestic films (see Sect. 3 for more details).

It is important to go beyond a mere statistical ascertainment. The fact that the Korean frequentation index is the highest for both overall and domestic demand is an important feature from an economic perspective.

Table 2 Korean film industry's performance (2018)

	Korea	*Japan*	*France*	*UK*	*US*	*China*
Demand: admissions in movie theater						
Overall demand (million admission)	217	169	197	177	1,346	1,720
Frequentation index (per capita)[a]	4.2	1.3	2.9	2.7	3.8	1.3
Domestic films (million admission)	109	93	78	66	1,300	1,070
Frequentation index (per capita)[a]	2.1	0.7	1.2	1.0	3.6	0.8
Market share domestic films (%)	50.2	54.8	39.5	37.4	96.6	62.2
Supply: production of domestic films[b]						
No. of produced films	494	594	300	285	660	874
Production index (per capita)[a]	9.6	4.7	4.5	4.4	1.9	0.6
State support[c]						
Financial support (million USD)[a]	148	n.a	629	767	1,652	n.a

Note b based on 2017
Source British Film Institute (BFI) (various issues), *Centre national du cinéma et de l'image animée* (CNC) (various issues), KOFIC (various issues), Motion Pictures Association of Japan (MPPAJ) (various issues), Motion Picture Association (MPA) (various issues); [a]authors' calculation based on data in Table 1; [b]UIS; [c]authors' calculation based on Table 1 in Chapter 4

It sends two messages: that the Korean film market is widely open and that Korean films are as attractive as Hollywood blockbusters.

Table 2 presents the market share of domestic films, which is the indicator most frequently mentioned in the public debate although it is ambiguous and easy to misinterpret. For instance, a large share is often understood as the sign of a successful film industry. However, as the market share is a percentage that does not show the actual market size, it can be large when the audience for domestic films is in actual fact low and the audience for foreign films is even lower. In this case, a large market share does reflect a serious lack of vitality of the film market for the country at stake. Similarly, a market share can be small when the audience for domestic films is high and the audience of foreign films is even higher—a situation that signals a very lively film market.

Indeed, the misinterpretation of the market share frequently emerges in international relations. For instance, the US request to Korea on cutting the screen quota during the negotiations of the Korea-US Free Trade Agreement (FTA) has been based on such a misinterpretation (see Chapter 3). The market share has additionally fueled hot debates about the impact of the screen quota cut as Korean films did not perform so well with a market share of around 50% in 2016 compared to roughly 64% in

2013. This comparison misses the fact that the Korean film market has witnessed a significant increase in foreign films between 2013 and 2018: 183 Korean films and 722 foreign films were released in Korea in 2013, compared to 455 and 1,192, respectively, in 2018 (KOFIC 2019).

Finally, Table 2 shows that only the US, China, and Japan have larger market shares with their domestic films in terms of admission numbers when compared with Korea. However, China and the US should be dealt with differently as China's large domestic market share reflects the fact that its film industry is protected by a complex and tight set of barriers much higher than those existing in the other selected countries (Parc et al. 2021). For the US, there is a wider set of reasons, all related to the fact that the US audience is mostly attracted to watching US films—or more accurately Hollywood films. It should be noted that the audience for US independent films is generally estimated to be around 5% of the US total admissions. Exploring the reasons why independent films have a limited appeal is a feature that goes beyond the scope of this book.

2.2 *The Supply of Domestic Films*

The second dimension frequently used when assessing the performance of a film industry is the number of domestic films produced (see Table 2). This indicator deserves a strong methodological caveat, which is valid for all the selected countries to various degrees. It can be the result of unexpected or unintended effects brought on by various factors such as public policies, foreign investment, or runaway production. For instance, a generous film subsidy policy or certain import quotas can inflate the number of domestic films produced (Parc 2017, 2021; Messerlin and Parc 2020). Besides the number of films produced, there is also the number of films released, which is different due to two reasons. First, this discrepancy reflects the fact that some domestic films are simply unable to find a distributor for their own market. Second, technological advancement has made other outlets for films available, such as streaming services or other similar platforms.

As in the case of the demand dimension, the number of films produced depends on the size of the population in general as the market size is closely related to the number of moviegoers—hence that large countries are likely to have many producers of films. It makes thus sense to calculate the "production index," that is the number of domestic films produced per capita. Other factors could also be invoked. For instance, one could argue that the desire and skill to shoot movies are dependent upon the level of development of the country in question. The countries selected for Table 2 are all developed countries although one may argue that China is not a developed country. This point needs to be nuanced since the gap between the rich and poor Chinese provinces is huge, and several provinces—precisely those which are the most involved in film production—have a level of development not so different from the other selected countries. In fact, these rich provinces are the main consumers of films in China. Furthermore, under the current political climate, the Chinese government is strongly engaged in film production and is able to mobilize a lot of resources to produce films—putting the quality of films aside. By considering these assumptions, Korea outperforms the five other countries in this respect as shown in Table 2.

2.3 *The Needs of Public Policies*

Films can have a massive social impact upon the public. Therefore, a number of governments have thought of utilizing this medium for various reasons including political ones. The economic impact of the film industry is also larger than what one may have thought. For example, when film-making began in the early twentieth century, it was the second largest industry in France while in the US it was the fifth largest (Parc 2020). Although the share of the film industry has been much reduced as other industries have become more significant, it is still considered to be important, particularly with the emergence of soft power in international relations. Throughout history, governments have become more involved in this industry by using two tools historically: public support and domestic regulations. These two measures have been believed to promote one's film industry while protecting it from others.

Public support includes subsidies, tax relief schemes, and specialized financial funds and holds a preeminent place in the film policies of many countries. Table 2 shows the estimated amount of total support granted by the four countries—France, Korea, the UK, and the US (see Parc and Messerlin 2018 for further details). The Korean film industry emerges by far as the least subsidized, especially if one considers the fact that it is larger than the French and UK film industries. It is important though to know in more detail the effects of subsidies on the development of the film industry and how Korea has been able to generate its film industry without much subsidies. Furthermore, it is important to examine the evolution of subsidies throughout the history of the Korean film industry. All of which is examined in Chapter 4.

Regulations in the film industry consist of domestic laws and other legal texts regulating the operations of domestic and foreign participants in the domestic markets. The film industry uses a wide range of inputs such as directors, scriptwriters, actors, scenery, hi-tech capacities (or facilities) for special effects, specialized lawyers, and general film crews for production. It deals also with a large variety of specific activities: many layers of specific channels of distribution, large infrastructure of "brick and mortar" movie theaters, sophisticated financing schemes, and heavy investment in advertising.

As discussed before, in a country's film industry foreign films play an important role. Traditionally, these foreign film producers have been more interested in distributing their films by using local partners or their own subsidiaries. However, they have become additionally interested in producing films in foreign countries in order to maximize the utilization of production factors which can often be found in international business schemes such as foreign direct investment. These foreign film producers usually need to buy or rent inputs in foreign countries: these international relations are examined from different angles in all the chapters of this book. In these cases, some film companies look for the most suitable countries in order to take advantage of (or even abuse) the differences among national regulations which fit best their activities with the lowest costs for the quality needed—Hollywood studios are well-known for doing extensive "regulation shopping", as reported by Epstein (2012, p. 85).

Many countries have also implemented various regulations to hinder the business activities of foreign films and their producers, believing that these regulations can protect the domestic film industry. The Organisation for Economic Co-operation and Development (OECD) has compiled a list of these regulations and published them in the Services Trade Restrictiveness Index (STRI) database. When examining its contents, one can see that Korea is one of the countries which imposes the lowest level of restrictiveness on the business activities of foreign companies in Korea and it is further analyzed in Chapter 5.

To sum up, this brief overview of the two main elements of public policies in the film industry suggests strongly that the Korean outperformance in terms of demand and supply has not been obtained by artificial state support and thus constitutes the first condition toward using the term "outperformance."

2.4 The "Attractiveness" of Domestic Films

If the government offers a huge amount of subsidies to its domestic film industry and regulates foreign companies and their films, will these conditions promote one's domestic film industry? In fact, a number of existing studies show that there is no strong empirical or statistical evidence in this regard (Murschetz et al. 2018). This book shows that the most important element to revive or boost one's film industry is the better quality or attractiveness of domestic films that can meet the expectations among moviegoers.

The key question regarding this issue is as follows: can subsidies effectively improve the attractiveness or quality of domestic films or can this goal be achieved without subsidies? Analyzing these two points are of great interest when developing film policies. In this regard, the emergence of the Korean film industry delivers meaningful lessons as its government has offered a markedly lower level of subsidies while its trade barriers or regulations against foreign companies and their films are one of the lowest among the selected countries. More surprisingly though is that the attractiveness—as reflected by the number of admissions—of Korean films is even better than French films despite the fact that they hold a high reputation. That said, it is crucial to stress again that this book differentiates attractiveness and quality; Chapter 6 elaborates more on the quality issue of films.

To sum up, the empirical evidence accumulated so far is strong enough to conclude that, in 2018, the Korean film industry has clearly outperformed its largest competitors in almost all dimensions conceivable. What remains to be done in this chapter is to examine whether this outperformance has been limited to a few years or not and what has been its main differences with the evolution of the other largest film industries. This is the goal for the two next sections.

3 Korea in the Global Film Market

Using data from a specific year does not encompass all the characteristics and performance of a film industry as such data can represent an exceptional case. This then makes it very risky to draw meaningful conclusions in terms of the best film policy to follow—the task taken on by this book. Hence, there is a need to adopt a longer period for observation in order to grasp the whole picture of a country's outperformance, as well as to find out when it emerged and how it has evolved. Furthermore, evolutions in the film industry often occur in incremental steps, which are hard to notice if the study is limited to a few years, especially when they are blurred by the high volatility of the film markets. Despite this fact, many existing film studies rely on too short periods for delivering robust results: a shift of a couple of years at one end of a short period can easily lead to completely different conclusions.

The following sections in this chapter cover thus the last forty years or so (1980–2018), a period long enough to avoid significant shortfalls. It leaves aside only the first "golden age" of Korean cinema in the immediate aftermath of the Korean War, which occurred during the 1960s and was succeeded by more than a decade of decay that lasted up to the period examined in this book. As shown by Parc (2014, 2021), this decay was largely brought on by inadequate film policies which have been tremendously harmful to the Korean film industry and forced it to start again from scratch in the late 1980s when this book begins its analysis.

3.1 *Catching Up in Absolute Terms*

Box office revenues reflect the amount of money that (foreign and domestic) films gather through admissions. In order to conduct international comparisons over a long period, the national box office revenues of the selected countries have been expressed in constant 2018 USD, using the GDP deflators provided by the World Bank. The year 2018 has been chosen in order to make the results more intuitive to read: it makes the values of the box office revenues in 2018 the same in current and constant dollars across all the following figures.

Figure 1 shows the box office revenues of Korea and the five other largest national markets: China, France, Japan, the UK, and the US. Since 2000, these countries account on average for two-thirds of the world's overall demand. Even if one adds more countries (for instance, Germany, Italy, Spain, and Mexico) in order to cover three quarters of the world's overall demand, the results presented below remain the same. Figure 1 provides an illustration of Korea's "catching up": in 2018, the Korean overall market size based on box office revenues is now bigger than that of France, and it is getting very close to the UK one.

In fact, Fig. 1 offers an interesting perspective if one splits the six growth trajectories into three groups which exhibit very different time patterns: the US, the "traditional" export markets for Hollywood films,

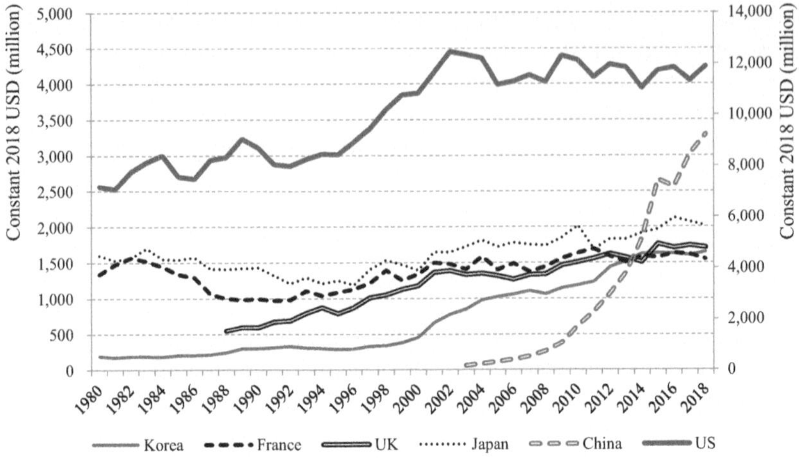

Fig. 1 Box office revenues: all films (1980–2018) (*Notes* Data for the US includes Canada; Box office revenues for Korea, France, UK, and Japan are shown on the left vertical axis; Box office revenues for China and the US are shown on the right vertical axis. *Sources* China-Korean Film Council [various issues] and Sohu [2019]; France-*Centre national du cinéma et de l'image animée* [CNC] [various issues]; UK-British Film Institute [BFI] [various issues] and CNC; Japan-Motion Pictures Association of Japan [MPPAJ] [various issues]; Korea-Korean Film Commission [KFC] [1992] and KOFIC [various issues]; US: Box Office Mojo; Authors' calculations)

specifically France, Japan, and the UK, and then the "new" US export markets, Korea and China.

The US box office revenues trajectory exhibits two very different growth periods for roughly the same length. Until 2002, the US film market was not only by far the largest market in the world, but also the most rapidly growing. However, the sharp ups and downs which occurred in the 1980s compelled the Hollywood studios to pressure the US government to negotiate the opening of several markets in order to counterbalance these short-term variations at home. With the Korea-US Film Agreements in 1985–1988, the Korean market became their first major target. By contrast, tense discussions with Canada in the late 1980s and the European Union Members States, most notably France, in the early-1990s did not lead to any concrete results.

After 2002, the situation changed dramatically with the stagnation of box office revenues in the US: in 2018 the revenues in constant USD are roughly six percent smaller than in 2002. Moreover, the post-2002 years have witnessed a much higher volatility of demand than during the 1990s—revealing a stronger dependence on mega-hits. Underlining the long stagnation of this increasingly volatile US market is crucial because it has had key consequences on the other film industries—especially Korea.

From a business perspective, the Hollywood studios have increasingly felt compelled to look toward foreign markets. While the box office revenues that the big six Hollywood studios generated overseas barely surpassed their domestic revenues in 1997, they have now reached almost 65% of their global box office revenues (Stephen Follows 2017). From the policy perspective, the Hollywood studios began to lobby again the US government in order to gain better access to foreign markets in the mid-1980s, which marked a change from the long pause in international film negotiations during the 1960s and 1970s. In fact it was reminiscent of the intensive negotiations during the 1950s—such as the Blum-Byrnes agreement between the US and France. Again, Korea has been a key target of these efforts when it began to negotiate the Korea-US Bilateral Investment Treaty and the Free Trade Agreement from the late 1990s to the mid-2000s (see Chapter 3).

There is an important reason why the Korean film market has been among the main targets for US trade policy, at least until the early 2010s. Simply, it is down to the fact that the "traditional export" markets for Hollywood—France, Japan, and the UK—have followed the same broad trajectory as the US: a modest growth followed by decline, though with different intensity and time pattern. The growth period has been much longer, roughly thirty years. However, it has consisted of lower growth in France and Japan than in the US, and better growth in the UK did not compensate enough for the poor performance of the other two markets. Altogether these three markets, which represent roughly 42% of the US market between 2002 and 2018, have grown by 17%—barely enough to compensate for the erosion of the US market. In addition, these sluggish evolutions have been followed by falling overall demand after their peak years with box office revenues decreasing substantially by 9, 5, and 3% in France, Japan, and the UK, respectively.

These evolutions stress the increasingly crucial role of the "new" export markets—Korea, then China—for Hollywood since the early 2000s. The US pivoting to the Asian film industries has been driven by the huge growth of these two film markets. In Korea, the box office revenues of the peak year (2018) are 8.5 times higher in constant USD than in 1980. In China, the revenues of the peak year (2018) are 56 times higher than those in 2003; the first year with reasonably robust data. Moreover, Fig. 1 shows that in both countries the growth has been much less volatile than in the US and in the traditional export film markets, offering the Hollywood studios much appreciated stability.

3.2 *Outperforming in Per Capita Terms*

While comparing the market size by using the total box office revenues is meaningful, it is also important to recognize that there are huge differences among the selected countries in terms of population, which is one of key determinants for market size. Hence, measuring the performance on a per capita basis helps to develop a more suitable picture. The box office revenues per capita for each country measures how much money the average inhabitant of a country spends on watching films in movie theaters throughout the year. This indicator is particularly important for Korea as it has the smallest population among the selected countries and for China which has by far the largest.

Indeed, Fig. 2 presents a sharply different picture from Fig. 1, which strongly suggests that Korean growth is not a mere "catching" up effort but rather an "outperforming" process. Since the early 2010s, Korean box office revenues per capita have outperformed by a large percentage the box office revenues per capita of Hollywood's traditional and new export film markets[2]: they are roughly 1.2 times higher than those of France and the UK, twice that of Japanese box office revenues per capita, and more than seven times the Chinese revenues per capita. Even more astonishingly, they are roughly on par in 2017 and 2018 with those prevailing in the US domestic market—a "first" since the US has been the undisputed leader in this respect of the global film industry since World War II.

Interestingly, Fig. 2 amplifies another important feature of the global film markets, which has not been observed in Fig. 1. Rather than a mere stagnation since the early 2000s, the US overall demand exhibits a notable

[2] It is important to recognize the shifting trend among moviegoers or audiences to streaming service providers such as Amazon Prime and Netflix, which may create a degree of stagnancy or decline in box office revenues per capita. However, this chapter focuses on the traditional film market and is represented by box office revenues (and admissions).

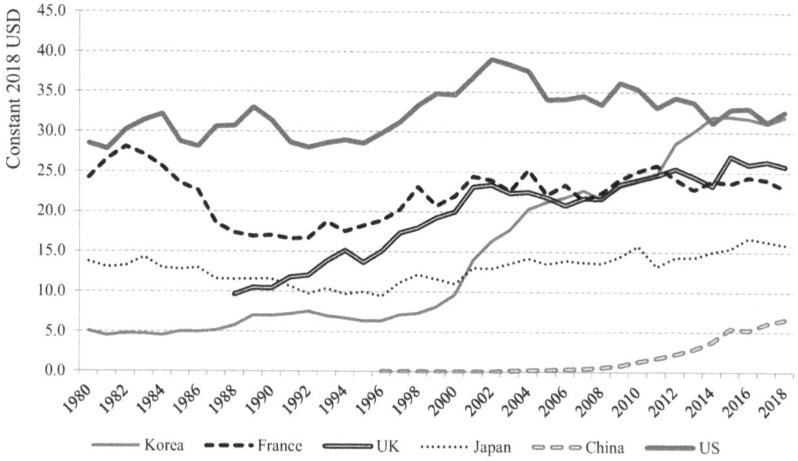

Fig. 2 Box office revenues per capita: all Films (1980–2018) (*Note* Data for the US includes Canada. *Source* Authors' calculations based on data for Fig. 1)

decline, one that presents a challenge for the Hollywood studios since this was basically the primary demand for their films. Such an adverse evolution is the key force that induces the US film industry to increase again its pressure to open foreign markets further—making the Hollywood studios and the US government more aggressive in international trade relations in the film industry.

4 Outperformance and Cultural Diversity

Deconstructing the overall demand into that for foreign films and that for domestic films gives a sense of whether Korea's success has been entirely driven by the demand for one type of film over the other. This question goes beyond a factual ascertainment: it sheds some preliminary light on the long-term sustainability of Korea's outperformance. If Korea's success had been dominated by domestic films, then such a trend would cast doubt on its sustainability in the long term. A healthy domestic market requires that films from all origins compete on a level playing field to attract the largest number of domestic moviegoers. This is also a key condition toward improving the cinematographic education among a country's audience as sophisticated moviegoers are one of the most important conditions toward improving the attractiveness (or quality) of the works produced by local directors. In short, a subtle balance between foreign and domestic films is the best way to ensure "cultural diversity" in the Korean film market.

Korea was the only country to exhibit high frequentation indexes for both domestic and foreign films in 2018 as shown in Table 1. This section examines whether this remarkable feature of a balanced growth in the number of domestic and foreign films in the Korean film market is recent or not.

4.1 *The Contribution of Domestic Films*

The information on the overall film market gives a sense of the size and growth of a country's moviegoers in a country is—in other words, the extent to which the film market is lively. However, this overall aspect is often neglected in the policy debate which narrowly focuses on the situation of domestic films—often in terms of the market share of box office revenues for domestic films among the total revenues of all the films screened in the country. Yet it has already been shown how the market share indicator is extremely difficult to interpret accurately. In this regard, what follows presents the information in absolute terms: thus, to what extent have domestic films generated box office revenues in each of the six countries? In order to avoid the bias of the absolute size of the six countries, Fig. 3 shows the evolution of the box office revenues per capita.

The first result drawn from Fig. 3 is that the box office revenues per capita of domestic films in Korea has been lagging behind that of other countries until the late 1990s but has been outperforming them since the mid-2000s—except for the US case. The degree of outperformance is remarkable. At the end of the period, Fig. 3 shows that the box office revenues per capita of Korean domestic films in Korea are between 1.4 to 1.9 times larger than that of domestic films in France, Japan, and the UK. The US exception needs to be more carefully interpreted. The vast proportion of films exhibited in the US market are produced by domestic studios: the frequent estimate is that it is roughly 95% of the box office revenues.

Second, Figs. 2 and 3 show a roughly similar growth trajectory for Korea's overall demands for both total films and domestic films, respectively. This similarity is crucial for the policy debate: it means that

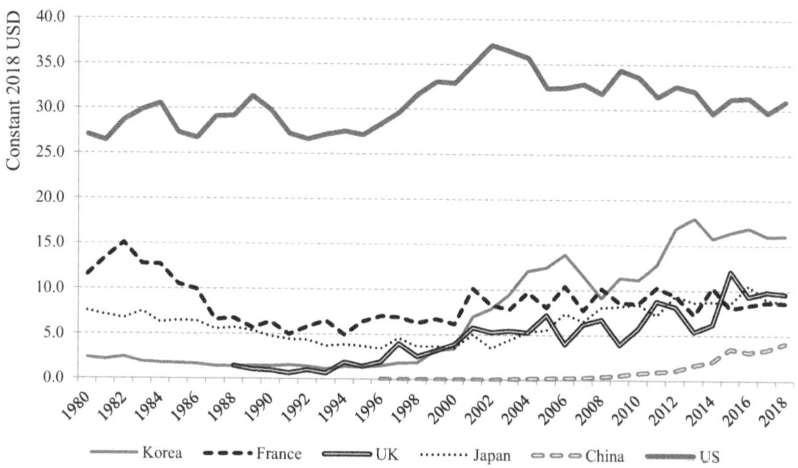

Fig. 3 Box office revenues per capita: domestic films (1980–2018) (*Note* Data for the US includes Canada. *Source* Authors' calculations based on data for Fig. 1)

"cultural diversity" has increased in the Korean film market as Korean films have become as competitive as Hollywood films. However, there is a notable difference between Figs. 2 and 3. The period 1986–1995 is almost flat in Fig. 3 while it is already showing an increasing trend in Fig. 2. This contrast reflects the different time length needed by Korean and foreign films to adjust to the opening of the Korean film market. In 1986 the foreign (US) studios could quickly increase their supply by tapping into their existing back catalogues, whereas Korean film companies have had to undergo a long restructuring process before being able to compete (see Chapter 2).

4.2 *The Contribution of US Films*

Figure 4 focuses on the box office revenues per capita of US films which reflect directly the reactions among moviegoers in these countries to Hollywood's dominance. As shown in Fig. 4, Korea outperforms all the other selected countries, except the UK with which it is on par in 2018. Moreover, Korea's growth trajectory for US films continues to grow until

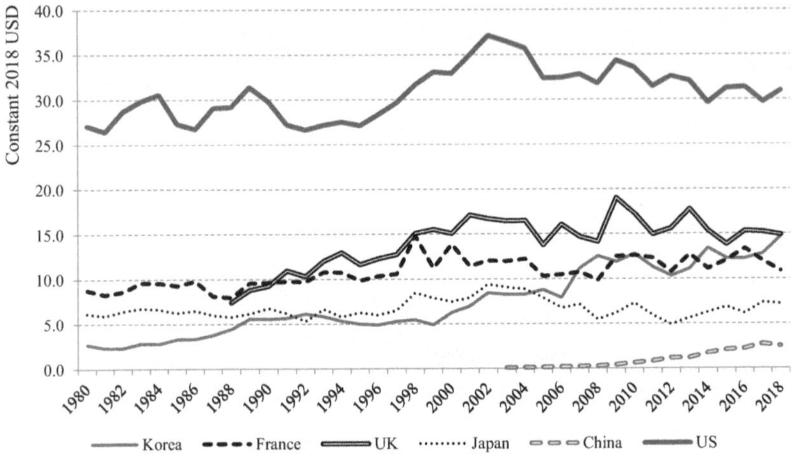

Fig. 4 Box office revenues per capita: us films (1980–2018, million) (*Note* Data for the US includes Canada. *Source* Authors' calculations based on data for Fig. 1)

2018, while the other trajectories are declining since the 2000s—especially in the US market. China's trajectory has some similarity with the Korean one.

4.3 *What Has Been Learnt by Looking at Growth Trajectories*

Examining Korean growth trajectories has added two results to those provided by the static view in 2018 as revealed in Sect. 1. First, the growth of the Korean film industry has been much less volatile—fewer ups and downs—than the growth shown in the other industrial countries covered. Second, even more importantly, the success of Korea's domestic films has not crowded out foreign films, an evolution which would have generated in the long run a risk of declining cultural diversity. In fact, as underlined before, this characteristic of balanced growth among domestic and foreign films should be highlighted as a key condition for the sustainability of the Korean film industry's growth: the large and continuous exposure of Hollywood films to the Korean audience is the best means to expose Korean filmmakers to their most challenging competitors at home—hence to induce them to be as competitive as possible.

5 Conclusion

This chapter has compared the performance of the Korean film industry to those of the largest film industries around the world. This comparison has been based on a long-term analysis covering forty years (1980–2018) in order to provide a robust overview of this period.

The results are surprising and impressive. When one defines the size of a national market by the total box office revenues in the country, the Korean market is now larger than the French market or on par with the UK one—by far the largest European markets. The box office revenues earned by domestic films in Korea are now much larger than their equivalents in the largest European film industries: they are 34% larger than French films and 46% larger than the UK films in each of their markets during the 2010s. The fact that French films have benefited from large subsidies over the past few decades and that UK films have enjoyed tax reliefs and close relations with the US film industry makes the outperformance of the Korean film industry even more remarkable.

Second, these results have underestimated the real situation because they have relied upon measures of performance among film industries which were systematically biased against countries with the smallest populations. Adjusting for the different size of the populations in order to reduce this bias has offered even more impressive results. The box office revenues per capita for all the films screened in a country have been larger in Korea than in any of the five other countries, including in the US. Furthermore, the box office revenues per capita of the screened domestic films has been larger in Korea than in any of the other countries, excluding the US.

Finally, the box office revenues per capita for US films screened in Korea has continued to grow, whereas it has stagnated or declined in the other countries. In other words, the success of Korea's domestic films has not crowded out its Hollywood competitors in Korea, an evolution which could have generated in the long run the risk of degrading the country's cultural diversity and therefore the robust attractiveness of Korean films. Based upon this example, this chapter suggests that market-driven cultural diversity that brings the Korean audience to Hollywood and non-US films has been one of the best means to expose Korean filmmakers to their most challenging competitors at home—it has induced them to be as creative as possible.

This aspect is a crucial element for the long-term sustainability of the Korean film industry, as vigorously highlighted by the CJ Group vice-Chairwoman and film producer Miky Lee during her acceptance speech at the 2020 Academy Awards Ceremony for the four-time winner *Parasite*: "… and specially I really, really, really want to thank our Korean film audience, all moviegoers, who have been really supporting all our movies and never hesitated to give a straightforward opinion on what they feel like their movies, and that made us really never been able to be complacent and keep pushing the directors, the creators, the envelopes and without you – our Korean film audience – we are not here."[3]

This chapter has highlighted the importance of Korea in the global film industry and its remarkable growth path over the last forty years. As a result, the Korean film industry has emerged as a good benchmark for in-depth research to extract policy implications. It has been much less volatile—fewer ups and downs—than the growth patterns in the other industrial countries covered. Why has this been the case and what have been the main causes for the shifts from one period to the next? Have they been related to changes in Korea's film policy? Have they been generated by new business strategies among Korean film companies? If these two causes have been at work, what have been their interactions and in what sequence? These questions are explored in the following Chapters 2 and 3, which unveil three forces at work: the opening of the Korean film market to foreign competition, the reaction of the Korean film industry, and the prudent Korean film policy.

References

Box Office Mojo. https://www.boxofficemojo.com/year/2019/?ref_=bo_yl_table_3.

British Film Institute (BFI). Various issues, *Statistical Yearbook*. http://www.bfi.org.uk/education-research/film-industry-statistics-research/statistical-yearbook.

Centre national du cinéma et de l'image animée (CNC), various issues, *Bilan*. https://www.cnc.fr/cinema/etudes-et-rapports/bilans/.

[3] Miky Lee is the granddaughter of Samsung's founder Lee Byung-chul. She has been a decisive force behind CJ Group, the largest Korean film producer and distributor; YouTube https://www.youtube.com/watch?v=ZmijJ7QnIRQ (1:39).

Epstein, E.J. 2012. *The Hollywood Economist 2.0: The Hidden Financial Reality behind the Movies*. Brooklyn, New York: Melville House.
Korean Film Commission (KFC). 1992. *Korean Cinema Yearbook 1991*. Seoul: Jipmundang (in Korean).
Korean Film Council (KOFIC). 2002. *Korean Cinema Yearbook 2001*. Seoul: Jipmundang (in Korean).
Korean Film Council (KOFIC). 2010. *Korean Cinema Yearbook 2009*. Seoul: Communication Books (in Korean).
Korean Film Council (KOFIC). 2019. *Korean Cinema Yearbook 2018*. Busan: KOFIC (in Korean). KOFIC 2020 Korean Cinema Yearbook 2019. Busan: KOFIC (in Korean).
Messerlin, P.A., and J. Parc. 2020. The Myth of Subsidies in the Film Industry: A Comparative Analysis of European and US Approaches. *Innovation: The European Journal of Social Science Research* 33 (4): 474–489.
Motion Picture Association (MPA). 2020. THEME Report. https://www.motionpictures.org/wp-content/uploads/2020/03/MPA-THEME-2019.pdf.
Motion Pictures Association of Japan (MPPAJ). various issues, Statistics of Film Industry in Japan. http://eiren.org/statistics_e/index.html.
Murschetz, P.C., R. Teichmann, and M. Karmasin. 2018. *Handbook of State Aid for Film*. Cham, Switzerland: Springer.
Organisation for Economic Co-operation and Development (OECD). 2020. Services Trade Restrictiveness Index Regulatory Database (STRI). https://qdd.oecd.org/subject.aspx?Subject=063bee63-475f-427c-8b50-c19bffa7392d.
Parc, J. 2014. *An Eclectic Approach to Enhancing the Competitive Advantage of Nations: Analyzing the Success Factors of East Asian Economies with a Focus on the Development of South Korea*. Thesis (PhD), Seoul National University and Université Paris Sorbonne.
Parc, J. 2017. The Effects of Protection in Cultural Industries: The Case of the Korean Film Policies. *International Journal of Cultural Policy* 23 (5): 618–633.
Parc, J. 2020. Between State-Led and Corporation-Led Co-Productions: How Has Film Co-Production Been Exploited by States in Europe. *Innovation: The European Journal of Social Science Research* 33 (4): 442–458.
Parc, J. 2021. Business Integration and its Impact on Film Industry: The Case of Korean Film Policies from the 1960s until the Present. *Business History* 63 (5): 850–867.
Parc, J., and P.A. Messerlin. 2018. In Search of an Effective Trade Policy for the Film Industry: Lessons from Korea. *Journal of World Trade* 52 (5): 745–764.
Parc J., P.A. Messerlin, and K. Kim. 2021, The Impact of Protectionism on Cultural Industries: The Effect of China's Film Policies on Market Access, mimeo.

Sohu. 2019. 2018nian quanguodianyingpiaofang, guanyingrenci, dianyingchanliang shujutongji, guochanpian chengwei ladong piaofang zengzhangde hexindongli [Statistics on the National Film Box Office, the Number of Audiences, and the Number of Films in 2018: Domestic Films Have Become the Key Driving Force for the Growth of the Box Office], *Sohu*. http://www.sohu.com/a/290898105_775892.

Stephen Follows. 2017. How Important Is International Box Office to Hollywood? https://stephenfollows.com/important-international-box-office-hollywood/.

UNESCO Institute for statistics (UIS). http://data.uis.unesco.org/.

World Bank, Indicators. http://data.worldbank.org/indicator/.

CHAPTER 2

Escaping the Import Quota and Why It Matters

In the 1980s, if you went to a movie theater in downtown Seoul, you would have been hard-pressed to find any domestic films on show as Hollywood films dominated the screens. In fact, these were not the latest titles but rather blockbusters that had already been successfully screened in the United States (US) and elsewhere. Still, they drew easily large crowds.

The contrast could not be more striking with the situation prevailing thirty years before. When Korea emerged out of the ashes of the Korean War in 1953, the film industry was one of the few activities that showed a degree of promise. It enjoyed a "golden age" which lasted until the early 1970s. Audience numbers were high as people flocked to view the latest attractive domestic films that could transport them away from the hardships of daily life. Of note during this time, there were import quotas that limited the number of foreign films imported to Korea. Among foreign films, those from Hollywood became popular in Korea for the same reasons—with their big stars, sophisticated plot lines, and dramatic special effects—that they were attractive for European audiences during the same time (Hayward 2005).

In fact, protectionism became a feature after the Korean War as a large number of US films were imported to Korea along with foreign aid that sought to help to foster the Korean economy. As was the case in Europe,

J. Parc and P. A. Messerlin, *The Untold Story of the Korean Film Industry*, Cultural Economics & the Creative Economy,
https://doi.org/10.1007/978-3-030-80342-1_2

the Korean government adopted an import quota in 1958 to curtail the dominant power of Hollywood films. In the early 1960s, the Korean government directly intervened in order to control the industry for a number of political and economic reasons. Specifically, this policy tool was supposed to boost the local film industry by limiting the number of foreign films that could be brought into the domestic market, but by the 1970s it was very clear that the opposite result had in fact occurred. Between 1979 and 1986, Korean film production had suffered a fall of 25% in its box office revenues (in constant 2018 USD) and had also witnessed a decline in the number of films produced (Parc 2017, 2020). Even worse, as will be shown later, the import quota created a number of vested interests in the Korean film industry who benefited from this trade restriction and formed strong opposition toward any effort aimed at initiating reform.

The only way out of such a stalemate was to experience a powerful external shock. This finally came when the Hollywood studios pressured Korea to sign two bilateral film agreements with the US in 1985 and 1988. As a result, the government pushed through legislation that eliminated the import quota and ensured that Hollywood films could enjoy unimpeded direct access to Korea's movie theaters. This would turn out to be a blessing in disguise for the Korean film industry.

Indeed, soon after the two film agreements were signed, the Korean film industry experienced its first positive change in growth trajectory in over a decade. Such an evolution raises three key questions that will be examined here. First, to what extent did the Film Agreements play a key role in this change of Korea's growth trajectory? Second, looking at the long-term picture, are there any other factors such as the Korean government's policies and/or the strategies among the film companies that can explain the much more marked growth that occurred in the late 1990s? Third, how does Korea's opening of its film market to the US compare with Mexico, a country which underwent a similar market opening process at around the same time? More specifically, what lessons can be extracted from Korea's experience that can help understand why Mexico's liberalization failed to boost its domestic film industry?

1 The Korean Import Quota: An Economic Analysis

Since its introduction, the Korean import quota has been modified many times reflecting the different policy objectives among successive governments (see Parc [2017, 2021] for further details). The first version set out in 1962 made the number of imported foreign films conditional upon the production and export of Korean films—in other words, it was conceived as a reward mechanism. Under this regime, Korean film companies could import lucrative foreign films, but only if they were capable of producing domestic films of "good quality" that could be exported to foreign markets. What seemed like an attractive incentive on paper, in particularly during the film industry's Golden Age, turned out quickly to have a major problem: it was impossible to define an efficient reward mechanism that everybody could agree upon. Enforcing this mechanism was made even more complicated by the fact that during this time Korea's industrial regulations considered producers and importers as part of the same integrated firms. Therefore, for simplicity sake, this chapter uses the generic term "importer" which covers both types depending on the period covered.

In 1966, the Korean government switched the definition for its quota regime to one based on quantitative terms: it dictated that simply producing three Korean films in domestic markets permitted the company to import one foreign film. This type of import quota is nothing new in the film business: it has prevailed in many countries around the world, including in Europe. However, without any proper analysis of the European import quotas and its consequences, the Korean government blindly adopted a similar regime. It is noteworthy that Japan also adopted its own import quota between 1952 and 1964, but the results were completely different from the case of Europe and Korea.

What factors lay behind Japan's import quota that produced less damaging effects on its domestic film industry? First, the ratio between foreign and domestic films as defined by Japan's quota regime was "more balanced" (one domestic film to one foreign film) than in Korea (three domestic films to one foreign film). Second, the import quota in Japan during its brief existence permitted a much larger number of foreign films to be brought in than in Korea: 215 films in 1952 and 275 in 1963, compared to the annual average of 26 films imported in Korea for the period 1970–1985. Third, these foreign films pushed the Japanese film companies to improve their own production.

1.1 *The Basic Flaws of an Import Quota: Ineffective and Divisive*

An import quota has a unavoidable flaw: it can artificially restrict the number of foreign films imported into the market, but it cannot limit how many moviegoers go to watch them. In this respect, it can be said that an import quota is ineffective. The Korean import quota was no exception (Parc 2017). With a limited number of foreign films allowed, Korean importers have been careful to select only the most attractive foreign films that can draw in the highest number of moviegoers. Thus, you have a situation where most people flock to watch a few selected foreign films while largely ignoring the countless domestic films on account of their poor quality.

The bulk of imported films were made up of Hollywood movies that had already proven to be successful in many markets around the world. Such a selective approach has two consequences. Not only does it generate more revenue from screening a single Hollywood film than from exhibiting many local productions; but it also further helps to avoid the risk of screening unsuccessful films, one of the main sources of losses in the highly unpredictable film business. The annual number of US films imported in Korea between 1975 and 1985 fluctuated between 16 and 28. It should be noted that Hollywood's general policy at that time was to sell proven titles at low prices in foreign markets since most of the production costs of these films had already been recouped in the US market. Such films may not have been the latest releases, but they were "cheap" to import and had a proven record of success—all attractive features for Korean importers who had relatively limited funds for buying foreign films during this period. For example, *ET: The Extra-Terrestrial* was not released in Korea until 1984, two years after its original release in the US, and *Star Wars: Return of the Jedi* was not released until 1987, four years after its US release. Both films had already enjoyed huge box office success in the US before they came to Korea.

While the import quota created an environment where foreign films became very lucrative for Korean importers, it had at the same time a very negative effect on domestic film production. In this respect, a quota can be said to be divisive. First and foremost, it put domestic movies in direct competition with the most attractive foreign films in Korean movie theaters. In such an "unbalanced" environment, Korean productions would always appear to be of poor quality to the domestic audience. This form of "unfair" competition was self-inflicted by the import quota. It has been amplified by Korean film producers who during this period increasingly resorted to producing "quota quickies"—the term given to Korean movies hastily made so that they could bring in more foreign films.[1] Out of this, a vicious cycle emerged: as frustrated moviegoers shunned away from watching these films, the resulting low revenues from the box office led to fewer resources for Korean filmmakers and thus created less incentives to invest in the production of new domestic films. To sum up, for two decades this import quota has systematically deteriorated the quality of Korean films and distorted the overall demand among Korean moviegoers in favor of already successful foreign films at the expense of domestic films.

Needless to say, this unfair competition for Korean film producers in their own domestic market stands in marked contrast to the official discourse that has claimed to protect domestic production.

1.2 Quota and Rents

Throughout the period from the 1970s to the 1980s, there was little understanding in Korea that this disastrous decline of the domestic film industry was primarily the result of the import quota. In fact, the participants in the Korean film market were all convinced that they benefited from imposing the quota. That was naturally the case of the Korean importers—those who were permitted to import and distribute foreign films and who were eager to maintain this measure as it allowed them to extract huge profits from the foreign films they had acquired for the domestic market. At the same time, the Korean film producers believed that strengthening the quota regime to restrict number of foreign films imported to Korea would help them to produce more films of better quality. More importantly, Korean moviegoers were mostly interested in the quality of the films regardless of their nationality and did not realize

[1] It is reported that quickies were made within a few weeks, and that the most prolific filmmakers could make up to six to eight films a year. Such a term actually originated with the "low-cost B-grade" movies that were produced in the UK in order to meet the basic requirements under the quota system introduced there in 1927 (Parc 2020).

that the import quota was the reason why so few foreign films and so many poorly made Korean movies were screened.

In short, there was no domestic voice in Korea that advocated for a radical reform of this import quota—hence the need for external pressure to push for reform. The next section explores these negotiations and how they were able to break down the barriers to entry into the Korean film market.

Box 1 Economic Analysis of an Import Quota

The figure below presents the simplest case of an import quota: the importer pays directly the foreign supplier for the purchase of their films and sells them directly to the consumer in the domestic market. It thus ignores all the intermediaries, distributors, or movie theaters for the sake of simplicity. The supply of foreign films is represented by the upward sloping curve SS, and the demand of foreign films by the downward sloping curve DD. In the absence of restrictions, demand meets supply at point E, which defines the number of foreign films to be imported OA and their "unit price" Oa—assuming for simplicity sake that all films are of similar quality.

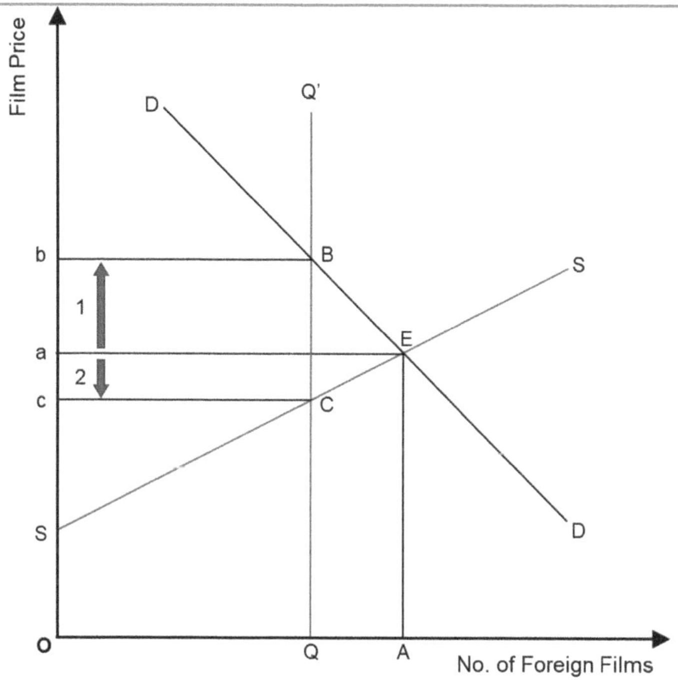

If the import quota OQ is imposed, the supply curve for foreign films becomes SCBQ', since it is forbidden to import more films than the number OQ. Importers can now sell imported foreign films to domestic consumers at price Ob (higher than Oa) which is the price where the quota-constrained supply of foreign films (QQ') meets domestic demand (DD). At the same time, the importers pay only price Oc to the foreign suppliers. This is the price where the quota-constrained supply of foreign films (QQ') meets foreign supply (SS). The difference cb between these two prices is the "rent" per film generated by the quota regime. The total rent created by the quota OQ in the whole market is illustrated by the area cCBb.

The crucial question is: Who receives the rent? The answer depends on a host of conditions which are shaped by the legal, institutional, and political environment of the import market at stake and by the specific regulations that established the quota. Parc (2018, 2020) describes in detail how the Korean regulations have defined these conditions in the case of the film industry. Most often, the rent-beneficiaries are the importers: their close access to the officials who deliver the licenses to import gives them a leverage in their negotiations with the foreign companies—allowing them to get the low price Oc—as well as in their negotiations with the movie theaters—allowing them to impose the high price Ob. This analysis is essential because it allows one to understand why quotas are often said to be the "mother of all corruption." The beneficiaries of the quotas can use their rents to maintain their privileged position by bribing officials or other market participants. This corruption amplifies enormously the final costs of the quota because it increases the distortions in the market at stake.

2 The Negotiations of the Film Agreements

After years of tense negotiations, two Film Agreements were eventually signed in October 1985 and December 1988, respectively. They led to the Korean import quota regime being abolished (for a thorough analysis see Parc [2018, 2020]). In 1985, the Motion Picture Export Association of America (MPEAA) filed a Section 301 complaint against Korea for its failure to allow US film companies to distribute their films directly in Korea. It was the end to a long saga. Since the early 1970s, the lobbying arm of the main Hollywood studios, the Motion Picture Association of America—MPAA (nowadays known by the acronym MPA)—had been pressuring the Korean government to open up their film market. The MPA was concerned that the Korean film market could evolve and end up like Japan: a market dominated by less than five domestic firms with vertically integrated operations which gave them considerable market power.

The MPA has always been an extremely influential voice in Washington—justifying its nickname as the "little State Department" (Lee 2008). It has accumulated a vast expertise in international trade affairs involving film industries: in particular, it has been involved in all the discussions on the film industry between the US and European countries since the 1920s and even today. In 1985, the MPA convinced the Office of the US Trade Representative to begin legal proceedings against Korea over unfair import regulations. This action pressured Korea into signing the First Agreement in 1985 to abolish the import quota. One notable outcome was that foreign studios were permitted to directly distribute their films in Korea.

2.1 *The 1988 US Lobbying Campaign: Breaking the Windowpane*

However, some barriers—such as the need for a review process of film prints and import taxes—were kept in place even after 1985 to the frustration of the MPA. In order to solve this problem, MPA President Jack Valenti decided to initiate a new lobbying campaign in 1988 to eliminate the last remaining barriers to the Korean film market which in his words were still "leaving the Americans outside with their nose pressed against the windowpane" (Valenti 2007, p. 379). As a former special assistant to US President Lyndon B. Johnson, Valenti was well connected to senior US policymakers and was also well versed in the intricacies of US trade law and regulations—particularly Section 301 of the Trade Act 1974. This provision was very much feared by all US trade partners as it could be triggered easily by the federal government and could lead to additional high tariffs on foreign goods entering the huge, dynamic, and lucrative US market.

During discussions with his Korean counterparts, Valenti made it clear that if Korea were to continue to hold out from fully implementing the first Film Agreement, its exports of made-in-Korea goods would be subjected to a Section 301 investigation leading to additional duties when entering the US market. This was a serious threat given that Korea as a brand was still trying to establish its position in the US market. Furthermore, Korea was already faced with many ad hoc US protectionist measures against its industrial exports (mostly anti-dumping actions in steel, chemicals, and electronic products) and had to deal with stiff competition from Japanese goods which enjoyed a strong presence in the US market.

To his surprise, Jack Valenti did not receive immediate support in the US for triggering a Section 301 case against Korea. First, not all members of the MPA favored such an aggressive approach. The most determined studio to take a strong stance was United International Pictures (UIP), a joint venture of Paramount and Universal. However, when talking to the other MPA members, Valenti (2007) notes that "oddly there were a few who were not that ready to fight" (p. 379). These differences were probably due to the fact that the Korean film market was not yet seen as a promising market by all MPA members. Second, the US government was divided between the Office of the US Trade Representative which was receptive to Valenti's goal and the State Department that favored more Korea as it was still in the process of democratic transition and becoming economically and politically important for the whole East Asia region. There was also precedent with the negotiations for the Canada-US free trade agreement in the mid-1980s. In this case, President Reagan set aside the vested interests of Hollywood in favor of US national interests despite the fact that he was himself a former President of the Screen Actors Guild (see the section on Mexico).

Undeterred, Valenti persisted with his lobbying efforts until he was able to convince the MPA and the US government to initiate a Section 301 investigation. This was quite an achievement given the political sensitivities surrounding the upcoming 1988 Seoul Olympics. Within days, the Korean government agreed to the US request by removing the remaining barriers that made direct distribution in Korea difficult. It is no surprise here that the Korean government would not endanger the country's emerging industrial base for a film industry that was already in a bad shape and seemed to offer little prospect for the overall economy.

2.2 *Estimating the Size of the Rents*[2]

This brief overview of the negotiations between the US and Korea raises an important question. Why was it so difficult for Korea to eliminate the import quota? In other words, who had the most to lose with the Film Agreements? As mentioned before and shown in detail in Box 1, the greatest losers were the Korean importers who lost the huge rents associated with their licenses to import US films.

A rough estimate of these rents can be calculated by using the official records on the import price of each US film imported. We cover only two years 1982 and 1983 as they are the years before the import quota abolition when the MPEAA raised issues with the Korea's import quota issues. During these two years, the total box office revenues of the US films amounted to USD 194 million. The official records show that Korean importers have spent USD 15 million in buying US films—that is, 8% of the total revenues of these US films in Korea. This is very modest compared to what US studios usually earn in the overseas market—at least 30% of the total revenues they gained with their films all over the world. In other words, absent the import quota, Korean importers would have normally paid about USD 58 million (USD 194

[2] All figures related to revenues and prices are in constant 2018 USD.

million times 0.30) to import these US films. The difference of USD 43 million (USD 58 million minus USD 15 million) is a rough estimate of the Korean distributors' rents for these two years.

This huge difference has two major interpretations. From the Korean perspective, it explains why Korean importers were so adamantly opposed to the elimination of the import quota regime, despite the severe harm that this regime had induced upon Korean film production and more broadly to the nation's culture. This is even more visible when one compares the quota rents and the box office revenues of the Korean films during these two years—USD 171 million. The quota rents alone were thus equivalent to one-fourth of the revenues of all the Korean films. From the US perspective, these rents amounted to substantial losses—at least for observers like Valenti who recognized early the growth potential of an increasingly affluent Korean economy, and of its dynamic film market.

The more one looks at the sheer size of the revenue that could be earned from film imports, the clearer it becomes on why it was so hard for the government to institute any type of reform of the quota system.[3] Indeed, the threat of a Section 301 investigation hanging over their heads was intended to put firmly the large industrial Korean firms in the camp of those who wanted to open the Korean film market.

This discussion deserves two final remarks. From the Korean side, the lifting of the import quota has had a significant impact upon Korean importers; in particular the adventurous but active participation of the large Korean conglomerates or *chaebol* in the industry which has changed the landscape of the Korean film industry completely, as shown below. From the Hollywood studios side, the amount they lost by not picking up the full amount of the box office revenues they could expect in Korea was modest compared to their total global revenues. For instance, it represented less than one percent of the box office revenues earnt by US film companies across the whole world for the same years. This may explain

[3] Some may argue that military governments were authoritative and not willing to reform the quota system. In fact, during Park Chung-hee regime (1963–1979), the Motion Picture Law had been amended four times. The way this law had been amended was inconsistent while the quota system had been maintained. Chun Doo-hwan (1980–1988) amended the law three times, but two were related to the two Korea-US Film Agreements.

the initial hesitation among some MPA members to follow Valenti's aggressive perception of Korea's potential.

3 The Effects of the Korea-US Film Agreements for the Short to Long Term

When examining these agreements on the Korean film market, their effects can be divided into two periods. There were the immediate short-term ones—between 1985 and 1995. Interestingly, these effects were in line with the pessimistic predictions among Korean filmmakers, but not with the optimistic expectations held by US film producers. Then there were the long-term effects after 1995 which have been dramatically different from what everyone expected, specifically the rapid and strong take-off of the Korean film industry and the disappointing performance of US films in Korea.

For a clearer understanding, it is noteworthy to point out a peculiarity within the film industry. In general, producing a large number of films is considered to be a desirable outcome, but producing too many films would automatically, sooner or later, result in deterioration of film quality and attractiveness due to the increasing financial burdens it entails. Film companies are well aware of these conflicting forces. Yet, at the same time they are averse to risk and it is this aspect that could induce them to produce a too large number of films (De Vany 2004). Thus, the optimal point between the number of films and their attractiveness requires a sophisticated business approach.

All these interactions suggest the following reasonable proposition: the higher the number of films, sooner or later the lower their average level of attractiveness. Connecting these two complementary perspectives—number of films and average box office revenues—allows to interpret the dramatic changes faced by Korean and US films in the Korean film market in the late 1980s–mid-2000s.

3.1 The Film Agreements: Short-Term Effects (1985–1995)

Figure 1 covers the period 1975–2005, a duration long enough to provide a comprehensive and robust analysis of the Korean film industry's transformation—long before the Film Agreements were negotiated and going up to the time long after their implementation when their effects were keenly felt. It shows a steady decline in the number of Korean

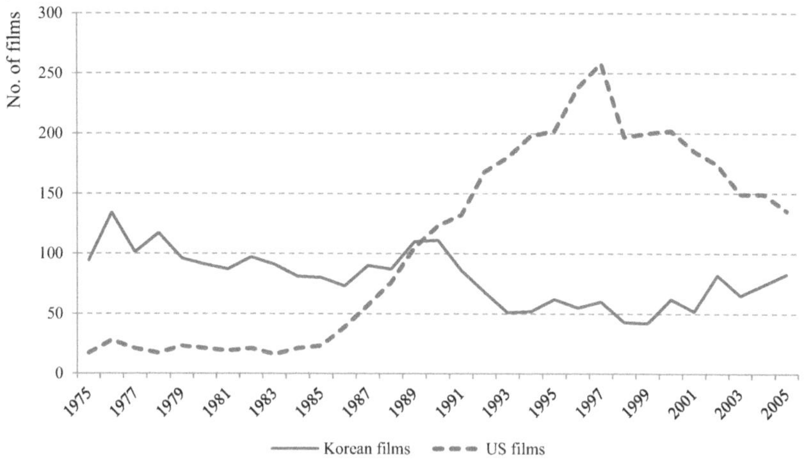

Fig. 1 The number of films in the Korean film market (1975–2005) (*Sources* Parc [2014], KOBIS)

films released until the mid-1980s. This drop-in numbers was the key consequence of imposing the import quota over such a long period: exhibiting Korean films was becoming less profitable, hence the incentives to produce new domestic films were declining steadily throughout this period (Parc 2017, 2021).

Turning to the number of US films, it was artificially constrained by the import quota until 1985. As soon as the first Film Agreement was signed, the number of US films increased sharply (see Fig. 1). The fear of a flood of US films raised by the Korean opponents to the elimination of the import quota seemed to materialize.

Regarding the average revenue per film, Fig. 2 reveals the key driving forces in action. Up until the end of the quota regime, the average revenues for US films have been very high, reflecting the strong attractiveness among the few Hollywood films. Yet once the restrictions on imports were lifted and US films were able to enter the Korean film market freely, their average revenues declined sharply—revealing a decreasing average attractiveness among the much larger number of imported US films. For the US film producers, that was a totally unexpected outcome from the opening of the Korean film market.

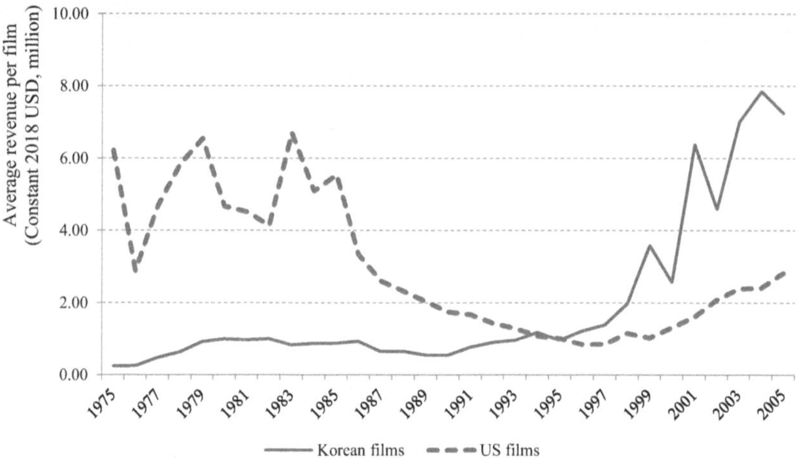

Fig. 2 The Korean film market: average revenues per film (1975–2005) (*Sources* Parc [2014], KOBIS)

Why did US films perform so badly after the opening of the Korean market? Given the incredible success enjoyed every year by just a handful of films in Korea, the Hollywood studios naturally assumed that all their productions would receive the same warm welcome in Korea. As a result, when the import quota was lifted, both Korean companies and Hollywood studios increased greatly the number of US films imported and distributed in Korea. In 1996, the number of US films released in Korea was up by six times from 1986. The resulting post-1988 decline in the attractiveness of US films for Korean audiences lasted more than a decade: the pre-1987 average revenue per US film was unsurpassed until 2005. This "attractiveness depression" reflected the profound changes in the views among Korean moviegoers toward US films—as well as toward the Korean films produced by a rejuvenated domestic film industry.

Turning to Korean films, the evolution of their average revenues throughout the whole period has been somewhat more complex. The stagnant numbers from 1979 to 1986 represent the impact of the "quota quickies," while the further deterioration shown from 1987 to 1990 mirrors the short-lived effort by existing Korean film producers to compete with the rising number of foreign films (see Fig. 1). In response to the increased number of Hollywood films, they adopted a strategy to ramp up their own production but by 1990 this effort had mostly failed: the average revenues per Korean film had decreased further. Facing a dire situation, Korean film producers were forced to cut the number of films produced—leading to a modest increase in the average revenues since the early 1990s (see Fig. 2). Some might argue that there is no wonder about the increase of average revenues per Korean film as the number of Korean films produced was significantly reduced. However, the general trend of Korean production is rather steady throughout the period from the mid-1990s to the mid-2000s.

3.2 *The Film Agreements: Long-Term Effects (1995–2005)*[4]

It took roughly a decade for the Korean film industry—and for Korean moviegoers—to reap the benefits from the Film Agreements. This long delay was reflective of the fact that the Korean film industry had to undergo profound restructuring in its composition, mainly with the emergence of *chaebols* and the entry of a new generation of film producers as the new players. This consequently led to profound changes in the Korean film industry's industrial strategies of production and distribution that could not be done overnight. Much of this stands in sharp contrast with the Hollywood studios who could rapidly increase the number of their films distributed in Korea by simply taping into their large stock of past and present films.

Indeed, the Korean companies operating before the Film Agreements did not realize the full scale of the changes required by a much more open market. As shown in Fig. 1, up until 1990 their response was simply to increase the number of their own films without improving upon enough their attractiveness. It was only after 1990 that an entry of new participants in the market—the subsidiaries of the *chaebols*—introduced a new strategy based on fewer but more attractive films. This attractiveness grew slowly between 1991 and 1994, then accelerated between 1994 and 1998 before reaching the second inflection point of 1998–1999 as noted in Chapter 1 (Fig. 2). From 1998 to 2005, growth then skyrockets (the years after 2005 are examined in the next chapter).

This evolution can be captured by comparing the averages during the two periods: 1975–1985 and 1985–2005—the longer period after the

[4] All figures related to revenues and prices are in constant 2018 USD.

Korea-US Film Agreements indicative of the lengthy time required for Korean producers to change their strategy. During the decade 1975–1985, there were on average 97 Korean films exhibited every year, which brought in roughly USD 68 million—a revenue of USD 0.7 million per film. By contrast, there were on average 21 US movies screened in Korea bringing in roughly USD 104 million—a revenue of USD 5.1 million per foreign film or seven times more than the average Korean film. During the period 1986–2005, 70 Korean films were exhibited on average every year and earned roughly USD 174 million—a revenue of USD 2.6 million per film. By contrast, the 158 US films exhibited on average every year earned roughly USD 243 million—a revenue of USD 1.7 million per film—only 65% of the average Korean film.

Last but not least, Korean moviegoers have been the biggest winners from the opening of the domestic film market over these two decades. In 2008, twenty years after the signature of the Second Film Agreement, the size of the overall Korean film market was four times larger than in 1988 while the seat price increased by only 1.5 times. The box office revenues were multiplied by eight and three times for Korean and US films, respectively, a sign of the huge increase in the variety of the films exhibited in Korea.

4 The Driving Forces Behind the Long-Term Effects: Korea's "Golden Duo"

While the two Film Agreements have been a crucial factor in rejuvenating the market and breaking the grip of vested interests, they were for the most part a trigger for broader change; in other words, they were a necessity but not the only condition. To understand more on how Korea developed its film industry it is crucial to consider two other main factors which have interacted without interruption throughout this period: the hands-off approach of the government and the strategies in the industry. Together, these two forces make up the "golden duo" for an effective film industry.

4.1 The Korean Government's Less-Interventionist Approach

A very frequent fate of policies that seek to open a market is to be reversed at a later stage. This is because governments often adopt measures that attempt to diminish the pain from the industrial adjustments required by a more open market. When doing this, it is rare then that governments will have recourse to policies that would directly facilitate the adjustment process as the market opens, such as training programs to help workers acquire new skills. This is because such policies are difficult to devise and to implement and are slow to bear results. As a result, governments tend to rely on new protectionist measures which are likely to be on a collision course with the market opening measures implemented previously. Such inconsistent measures—opening then closing—are very costly as they create uncertainty over the future evolution of the market in question.

The Korean government did not embark upon such a challenging path. In fact, in contrast to what might be expected after twenty years of its tight grip on the film market, it maintained a less-interventionist approach toward the film industry after the import quota was lifted. In particular, it did not seek any new or alternative measures to restrict access to the domestic film market nor did it backtrack on its commitments in the two Agreements. This restraint has been absolutely essential for the long-term success of the Korean film industry: it placed Korean film companies in a stable and consistent legal policy environment, ensuring that they could make long-term strategic choices. The comparison with the Mexican case examined at the end of this chapter presents clear evidence in this regard.

It should be noted that this restrained approach taken by the Korean government was neither due to it being in a weak position nor lacking the resources to do so. While it is fair to say that the option not to reintroduce the import quota or a similar instrument was driven by a fear of triggering a harsh US response, it is important to recognize that the Korean government had many other protectionist tools in its hands. For instance, it could have invoked legislation to restrict imports under the label of "protection of public morals" which is allowed under Article XX of the General Agreement on Trade and Tariffs (GATT)—one of the few "general exceptions" to freer trade accepted by the entire global community. Such an approach though was not adopted and the Korean government refrained from intervening in its film industry.

This less-interventionist approach was considerably helped by a pragmatic decision made by the Korean government. It was able to offset domestic opposition to market opening by being careful enough to keep in place the other protectionist measure—the screen quota which was introduced in 1966 as part of the second amendment of the Motion Picture Law. This policy instrument guarantees a minimum number of days (146 days in 1986) to exhibit Korean films in movie theaters. With the elimination of the import quota, it was widely seen in Korea as the safeguard needed by the domestic film industry to offset any excessive dominance by Hollywood films. In fact, as shown in Chapter 3, the screen quota was actually a paper tiger: it has had no noticeable impact on the Korean film market since it was established. As a result, keeping it was de facto economically harmless for the US films and politically clever for the Korean government.

In the subsequent decade after the Film Agreements, two further factors were crucial in explaining why the Korean government was able to maintain such a less-interventionist approach. First, the unexpected but remarkable success of the Korean film industry after 1999 did help to reduce the pressure on the government from the protectionist-minded interests in the film industry—though it should be noted that these voices have never completely faded away as one should expect in the real world (this is analyzed further in Chapters 4–7). Second, despite the 1997 Asian financial crisis, the Korean governments still believed in the massive benefits offered by globalization for the whole economy. This came in the shape of rapid growth in the average income per capita, an increasingly powerful export-oriented industrial basis, and the emergence of large domestic multinationals that began to make significant investments abroad. Simply, successive Korean governments did not want to jeopardize these massive benefits for the sake of the still marginal film industry.

4.2 *The Industrial Strategy of a New Generation of Korean Film Companies, Chaebols*

Within the context of the less-interventionist approach adopted in Korea, the strategies pursued by the country's film companies were able to emerge as a key driving force behind the industry's long-term success. As this topic is beyond the scope of this book which focuses on the international aspects of the Korean film industry and its policies, what follows presents only a brief analysis of the adjustment process in the Korean film industry.

What makes the Korean case unique in the global film industry has been the entry in the mid-1990s of *chaebols* such as Samsung, Lotte, and Daewoo who previously did not have any major stake in the film industry. In particular, no other Asian country has witnessed this kind of evolution.

In Japan, large entertainment firms have long dominated the domestic film industry while Taiwan has witnessed some attempts to replicate the Korean case but these efforts have not come to any fruition. And Hong Kong film producers have mostly pursued co-production projects with Mainland producers.

Since the late 1980s, the *chaebols* have been the backbone of Korea's industrial growth and development. Although some had brief experiences with entertainment-related activities (film rentals, TV channels, and even music labels), none have shown any explicit interest in the film industry per se, except in the low-level distribution of films produced by small US studios. As the *chaebols* became progressively aware of the huge potential profits that could be earned from the film industry, they had to transform their internal organization. This came at a time when these organizations were already undergoing restructuring given their increasingly large size and diversified products. Out of this emerged the subsidiaries that specialized in "entertainment," where activities in the film industry could be easily included.

Although not all participating *chaebols* were able to achieve much success when entering the film industry and some had to close their film business, they have collectively made a huge contribution to the success of the Korean film industry as a whole. This is partly due to the way in which they have inspired the need for change within the whole industry. In particular, they have combined several qualities that were missing among the Korean firms operating in the film industry before 1988: boldness and innovation combined with a broad range of business experience acquired in other economic activities. This is best illustrated by the case of CheilJedang (CJ), one of Samsung's subsidiaries.

First, CJs founders were bold and innovative in the Korean film industry which was mostly focused on rent-seeking activities through distribution and exhibition. As soon as CJ was separated from Samsung, its management decided to invest in one of the most innovative and iconic US studios, DreamWorks. Initially, they sought to finance films that could be distributed in Korea, but they were soon keen to learn more about how to run a modern film production company. This was a bold move for a new company from what was then a developing country and without much experience in the film business. Indeed, it was not easy for CJ to get the authorization from the Korean government to invest the USD 300 million needed to buy a stake in DreamWorks given the country's developing status at the time (Russel 2008). Initially, the Korean government was far from being supportive as it viewed this investment as a drain of funds from the country toward the US, not as an opportunity to acquire skills and other assets. This was reflective of the traditional approach toward international investment among developing countries at this time (Parc 2017, 2021).

Second, CJ's management benefited from Samsung's business experiences accumulated from its other activities. They generated and organized many skills, such as marketing, finance, and accounting, that were lacking in the Korean film industry at that time. Crucially, they brought with them Samsung's approach to vertical integration of business operations which led them to be active in all segments of the film industry (production, distribution, and exhibition). Such vertical integration offers strategic advantages like access to information on what is going on across the whole industry as well as alternative options for the reallocation of internal resources in case of external shocks.

This intimate knowledge of the film business via vertical integration further reduces the risk of bottlenecks as illustrated in Fig. 3. It shows the almost "synchronized" growth in the number of screens and the size of the audiences for Korean blockbusters up to 2007. Coupled with

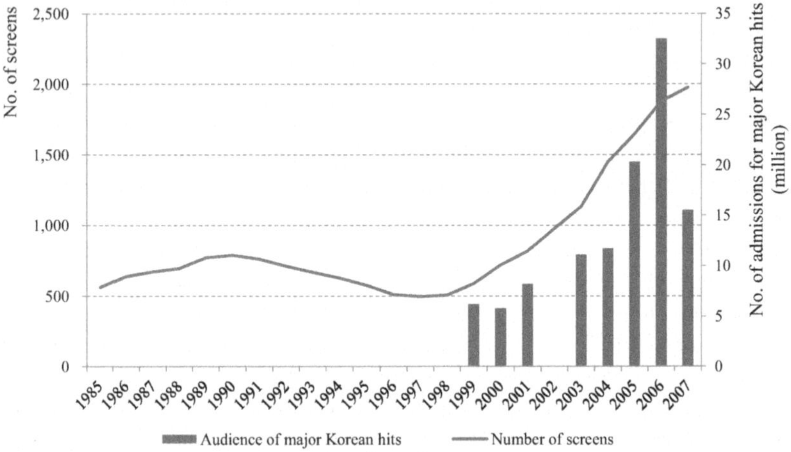

Fig. 3 Korean screens and Korean mega hits (1985–2007) (*Sources* Parc [2014] and KOBIS)

improved quality of Korean films and the introduction of the multiplex (a movie theater with multiple screens housed in a single building) these changes helped to accelerate the influx of Korean moviegoers to watch domestic mega hits. It grew by an even faster rate from 2004 to 2007 with an impressive list of regular hits.

That said, it is important to underline that the success of the Korean film industry was not a smooth process. It was led by the large, powerful, and aggressively competitive *chaebols*, who were very quick to make alliances or mergers and could rapidly change their strategies if they did not work well. These features were exacerbated by external disturbances, in particular the 1997 Asian financial crisis which led to some of these investments failing to succeed and a few *chaebols* even withdrew from the film industry altogether (Parc 2017, 2018). However, despite them pulling out, the Korean film industry as a whole managed to adopt the modern way to produce and distribute films, a process that helped them to become more globalized and competitive.

5 Why Mexico Failed While Korea Thrived

The benefits from the approaches adopted by the "Golden Duo" are even more evident when examining how Mexico's government initiated a major overhaul of its film policies between 1988 and 1994, almost at the same time that Korea was opening its film market. The situation looked initially more favorable for Mexico than Korea: in contrast with the Korean government's reluctance to liberalize its domestic film market, the Mexican government was eager to adopt reforms and improve the situation for its film industry. Although the Mexican film industry was once the world's third largest in the 1940s, it went into a steady decline since and already reached a poor state by the 1960s. Opening the market seemed an attractive option and the environment looked ripe for success following the launch of negotiations for the North American Free Trade Agreement (hereafter NAFTA) with the US and Canada in 1991. With its successful conclusion in 1994, there was a growing appetite for globalization in Mexico, reflecting the trend among many countries around the world at the time.

Despite this favorable background, the outcome of Mexico's liberalization efforts for its film industry has not been as successful as Korea. While it has achieved success in the distribution and exhibition segments, it has had very disappointing results with film production where the attractiveness of Mexican films in the post-liberalization era has not met the tastes of audiences. This particular outcome can be considered as a major failure by the audience from a cultural creativity and diversity perspective. The fact that Mexico was eager to open its film industry but was unable to achieve a similar level of success as Korea whose government was reluctant to open its film industry is a paradox which deserves to be examined.

One explanation here is that Mexico was mostly interested in advancing its TV and audiovisual sector during NAFTA negotiations as its "telenovelas" were very successful among the Spanish-speaking population in the US. Another possible reason is that Mexico did not adopt the best policies toward opening up its film industry. As this book deals with the film industry, this section focuses on this second reason by comparing the measures adopted by Mexico and Korea in opening their respective domestic film markets. This comparison is possible because these two countries are remarkably similar: they had roughly the same income per capita when they opened their film markets during the late 1980s and early 1990s; their film industries faced the same broad economic, social, and technological factors and history; and both were confronted by the same high share (around 70%) of US films in their domestic film market before their liberalization.

More precisely, this section examines whether the absence in Mexico of the "Golden Duo" that has been shown to be so critical for Korea's success has had a detrimental effect. In particular, was the Mexican government able to ensure a stable and economically sound environment that allowed film companies to develop their best industrial strategies? If this is not the case, then the delicate balance between public policy and private strategies observed in Korea emerges as a good anchor point toward identifying the "ideal" film policy for developing film industries with cultural creativity and diversity as the main goal.

5.1 NAFTA vs. Korea-US Film Agreements

The opening of the Mexican film industry under the auspices of NAFTA has often been perceived as a key factor behind the disappointing results of the Mexican film industry since the 1990s; in other words, globalization has often been blamed (Gomez 2006, p. 123). In contrast to such thinking though, Fig. 4 shows that this linkage is not convincing: since 1980—almost fifteen years before the signature of NAFTA in 1994—the number of Mexican films produced began to experience a rapid decline.

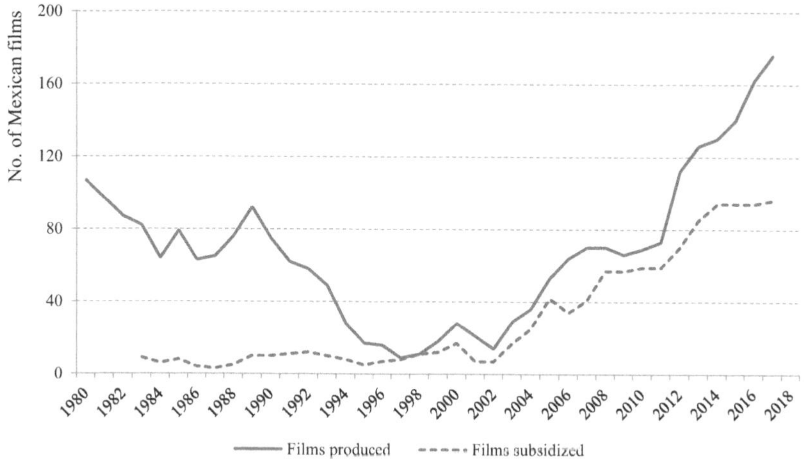

Fig. 4 Mexican film production (since 1980) (*Sources* Piva et al. [2011] for 1980–1999; CNC (various issues) for years 2000–2018)

A thorough comparison of NAFTA with the Korea-US Film Agreements confirms this first assessment: in a nutshell, NAFTA has been much less demanding on Mexico in terms of opening measures in the film industry than the Korea-US Film Agreements. When Canada negotiated its wide-ranging free trade agreement with the US in 1987 (the Canada-US Free Trade Agreement), it was able to guarantee its TV quota that ensures 50–60% of transmitted audiovisual works are "certified Canadian content." When Mexico approached the US to conclude a bilateral agreement in 1990, it expressed little interest in a similar provision that would ensure a "cultural exception" for its film industry (Larroa and Garcia 2011). Moreover, it promptly agreed to eliminate the 10% tariff on films imported from the US, a measure that was incorporated into the text of NAFTA.

This NAFTA commitment on tariffs is considerably more limited than the elimination of the tight import quota required by the Korea-US Film Agreements. Moreover, these Agreements have imposed a strong "binding" clause on Korea in the shape of a threat of a US Section 301 action, which would be implemented if the terms of the agreement were reneged upon. Binding is a key legal feature of international trade treaties. It means that if, for whatever reason, a country wants to reintroduce a barrier previously eliminated in a treaty—say an import quota or a tariff—it could not do so without having to pay "proportional" compensation to its partner. Clearly, the compensation costs to be paid to the US by Mexico if it were to reintroduce a 10% tariff on Mexican imports of US films would have been much smaller than those to be paid by Korea if it would have reintroduced its tight import quota.

5.2 *Picking on the Wrong Target: The Screen Quota*

The Mexican tariff cut under NAFTA was so limited that its impact on the country's film industry was negligible. This suggests that the reasons for the negative outcome following the opening of the Mexican film industry are to be found elsewhere, specifically among the many regulations that were implemented by Mexico during this period. Among all the instruments in Mexico, the screen quota which guaranteed 50% of the screen time to domestic movies was the most blatant protectionist device and was emblematic of Mexico's past film policies. Adopted in 1936, it was the first measure of protection in the Mexican film market and has been widely credited for having been instrumental in the emergence of the *Época de Oro del Cine Méxicano* or the golden age of the Mexican film industry in the 1940s and 1950s. In 1992, after much debate, the new Federal Cinematographic Law was brought in and imposed for the first time a cut from 50 to 30% of the screen time guaranteed by the quota. This was expected to be followed by more unilateral cuts resulting in a screen quota of only 10% (Ley federal de cinematografia 2020).

The government's decision to focus solely on the screen quota was an economic and political miscalculation. From an economic point of view, a screen quota is a very porous barrier, which can be easily circumvented (see Chapter 3). Therefore, its reduction could be qualified as "notional" and is unlikely to bring about any notable economic gains. And with the case of Mexico, gains were even more unlikely because the initial target of a 30% screen quota was unrealistic given the poor productivity of the Mexican film industry. For many years, it has never been capable of producing enough films that can attract more than 10% of the Mexican audience, as outlined below.

From a political viewpoint, this unilateral cut of the screen quota has generated huge costs. It was perceived as a surrender to US pressures and therefore instantly generated strong and long-lasting opposition among those with vested interests in the domestic film industry. This decision ignited so fierce debates in Mexico City that the government feared the legal text required for implementing the new Federal Law could be reversed at a later date. To prevent such an outcome, the government decided to strengthen the screen quota cut by including it in the text of NAFTA. Although this commitment was written in loose legal terms, this decision made the political situation worse: it has been widely interpreted by the Mexican film industry and the public as a further opening of the domestic market under US pressure.[5]

The Korean government's approach to its own barriers on foreign films has been the opposite of Mexico. First, Korea eliminated the import quota—a much more restrictive measure—bringing in huge economic gains by getting rid of unjustified rents while increasing the level of competition in the domestic film market. Second, as mentioned above, the Korean government was careful to leave in place the screen quota. In the end, this was a key decision from a political perspective: it has decreased the political costs of opening the market by generating the impression in Korea that there was still a substantial safeguard in place, particularly if the elimination of the import quota would turn bad. This decision has greatly facilitated the Korean government to adopt its less-interventionist policy—whereas the Mexican government has been bogged down in bitter domestic fights over the level of its screen quota for many years after its reduction.

5.3 *Mismanaging the Right Target: The Privatization Process*

The Mexican government sought to address the long decline of its film industry between the 1960s and the 1980s by adopting a long list of measures which unfortunately have further reduced the level of healthy competition in Mexico's film markets. Two characteristics in this regard deserve specific attention. The first one is that a large portion of the distribution and exhibition segments were owned by the state while the second is that the labor markets across all segments of the film industry

[5] NAFTA Annex I, Mexico, reads: "Thirty percent of the screen time of every theater, assessed on an annual basis, may be reserved for films produced by Mexican persons either within or outside the territory of Mexico." The vague "may" was used instead of "should" or "shall," the latter term being the only one implying a hard commitment in international law. For further details, see Foreign Trade Information System (http://www.sice.oas.org/Trade/NAFTA/anx1amex.asp).

were dominated by powerful trade unions—including at the level of film directors. Combined, these two factors played the role of a de facto import quota: foreign films could not be exhibited in Mexican movie theaters without the agreement of state-owned distribution companies or the permission from the powerful trade unions (Paxman 2018). These internal barriers have been much more detrimental to the Mexican film industry than the screen quota per se.

As was so often the case during the 1980s, privatization was seen as the silver bullet that could eliminate these internal barriers in one shot. In 1988, the Mexican government initiated a program for the privatization of the film industry, which indeed led to positive effects in the distribution and exhibition segments of the Mexican film market although the beneficiaries have been mostly US films, not Mexican. As illustrated by Fig. 5, the number of overall admissions in the late 2010s is four to five times the number in the mid-1990s. For 2019, the total box office revenues in Mexico amounted to USD 1 billion, making it the eighth largest film market in the world.

A very different picture emerges with the production segment. Figure 5 shows that during the 2000s admissions for Mexican films have remained at a very low level. Their share in overall admissions has never

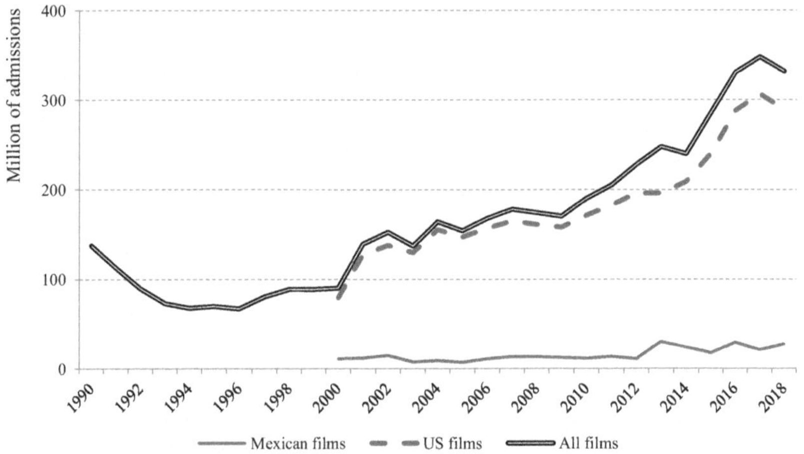

Fig. 5 The Mexican film market (since 1990) (*Sources* Piva et al. [2011] for 1980–1999; CNC (various issues) for years 2000–2018)

(but for one year) been larger than 10% which is a much lower share than the 50–65% observed in Korea since 2000. Another way to stress this sharp contrast is to note that in 2018, the average box office revenue per capita for domestic films amounted to USD 0.55 (55 US cents) in Mexico, compared to USD 16 in Korea.

What accounts for this specific failure brought on by Mexico's policies to open up its film market? Paradoxically, the way the privatization process was conceived and implemented bears a large responsibility for this outcome. More precisely, it has prevented the development of vertically integrated Mexican film companies that could have been comparable to Korea's *chaebols*. The Mexican government has had no difficulty to find private companies eager to run distribution networks and movie theaters because these firms could expect rapid and relatively stable profits by importing attractive US films and exhibiting them in their renovated movie theaters. However, these companies have not been so eager to invest in the much riskier film production segment. This situation was the exact opposite of the Korean case where the leading role in market restructuring was played by the *chaebols* with their vertically integrated structure and their increasingly efficient production units. Ironically, the privatization process in Mexico led to a situation reminiscent of the one prevailing in the 1960s where an American-owned distribution company—the Jenkins Group—was notorious for its anti-competitive behavior and its strategy of exhibiting big-budget US films while producing cheap but much less attractive Mexican films (Paxman 2018).

Finally, the situation in Mexico was particularly difficult due to two self-reinforcing factors. First, the production segment in Mexico was plagued by long-lasting internal political and ideological fights between established film directors and promising younger filmmakers which led to an increasingly ossified Mexican film industry. Second, there were no Mexican companies that were eager to enter the film market and/or took the lead in restructuring the film business with an entrepreneurial spirit like Samsung or Lotte in Korea.

To conclude, the crucial lesson from comparing Mexico and Korea is the complementarity between a strong film industrial basis and the dynamic cultural creativity and diversity in the film sector. Industry and art should not be artificially opposed to one another. This is best illustrated by the fact that once the markets opened in Mexico and Korea, a number of promising young directors have emerged in both countries. However, prominent Mexican directors such as Alfonso Cuarón, Alejandro G. Iñárritu, and Guillermo del Toro were unable to make their voices heard in Mexico and ultimately had to leave the country for Hollywood, depriving the Mexican film industry of its key cultural assets. By contrast, many prominent Korean filmmakers, such as Bong Joon-ho, Kang Je-gyu, Lee Joon-ik, or Park Chan-wook, have been able to work with Korean film companies which have contributed to cultural creativity and diversity at home. This aspect was all the more important for Korean filmmakers who had to face language and distance barriers much greater than their Mexican counterparts.

5.4 *Giving Up: The Return to Subsidies*

The persistent lack of entrepreneurship in the film industry induced the Mexican government to quickly resort again to the use of the final remaining instrument of protection inherited from the 1940s: subsidies to filmmakers. In 1942, the Mexican government established the National Film Bank as the agency to provide loans to the film industry at special interest rates—hence they were de facto subsidies. As shown in Fig. 4, the Mexican government reactivated this old policy in the early 2000s as part of despaired efforts to boost domestic production. However, as shown by Fig. 5, this policy has not been any more successful than it was during the period from 1960 to 1999: the increasing number of subsidized films did not have a notable impact on admissions to Mexican films.

The return to subsidies stands in contrast to Korea's film policies. As documented in more detail in Chapter 4, one of the main characteristics of the Korean government's policy has been the very low level of subsidies granted to the domestic film industry from the 1990s to the late 2000s, that is, throughout the hardest period of industrial reorganization in the Korean film industry.

6 Conclusion

First of all, this chapter has provided a fresh perspective on the complex relations between diplomacy and economics. At first glance, the two Korea-US Film Agreements would seem to have represented a severe diplomatic setback for Korea as it was forced to accept US conditions on the opening of its film market. However, the outcome of these Agreements has turned out to be the source for a major Korean economic success story as the film companies and the government have implemented complementary strategies, the "golden duo," capable of taking on the challenges presented by the elimination of the import quota. At the same time, these Agreements have resulted in a disappointing outcome for the Hollywood studios who overestimated the attractiveness of their movies in the open Korean market. In short, diplomacy and economics rarely obey the same logic.

Second, this chapter has stressed that success requires a subtle articulation of the domestic strategies between the government and film companies. The government sets the broad economic environment promoting a sound and stable legal regime that is required by film companies. On this basis, film companies develop their business strategies, in particular they take the high risks inherent with this industry. If one of these two pillars takes on a role that is either too big or too small, then the whole national film industry will endure economic hardships and eventually will have a limited impact on cultural diversity.

From a state policy perspective, this chapter has provided three main lessons. First, the government should clearly show its intent to respect the market opening that it has agreed to. An easy way to achieve this goal is to be credibly bound by an international agreement. In this respect, it is fair to say that the Korea-US Film Agreements did not leave much choice for the Korean government: the import quota had to be eliminated or there was the very high risk of US retaliation in other valuable sectors of the Korean economy. Second, the government should avoid adopting alternative measures of protection that would unravel—indirectly but irremediably—the impact of the initial market opening. To some extent, the Korean government has been politically prudent in this regard since it has kept in place the screen quota when it eliminated the import quota. Fortunately, the screen quota, which was wrongly believed to be a strong safeguard in the late 1980s, has in fact been an ineffective measure of protection. In the case of Korea, it has had little if any effect at all. That said, the Korean government has refrained from using other "escape" clauses that international trade law would have permitted in order to re-protect its film market.

Finally—and this is by far the most delicate and complex aspect in opening a film market—the government has to take into consideration the adequacy between the industrial structure of its film industry and the goals of liberalization that it supports. In this regard, it should be asked about how involved the government should be in the film industry.

Should the government pursue the limited goal of making more efficient only the segments of distribution and exhibition of films? Or should it also promote the emergence of a creative domestic film production segment? The latter goal is much more ambitious and difficult to achieve since it relies largely on the existence of dynamic firms ready to take risks in the domestic film market. Hence it may well be beyond the reach of governments for both economic and cultural reasons.

From the perspective of the film companies, the key point has been their ability to learn how to run an efficient business and to produce attractive films in a more open film market. These conditions have been hard to achieve without a renewal of the film companies operating previously in a protected market. By definition, the incumbent firms have not been exposed to foreign competition, hence are likely to have lost touch with "up-to-date" business practices. A fascinating lesson from the Korean case has been that this renewal process can involve domestic firms from other industries initially far away from the film industry. This is the opposite of the views of most people—from the industry as well as from the public at large: opening a market is often seen as the fact that existing domestic firms have to leave the market. The opening of the Korean film market has shown a much more complex flow among Korean firms: some have had to leave, other have been attracted to enter.

Another surprising lesson has been that foreign film companies must adjust to a more open market regardless of whether they enjoyed success before the opening. The Korean case has illustrated clearly the costly consequences brought on by the overly optimistic expectations among the Hollywood studios on their sales in Korea after the Film Agreements came into effect. Opening a market means that the market will change for "all" the existing participants, both domestic and foreign. In short, market opening generates a dynamic process: by creating more competitive domestic films, it challenges foreign incumbents.

Finally, from an international perspective, the stark contrast between the opening of the Korean and Mexican film markets has underlined the fact that concluding trade agreements—be it enthusiastically (Mexico) or reluctantly (Korea)—provide only opportunities. They do not guarantee outcomes. The role of businesses and governments is precisely to morph these opportunities into concrete results—successes if businesses and governments adopt sound strategies and policies, failures if they do not. This essential point is too often forgotten—leading to the excessive importance given to trade agreements per se, and to a serious oversight of the policies that accompany these agreements. This point features in the next chapter which is devoted to the preferential trade agreements in the film industry negotiated and concluded in the late 2000s and early 2010s.

References

Centre national du cinéma et de l'image animée (CNC). Various issues, *Bilan*. https://www.cnc.fr/cinema/etudes-et-rapports/bilans/.

De Vany, A. 2004. *Hollywood Economics: How Extreme Uncertainty Shapes the Film Industry*. New York: Routledge.

Gomez G.R. 2006. *El Impacto del Tratado de Libre Comercio de America del Norte (TCLAN) en la indutria audivisual mxicana (1994–2002)*. Thesis (PhD), Univrsidad Autonoma de Barcelona.

Hayward, S. 2005. *French National Cinema*. London and New York: Routledge.

Korea Box-Office Information System (KOBIS). https://www.kobis.or.kr/kobis/business/main/main.do.

Larroa, A., and R.G. Garcia. 2011. Analysis of the Film Production District in Mexico City. *International Journal of Communication* 5: 844–874.

Lee, K. 2008. 'The Little State Department': Hollywood and the MPAA's Influence on U.S. Trade Relations. *Northwestern Journal of International Law and Business* 28 (2): 371–397.

Ley federal de cinematografia. 2020. *Nueva ley publicada en el diario oficial de la federación el 29 de diciembre de 1992*. http://www.diputados.gob.mx/LeyesBiblio/pdf/103_061120.pdf.

Parc, J. 2014. *An Eclectic Approach to Enhancing the Competitive Advantage of Nations: Analyzing the Success Factors of East Asian Economies with a Focus on the Development of South Korea*. Thesis (PhD), Seoul National University and Université Paris Sorbonne.

Parc, J. 2017. The Effects of Protection in Cultural Industries: The Case of the Korean Film Policies. *International Journal of Cultural Policy* 23 (5): 618–633.

Parc, J. 2018. Evaluating the Effects of Protectionism on the Film Industry: A Case Study Analysis of Korea. In *Handbook of State Aid for Film*, ed. P. Murschetz, R. Teichmann, and M. Karmasin, 349–366. Springer, Cham: Switzerland.

Parc, J. 2020. Between State-led and Corporation-led Co-Productions: How Has Film Co-Production Been Exploited by States in Europe. *Innovation: The European Journal of Social Science Research* 33 (4): 442–458.

Parc, J. 2021. Business Integration and its Impact on Film Industry: The Case of Korean Film Policies from the 1960s until the Present. *Business History* 63 (5): 850–867.

Paxman, A. 2018. Who Killed the Mexican Film Industry? The Decline of the Golden Age, 1946–1960. *Estudios Interdisciplinarios De América Latina Y El Caribe* 29 (1): 9–33. http://eial.tau.ac.il/index.php/eial/article/view/1556.

Piva, J., R. Perez, C. Perez, and V. Montoya. 2011. *The Mexican Film Industry and Its Participation in the Global Value Chain*. United Nations, Mexico City. https://repositorio.cepal.org/bitstream/handle/11362/4916/1/S2011039_en.pdf.

Russel, M.J. 2008. *Pop Goes Korea: Behind the Revolution in Movies, Music and Internet Culture* . Berkeley, CA: Stone Bridge Press.

Valenti, J. 2007. *This Time, This Place. My Life in War, the White House, and Hollywood*. New York: Three Rivers Press.

CHAPTER 3

From the Screen Quota to Cultural Cooperation: Preferential Trade Agreements

After a long and turbulent period at the box office, the Korean film industry began to enjoy incredible success throughout the first half of the 2000s. During this period, every year witnessed the release of several local blockbusters, most of which earned widespread acclaim in Asia, notably in China, Japan, and Southeast Asian countries. Yet anytime a film flopped, speculation would mount as to whether or not this signaled the beginning of a decline. This became very evident when Korean films did indeed experience a sudden sharp fall in admissions following the screen quota cut in 2006, which seemed to prove that this policy instrument was essential for the health of the Korean film industry. With such perceived vulnerability, critics were quick to claim that the Korean film industry's success was just a flash in the pan. However, they had jumped the gun as this downfall was quickly followed by a rebound from 2009 that ushered in a new period of growth as the Korean film industry would go on to outperform its rivals for the next decade.

These fears among Korean observers toward their film industry cannot be fully understood without taking into consideration the context of the international environment at the time. Korea was hit badly by the Asian financial crisis in 1997–1998, which triggered its worst recession since the Korean War in the early 1950s. A year later, the Korean economy was back on track; but after such a huge shock, domestic confidence was

J. Parc and P. A. Messerlin, *The Untold Story of the Korean Film Industry*, Cultural Economics & the Creative Economy,
https://doi.org/10.1007/978-3-030-80342-1_3

limited, all the more because the post-1999 annual domestic growth rate had declined to around 5% in the 2000s and then to 3% in the 2010s. Although this was highly enviable by European standards, it was a far cry from the average annual growth rate in both the 1980s (9%) and the 1990s (7%).

Amplifying these profound domestic changes, the open multilateral trade environment to which Korea's economic success owes so much began to face its own difficulties. In 1994, the outcome of the Uruguay Round was heralded as a successful breakthrough for international trade as it led to the establishment of the ambitious World Trade Organization (WTO). But this forum quickly went on to fuel a number of bitter conflicts toward the late 1990s, such as the dispute over whether developing countries could gain easy access to generic drugs. This then had the knock-on effect of reopening the fresh and profound scar left by the failure to get an agreement on the film industry during the Uruguay Round.

Such trade disputes generated rising skepticism on both sides of the Atlantic toward the potential benefits of globalization throughout the 2000s. Although the support for multilateralism and globalization remained strong in the Asia Pacific region, the absence of strong political will in the United States (US) and the European Union (EU) was enough to lead to the de facto collapse of the Doha Round in 2005. With China's growing influence in the WTO from the mid-2000s, the US responded by undertaking an irreversible shift from its traditional benevolent multilateral approach to a bilateral one based on preferential trade agreements (PTAs) where it could use its maximum leverage when negotiating with each partner. The EU and the other developed countries followed this path.

This transformation of the global trade architecture in the early 2000s forced Korea to consider how to change its trade strategy given that it was one of the very few countries that had not yet concluded a single PTA by this point. Once it had made the decision to pursue a PTA policy in 2002, Korea progressed at an amazing speed. By the early 2010s, it had reached "deep and comprehensive" agreements with both the EU and the US—a goal achieved by very few countries still today. In each of these negotiations, the Korean film industry was one of the key issues—as best illustrated by the US pushing to lift the Korean screen quota as a non-negotiable condition for opening talks on the Korea-US Free Trade Agreement (hereafter KORUS FTA). At the same time, Korea entered into negotiations on the Korea-EU Free Trade Agreement (hereafter KOREU FTA) where it had to work out provisions—the so-called Protocol on Cultural Cooperation—on the film industry that needed to be radically different from the one in the KORUS FTA. This was necessary because the EU was adamantly opposed to any outcome that would allow easier access to its film markets—the exact opposite of the US negotiating precondition. Since then, most of Korea's PTAs have provisions on the film industry including similar "protocols" with countries that have large film markets. This chapter explores how Korea has been able to successfully find its way amidst these divergent requests from its powerful trading partners.

1 Facing a New World: US Pressures on Film Markets Opening

Since the 2000s, a curious and somewhat contradictory picture has emerged with the US film industry. On the one hand, Hollywood's enduring dominance seems more robust than ever as best illustrated by its huge recent inroads into the Chinese market. Yet on the other hand, the US government has adopted an unyielding approach toward opening foreign markets by pursuing face-to-face bilateral PTAs where it held the advantage. The following section outlines the major factors that explain this contrast between a flourishing business and a "tough" trade policy.

1.1 US Disappointment Over its Past Film Policies

Since the mid-1990s, US businesses and governments have been confronted by an increasingly more complex world where a larger number of competitors have rapidly emerged. This evolution which is still going on today has led to the wide-spread conviction in the US that they "gave away trade concessions and collected few in return" (Bhagwati 1993). Such a disappointment over its previous trade policies has prompted a US return to a more mercantilist approach after the mid-1990s.

Until this change in attitude, Washington had by and large pursued a "benevolent" attitude toward trade negotiations. In 1947, the US conceived the General Agreement on Tariffs and Trade (GATT) as a multilateral forum—renouncing by the same token the pre-World War II system of bilateral deals which would have actually benefitted the US given its superior negotiating power. Still, it should be understood that by most judgments, this benevolent approach has been fruitful for the US as well as for the rest of the world. Indeed, until the mid-1990s, the US rarely, and somewhat wisely, used its leverage in bilateral deals. It targeted foreign barriers that prevented the access of US products to overseas markets but that were also clearly detrimental to the welfare of its partners. The best illustration in this regard is the Korea-US Film Agreements. As shown in Chapter 2, the elimination of the import quota has had a huge positive impact on the welfare of Korean moviegoers: within fifteen years (1988–2003), it boosted both the revenues of the Korean and the US films in Korea—by eight and two times more than before, respectively.

Since its shift to a trade policy increasingly dominated by PTAs, the US has progressively lost the view of the mutual benefits from trade liberalization. With such a narrower view, Washington has increasingly focused on economic indicators which are easy to misinterpret, such as the market share of US films in Korea that has declined from roughly 77% in 1988 to 46% in 2003. As dramatic as these figures may seem, they do not take into consideration the huge growth of the whole Korean film market where US film revenues have actually increased from US 186 million in 1988 to US 396 million in 2003 (in constant 2018 USD). This biased presentation was enough to set the US film industry and the US government on a course toward seeking to eliminate the Korean screen quota, a political and economic mistake as analyzed below.

The attempt by the US to eliminate foreign barriers on a bilateral basis before the 2000s has not been limited to Korea. It also targeted its neighbors Canada and Mexico with the North American Free Trade Agreement (NAFTA) that has generated a degree of disappointment in the US film industry. In particular, the Hollywood studios were utterly frustrated by the fact that the US government recognized the principle of "cultural exemption" tabled by Canada in NAFTA, hence it did not provide them with increased access to the Canadian film market. What the studios had failed to recognize though was the fact that with the conclusion of NAFTA, they enjoyed more privileged access to the Canadian markets when compared to those available to non-US film companies, as illustrated by the Polygram case.[1] Meanwhile, the Hollywood studios kept

[1] In 1988, a new Canadian law restricted foreign investment in the local film distribution sector to non-Canadian investors that either possess worldwide distribution rights or

quiet about the fact that Mexico was unable to build up a film production segment comparable to the one prospering in Korea, leaving a huge share of the Mexican film market to US films (see Chapter 2). The overall lesson that the US film industry has drawn from these two NAFTA partners is that it pays to be aggressive in bilateral negotiations—and the more aggressive, the better.

The US shift away from multilateralism toward bilateralism became well entrenched after Washington failed to open up the global audiovisual markets at the end of the Uruguay Round. Most studies explain this failure as caused by international tensions between the US and the EU. Such perspectives though ignore one additional—but key—aspect: the US film industry had a hard time to decide upon its own negotiating priorities during the Uruguay Round for reasons that will be explained in detail later. This struggle left the US government with no clear guidelines on what Hollywood actually wanted. In the complex world of multilateral negotiations involving a host of goods and services, it is critical that national goals are clearly defined and prioritized at the earliest stages to ensure success. The hesitation shown by Hollywood opened the door toward the erratic negotiating positions shown by the US government which was then carefully exploited by the "anti-American" camp among some EU film industries—with strong support from a few corners of the Korean film industry.

1.2 *Facing Unprecedented Challenges*

Since the early 2000s, the US film industry has been confronted by a new challenge: the *relative* shrinking of its domestic film market over the long term compared to the rest of the world (see Chapter 1). From a purely economic point of view, such a decrease is not necessarily bad news: rapid growth in other countries around the world can be a source of profitable opportunities for the Hollywood giants—as best illustrated by the amazing growth of their box office revenues in China since the 2000s.

have contributed to more than fifty percent of the production costs of the films to be distributed. Thanks to NAFTA, this law did not prevent the US studios from building up their business in Canada on the basis of the less restrictive laws in force before 1988. These studios thus enjoyed preferential access to the Canadian market compared to film companies trying to enter the Canadian market after 1988, such as the British-Dutch company Polygram (Fong 1997).

However, focusing on this economic aspect ignores broader political, social, and psychological effects and reactions.

It is important to understand the true scale of the US film industry's decline in relative terms if one wants to take into consideration these reactions. First, the sheer size of the long-term changes in the global film markets can be captured by comparing the box office revenues and admissions in markets around the world to those in the US domestic market—that is, by calculating the *relative* evolution of the US box office revenues and admissions in the overseas markets compared to those in the US domestic market.

These calculations are presented in Fig. 1 which relies upon ten countries: the US and the nine other largest markets (China, France, Germany, Italy, Japan, Korea, Mexico, Spain, and the UK) covered in this book. Altogether, the US and these nine markets represent 73% of the estimated global box office revenues in 2018. Figure 1 shows two distinct comparisons for admissions and for box office revenues: the US with respect to its counterparts excluding China with dotted lines and the US with respect to the other countries including China with solid lines.

In Fig. 1, it is clearly noticeable that the US film industry has become a "diminished giant" in relative terms—again in absolute values, it remains the largest industry in the world. Focusing first on the admissions excluding China, the US film market was 1.6 times larger than the total admissions of eight other markets in 1995, but it becomes only 0.9 times of today's total admissions (see the line for Admissions of 8 on the right axis). This relative shrinking of the US market is vastly amplified when one adds China: then the relative size of the US market in 2018 is roughly 0.4 times the size of the combined nine markets in 2002 (see the line for Admission of 9 on the right axis).

Furthermore, Fig. 1 provides a sense of the increased dependency of the US film industry upon the preferences among foreign audiences. It shows the relative evolution of the box office revenues generated by US films in the domestic market and in foreign markets (see the lines for Revenues of 8 and Revenues of 9 at the left vertical axis). When one excludes China and focuses on the traditional export markets for US films, the box office revenues that they have earned in these markets compared to those collected in the domestic market are declining: their 1993–1995 peak is followed by a declining trend, albeit with some ups and downs. They amount to roughly 55% in 2018, compared to their 1993 peak of 70%.

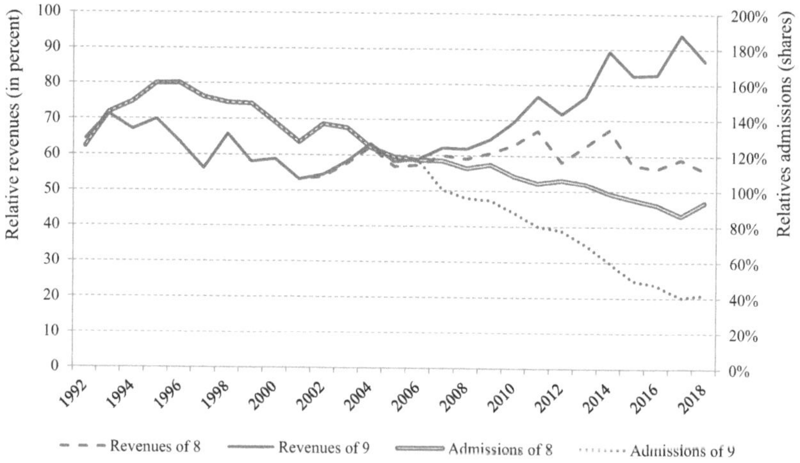

Fig. 1 Comparing the US and the other largest markets (*Notes* Admissions are for all films [foreign and domestic] shown in the countries covered; the ratios of the US compared to the eight or nine other countries are shown on the right axis; Revenues are those for US films only; the shares of the US market in the eight or nine other markets are shown on the left axis; "8" refers to data without China (France, Germany, Italy, Japan, Korea, Mexico, Spain, and UK) and "9" to data with China [only after 2002], respectively; The lines for China only begin in 2002 because data on the Chinese film market before this year are not robust enough. *Sources* Authors' calculations based on MPA [various issues] for US, CNC [various issues], KOFIC [various issues], MPPAJ [various issues])

By contrast, when one includes China, the box office revenues for Hollywood films in the foreign markets have increased from 60% to more than 80% between 2002 and 2018 (China's share before 2002 is barely noticeable). This result highlights the increasing dependency of the US film industry upon Chinese demand, a situation which is likely to induce a tougher position from Washington in its negotiations with Beijing to open its market further as well as with other countries like Korea to offset such dependency on China.

The magnitude of these evolutions depends very much on what happens in the rest of the world. As Fig. 1 presents relative evolutions, it should be carefully interpreted. The lines in Fig. 1 do not mean that the US film market per se is diminishing or declining, but it signifies the noticeable increase of the other markets compared to the US one.

These evolutions have an important corollary: they show the potential of the greater benefits that the US film industry can obtain from the larger overseas markets; in fact, the bigger these evolutions, the more potential gains there will be. In other words, by exporting more films to increasingly larger (in relative terms) markets in other countries, the US film industry can boost its revenues while maintaining its own so far undisputed dominance in its domestic market.

1.3 An Increasingly Complex Industry

These changes have put Hollywood firmly behind the US government's shift toward bilateral trade agreements where it can exert its maximum negotiating power and leverage. The US has pushed a number of countries, particularly European countries as well as Canada and Mexico, to open their markets more toward Hollywood films, yet the success of the US strategy has been uneven, to say the least. How has such an outcome emerged?

When negotiating on a given topic, a government must first define a clear goal and outline a coherent strategy if it wishes to negotiate a successful agreement with its trade partners. This condition largely depends on whether a government can rely upon robust support from among its domestic industry. This in turn requires that this industry is capable of collectively defining a realistic outcome it would be happy with, and to adjust its target and strategy if needed during the process of negotiations. At a first glance, the presence of the Motion Picture Association (MPA) with only a handful of members—the six large Hollywood studios—would suggest the existence of a carefully prepared strategy for the US film industry to pursue. The reality though is different because over the years the MPA membership has represented widely different interests—from the film industry to home entertainment as can be seen in Fig. 2, which illustrates the profound transformations on the basis of the MPA's revenues.

Divisions among the MPA members were not uncommon before the 1990s. As mentioned in Chapter 2, Korea witnessed such a case in 1988 when the MPA members did not show unified support for a tougher stance during negotiations for the second Korea-US Film Agreements. A few years later, during the most critical years of negotiations for the Uruguay Round (1990–1993), Korea and the other film-producing countries could again measure the extent to which the MPA members were

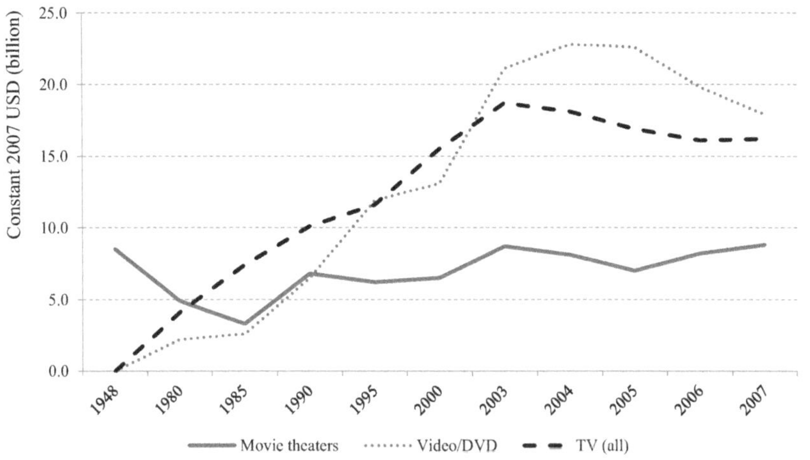

Fig. 2 The MPA revenues: From film industry to home entertainment (*Source* Epstein [2012, p. 100]; based on worldwide MPA studios receipts)

unprepared and divided.[2] The US came very much unrehearsed to the negotiating table, thus generating delays, hesitations, and turnarounds as described in depth by Grantham (2003, pp. 106–114). The overall result was that the WTO negotiations on market access for the whole audiovisual sector (film and TV) were de facto set aside.

This dramatic, yet often overlooked, precedent for the US film industry has triggered deep skepticism in the US on the value of multilateral negotiations. That said, in the context of this book, it also raises the following question for the future. Could one assume that the Hollywood studios will be united on the critical issues that are at the heart of future international negotiations in cultural industries: the fight against piracy, unrestricted market access, and a stronger control on subsidies? What follows suggests reasons that cast doubt on the ability of the MPA to adopt a common position.

The fight against piracy has probably been one of the most prominent topics for US trade officials to pursue when negotiating PTAs. Yet this

[2] Grantham, B. (2003) also documents similar problems on the EU side, with deep disagreements among EU Members (and even within some EU member states, such as France) on the exact intent and content of the Directive Television without Frontiers.

sacrosanct element has shown surprising cracks from within the US film industry itself which is best illustrated by the "screeners" issue reported by the MPA President Jack Valenti in his memoirs (Valenti 2007, p. 393). Screeners are copies of films that are regarded as having reasonable hope to be nominated for the Academy Awards. Every year, in the run up to the Awards, US studios send out screeners to a large number of recipients in the US and UK film industries.[3] During Valenti's time in charge, his staff at the MPA anti-piracy unit discovered that a large portion of these screeners had in fact fallen into the hands of "pirates" who sold them on the illegal markets as soon as the Awards winners were known. To Valenti's horror, these pirates were in fact US industry insiders: they were so powerful and this practice so well entrenched that, to his great regret, Valenti could not really address this problem.

The other top issue for US audiovisual companies is to gain better access to markets around the world, an important aspect since they are the world's largest exporters. The increasingly wide range of industrial interests depicted in Fig. 2 with the emergence of home entertainment in the 1980s, has profoundly reshaped the balance between the US film and TV industries, making it more difficult for the US government to establish the best balance among the interests of these two sectors during international negotiations. US trade negotiators have had to split their limited negotiating capital available for the whole audiovisual sector on two different agendas, movie theaters, and home entertainment—leading to a dispersion of the efforts by US economic diplomacy. This is best illustrated by the negotiations of the KORUS FTA that will be explained in more detail later. Such situations are likely to reemerge in the near future. Given the admission of Netflix to the MPA in January 2019 following Disney's acquisition of 20th Century Fox, there is likely to be an increase in the heterogeneity of interests among the various MPA members. However, this divergence will decline as and when all the MPA members will adopt a more similar business model.

[3] The recipients of the screeners were typically academy members, the special nominating committees of the Screen Actors Guild, the Directors Guild of America, the Writers Guild of America, the Hollywood Foreign Press Association, the British Academy of Film and Television Arts, independent filmmakers, and movie critics (Valenti 2007, p. 194).

1.4 An Important Caveat from an Economic Perspective

When exploring the economic consequences of the US shift to bilateral agreements, it is important to clarify the terminology used in this chapter. The official title used in all bilateral agreements that are examined here is "Free Trade Agreement (FTA)." While this term conveys a sense of political respectability, economically it is profoundly misleading. Opening one's markets to a partner country but not to the rest of the world is far from welfare-improving in terms of an economic perspective, hence this book elects to use the more accurate term of "preferential trade agreements (PTAs)."

Contrary to multilateral agreements, such as those concluded at the WTO forum, PTAs can be welfare-deteriorating when they favor the exports of a partner who is an inefficient producer of the good or service in question relative to other countries in the world. For instance, if Country A has a PTA with Country B that produces few attractive films while still discriminating against films from other countries, then the audiences in Country A will have their choices limited to the relatively unattractive titles imported from Country B. This is the opposite of a situation without any import restrictions where audiences can choose from the most attractive films on offer from all countries. Such an outcome explains the skeptical tone expressed in the literature regarding the existing provisions on audio-visuals in the PTAs shown in Box 1.

Box 1 The Value of Provisions on Audio-Visuals Within the PTAs: A Skeptical Tone

The literature examining the "economic value" of provisions on audio-visuals within PTAs can be split into two main groups. The first focuses on the analysis of the commitments taken by the signatories. This group expresses skepticism on the capacity of PTAs to bring about tangible results in the audio-visual sector when compared to those possibilities in the multilateral context (Bernier 2004; Pauwels and Loisen 2003; Roy et al. 2007). At first glance, this is surprising as these studies concentrate on PTAs concluded by the US, which has been leading the way to pressure countries for further market opening (Chase 2018; Gagné 2016; Roy 2008). The bleak conclusion of these studies is based on the observation that the audio-visual provisions in most of the PTAs covered remain limited in coverage and in the depth of legally-binding commitments. They also believe that PTAs with more meaningful commitments have usually resulted in aligning the laws and regulations of the partner country to US regulations. However, these studies show that this alignment has been voluntarily chosen by US partners who either have a limited interest and/or knowledge of the issues at stake, or are motivated by political interests, such as Australia who negotiated its PTA with the US during the Iraq War.

The second group of studies focuses on the economic and political forces at work in both countries during the process of negotiations. These studies concentrate on one or two negotiating countries: the US with Canada (Acheson and Maule 1999), the EU (Grantham 2003), France (Buchsbaume 2017), or Korea (Parc 2017, 2018, 2021; Yecies and Shim 2016). They reveal the many hesitations due to the internal divisions within the negotiating countries in question and explore the conflicts among their various domestic players in the film industry. This view echoes the analysis undertaken in the previous chapter on the conflicting interests among Korean firms with respect to the Korea-US Film Agreements. Moreover, this approach emphasizes changes among the domestic balance of forces within a film industry which can be deep and fast—leaving the slow process of negotiations out of touch with the economic reality of the country and/or of its film industry, hence likely to fail.

The capacity for PTAs to be detrimental to the welfare of the audience should not be understated in the case of films. This is because films are not standardized goods: each film is unique—hence they vary enormously in terms of attractiveness even if this country is seen as a producer of good films. To sum up, from an economic perspective, there is a crucial difference to be made between "preferential trade agreements" (PTAs) and "free trade agreements" (FTAs). In this book, PTA is considered as the more appropriate term as it does not prejudge the economic consequences of the preferential treatment on the welfare of moviegoers.

2 The Korea-US Agreement and the Screen Quota

In 1998, Korea approached the US about the possibility for negotiating a "bilateral investment treaty (BIT)." This initiative was an effort to restore the credibility of the Korean economy which had been heavily disrupted by the 1997 Asian Financial Crisis. At that time, countries were often using trade agreements with foreign countries as a way to buttress their own domestic reforms—as shown by Mexico with NAFTA (see Chapter 2). If the penalties associated with breaking the provisions of a treaty are stiff, it provides the perfect excuse for a government to state that its hands are tied. The US with its huge market size and strong focus on legal commitments was considered at this time by many countries as the most credible partner to lock their domestic reforms with.

The preliminary BIT discussions between US and Korean negotiators began immediately with the US request for the elimination of the Korean "screen quota." With no compromise shown by either side on this issue, the entire BIT talks soon collapsed in 2001. This aspect underlines the continued critical importance of the film issue in the economic relations between the two countries (Lee 2013, p.100). Initially, the Korean government was ready to abolish the quota, but the domestic film industry expressed such hostility that it derailed the talks. As a compromise, the government suggested a reduction of its screen quota instead of abolishing it, but it did not work in this instance.

It is important here to consider the context facing the Korean film industry at the time. The success and implications of the romantic comedy *Marriage Story* released in 1992—the first Korean film that copied the Hollywood studio's film production system—were only tentatively being felt. At this stage, it was still too early for the Korean film industry to recognize with confidence that it could produce attractive films on a regular basis using this formula. Under these circumstances, abandoning the screen quota only a decade or so after the import quota elimination was perceived by many domestic players in the film industry as too risky.

The situation remained quiet until February 2006 when the US and Korea announced the launch of the KORUS FTA that would go far beyond the usual tariff issues and would cover a wide scope of products, services, and other issues such as intellectual property rights. In fact, the process for negotiations began much earlier—specifically, in November 2004 when Korea and the US arranged a "joint feasibility study group" for such an agreement. It was during this early stage that the issue of the film industry was again placed on the table by US negotiators who insisted that Korea should abolish its screen quota prior to the commencement of formal negotiations on the FTA per se. In other words, it was again a non-negotiable precondition imposed on Korea.

In contrast to the previous rounds of negotiations on its film industries, Korea's negotiating position had markedly improved due to several factors. First, President Roh Moo-hyun knew what he wanted—a broad "free-trade pact" with the US—and his government spent the first two months of 2006 criticizing the Korean film industry for being "unduly self-serving" (Moon 2006). Second, the Korean film industry was in a stronger position than it was during the BIT negotiations. Since 1999, it had demonstrated its capacity to regularly produce blockbusters and enjoyed a domestic market share that is more than 40% (corresponding to the ratio of 146 days in a whole year) without having to rely upon an import quota. Last but not least, the US argument for cutting the screen quota was presented in a much less convincing way than when it sought to eliminate the import quota twenty years before. The US delegation led by Valenti came to Seoul with obsolete statistics as shown by the US State Department archives (Yeceis 2007)—and no robust economic rationale—contrary to what happened for the Korea-US Film Agreements. All of these factors allowed President Roh to give his personal word to the US government on cutting the quota by half while gaining some respite before making his commitment publicly known and then implementing it in July 2006 (Chang 2014; Moon 2006).

Indeed, the insistence of the US government and Hollywood studios on lifting the Korean screen quota is puzzling. The series of Korean mega-hits between 1999 and 2006–2007 clearly showed that reducing or eliminating the screen quota would be unlikely to improve the competitive position of US films in the Korean market. It was rather obvious that Korean films were firmly established in their domestic market, with a market share above 50–55% every year since 2001. This insistence on lifting the screen quota is even more intriguing when it is placed in the wider context of the ongoing negotiations between Korea and the US based on the same basic logic of give and take. In other words, the focus on the screen quota issue could have been a good excuse for Korea not to give in on another, possibly costlier, concession to the US.

Given these circumstances, it is important to scrutinize the US motives by presenting a brief economic analysis of the Korean screen quota and by analyzing the robustness of the US claims regarding the detrimental effect of the screen quota on US film exports to Korea during the late 1990s and early 2000s. This section then explores all the possible causes that can explain the sharp fall in the growth trajectory of the Korean film industry for the period 2007–2009, an outcome which was widely perceived in Korea as triggered by the quota cut.

2.1 *The Screen Quota: An Economic Analysis*

The Korean screen quota defines the minimum number of days that shall be reserved to show domestic films on screen at movie theaters including multiplexes (movie theaters with multiple screens) which appeared later. When introduced in 1966, the screen quota was set at 90 days per year but was increased six times over subsequent years before ending up at 146 days per year in 1985 during the negotiations on lifting the import quota. Since then, the screen quota was widely perceived in Korea as the ultimate "safeguard measure" to prevent a plunge in admissions under the pressure of foreign competition.

Such beliefs though are misguided as the screen quota only guarantees the number of days for which a Korean film can be screened, not the frequency of screenings within those set days. This loophole was used by Korean movie theaters who could reduce the number of screenings for Korean films while exhibiting foreign films as many times as possible. Associations among filmmakers—such as the Screen Quota Watch Group—sought to impose a strict implementation of the screen quota though without much success.

As a result, the effective impact of the Korean screen quota depends ultimately on the relative attractiveness of the domestic and foreign films exhibited. If the relative attractiveness of Korean films is poor, movie theaters will only show them once during off-peak hours in order to respect the screen quota while minimizing any possible losses. By contrast, in order to maximize profits, movie theaters will screen the relatively more attractive foreign films as many times possible per day, especially during the prime-time slots. By contrast, if the quality of Korean films is good, then movie theaters will show interest in screening them as many times as possible. In short, the Korean screen quota which is based on the number of days in a year has an obvious logical flaw, and it is thus odd that it has remained at the top of the US negotiating agenda with Korea up until 2006.

2.2 *The Screen Quota and the Bilateral Investment Treaty Negotiations*

The Korean request for talks on a Korea-US BIT offered the first opportunity for US negotiators to call for the existing screen quota to be cut as they believed it was limiting the box office revenues for US films in the Korean market. What follows seems to justify the US claims if one remains in the narrow time frame of the BIT talks (1998–2001). In order to rely on more robust grounds, however, Fig. 3 covers the period 1986–2006 which is longer than the period of the BIT talks—from the elimination of the import quota to the year where the screen quota was cut by half as the result of the KORUS FTA. The Korean screen quota is thus the same for the whole period covered by Fig. 3.

Figure 3 (right axis) shows that an increase in the market share (in terms of admissions) of US films in Korea since 1986 followed the lifting of the import quota. However, this trend reversed after 1993 though the whole period is under the unchanged screen quota regime. Figure 3 (left axis) also shows the box office revenues for both Korean and US films. The revenues of US films were on the increase until 1992, at which point they then entered a period of stagnation until 1999. Here they began to increase sharply until 2002 where they reached a new plateau. The revenues of Korean films were flat until 1998 before increasing sharply for the period up to 2006. In other words, it is the *relative* growth of the Korean and US box office revenues that explains the decline of the US market share—not the screen quota. Indeed, this relative growth is easy to interpret: Korean films exhibited during this period have been on average more attractive than US films in the Korean domestic market.

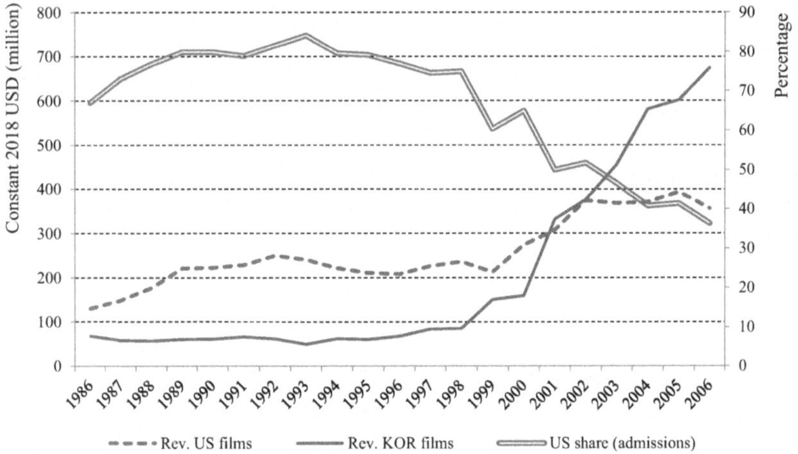

Fig. 3 The evolution of revenues in the Korean film market (1986–2006) (*Source* Authors' calculations based on KOFIC [various issues])

2.3 *The Screen Quota Cut: The Cause of the 2007–2009 Dip?*

In July 2006, the Korean government cut the screen quota by half—from 146 to 73 days per year. When the admissions and the box office revenues declined sharply in 2007 and 2008 (see Fig. 4), the general perception was that this dip was due to the screen quota cut. This conviction was reinforced by several studies released before 2007 which argued that the screen quota was responsible for the success of the Korean film industry (Lee 2005; Lee and Bae 2004). Yet these results are based on a period too short to take into consideration all of the consequences from the post-1988 industrial changes. By contrast, Fig. 4 based on Parc's (2017) analysis offers an overview of the main forces at stake over a long period. In order to provide a more robust explanation on what has happened, his analysis traces the evolution of four key variables: the number of admissions for Korean and foreign films, and the number of Korean and foreign films released.

Figure 4 shows that it is business as usual for all the variables except the admissions of Korean films: the trends among the three other lines do not show any notable changes until 2010. In his study, Parc interpreted this brief decline as the result of a shortage of lucrative and attractive Korean

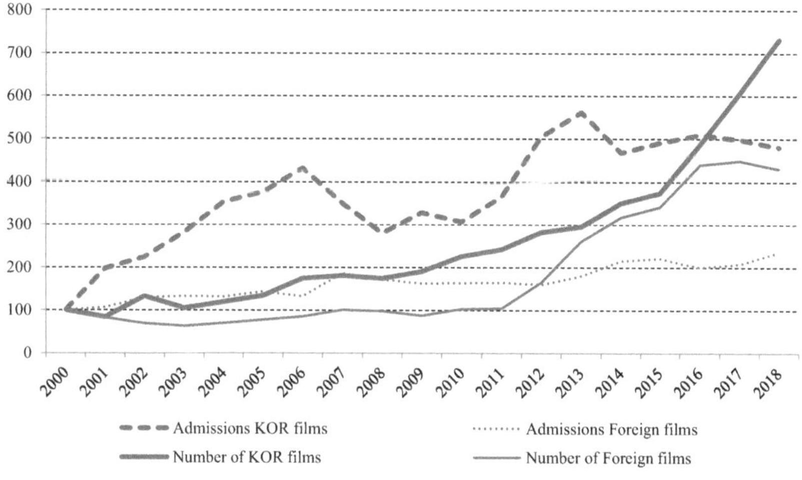

Fig. 4 A closer look: The Korean growth trajectory (2000–2018) (*Source* KOFIC [various issues] for 2014–2018 based on Parc [2014, 2017])

"blockbusters" to please domestic tastes. Despite no noticeable impact on the number of Korean films produced during the decade following 2006, there has been a sharp decline of average investments per film since 2003. As news about the negotiations on the elimination of the screen quota came out, Korean investors in the film industry tended to reduce their investment in order to minimize any possible risk. At this time, there were many films in the production pipeline that required a large amount of investment. Once there was more clarity over the situation, the Korean film industry was able to learn how to effectively utilize their limited investment, and then regained its previous growth trajectory up to 2013.

From a long-term perspective, Fig. 4 shows a clear change in the growth pattern of the film industry after 2014; the growth of admissions is somewhat stable while the growth in the number of Korean films increases, with a roughly similar evolution occurring for foreign films (see also Chapter 7).

2.4 KORUS FTA: The Broadcasting Sector

The above economic analysis of the screen quota suggests that US negotiators made a serious tactical mistake when they argued that this instrument was the key reason for Hollywood's difficulties in the Korean market. Cutting the screen quota down to 73 days per year was not the biggest or most urgent concession to ask from a Korean film industry that did not need such protection because of its sustained and robust growth. This misperception was not inconsequential: the US negotiators wasted a notable share of their overall bargaining chips when fighting for a non-negotiable cut of a screen quota that had little economic value. The fact that the Korean government had to deliver this cut as a precondition for negotiating the KORUS FTA—in fact five years before its final ratification—has increased its costs from a political perspective.

As a result, the US government was left with less negotiating capital to push for an opening of the other, more important, sector of interest for US companies: the broadcasting industry. Furthermore, the US strategy made it politically more difficult for the Korean government to sell to its public the prospect of opening up this sector. These converging forces explain the very limited Korean concessions in broadcasting shown in Table 1. If one looks at the opening of this sector to US investors, the market access concessions granted by Korea have been very marginal.

Table 1 KORUS FTA: Korean concessions in the film and broadcasting sectors

Genres	*Operators*	*Barriers*	*Old level*	*New level*
A. Film industry				
Movies		Screen quota	146 days	73 days
B. Broadcasting services				
Animation	Cable system operator, program provider, satellite broadcasting operator	Domestic content quota	35%	30%
	Terrestrial broadcasting	Domestic content quota	No change (45%)	
Movies	Cable system	Domestic	25%	20%
Movies	operator, program provider, satellite broadcasting operator	content quota		
	Terrestrial broadcasting	Domestic content quota	No change (25%)	
Animation & movies	Cable system operator, program provider, satellite broadcasting operator	Sub-quota on single country foreign content	60%	80%
Not MHN	Program provider	Maximum foreign ownership	0%	100%

Note MHN means multi-genre, home shopping, and news
Source Annex I Reservations: Maintenance and renewal of measures, Korea-US Free Trade Agreement

3 The Korea-EU Agreement: Between Ambition and Reality

Once Korea decided to adopt a systematic approach toward pursuing PTAs in the very early 2000s, the EU was one of its primary targets: it was the largest trading bloc in the world, the third most important outlet for Korean goods and services—and, last but not least, an opportunity "to simulate the negotiations with the US" as Korea's chief negotiator would remark (Lee 2013). Surprisingly though, when Seoul approached Brussels about initiating talks in 2003, it was turned down (Lee 2013, p. 17). The official reason given was that the EU had more urgent negotiating priorities: the WTO multilateral negotiations and a host of regional negotiations with Central European, Balkan, Mediterranean, and Mercosur countries. This reasoning may well be true, but it was a clear misjudgment of what could be realistically pursued with these negotiations. If one puts aside the excuse of talks with the Central European countries, all the others had achieved very little by the mid-2000s. Indeed, these failures forced the EU to rethink its own priorities in the pursuit of PTAs. In 2006, the EU Commission launched its "Global Europe" strategy which proposed a new list of countries that should be prioritized for its future trade deals. Korea was at the top of the list with India and the ASEAN countries. However, most of these potential negotiations encountered rapidly major obstacles—leaving Korea as the only candidate for a substantial and likely deal.

With Korea first in line, the EU was able to mobilize enough negotiators to match the large Korean team, making the KOREU FTA one of the most comprehensive trade agreements ever concluded by Brussels. For its part, Korea was in the enviable situation to benefit from some "rivalry" between the EU and the US on who would secure the more favorable deal. In fact, the KORUS FTA has largely shaped the broad content of the KOREU FTA—except in cases like the film industry—while the rapid progress in the KOREU FTA spurred on the completion of talks between the Korea and the US.

Regarding the film industry, these KOREU FTA negotiations did not witness any notable divergence of views among the two parties. Increased market access to the theatrical and entertainment markets was an issue that the EU routinely excludes from its trade negotiations as part of its policy of "cultural exception." In fact, this stance was broadly in line with Korea's own views and past actions in the United Nations Educational, Scientific and Cultural Organization (UNESCO)—the archrival of the WTO in cultural matters. At this multilateral forum, the Korean film industry lobby group "Coalition for Cultural Diversity in Moving Images" (CDMI) has been very active, especially during the screen quota negotiations with the US, urging UNESCO to remove culture from international trade and investment—an objective similar to the one defended by France and a few other EU Member States. Furthermore, during the 2005 UNESCO General Conference, the CDMI was also instrumental in using the Korean case as a prime illustration of the need to adopt the Convention on the Protection and Promotion of the Diversity of Cultural Expression which is the main inspiration for the KOREU Protocol on Cultural Cooperation for promoting international co-production.

3.1 *The Screen Quota and the KOREU FTA*

The fact that no provision on market access was included in the KOREU FTA was seen as a diplomatic success by the EU which argued that discussions on such issues would have created a precedent for future negotiations on the Trans-Atlantic Free Trade Agreement (TAFTA) with the US. This argument was misguided. As explained in the previous section, since the 2000s, the US film industry has had its own economic motives to follow a more confrontational PTA-based approach toward opening foreign film markets—and indeed, unsurprisingly, the US brought up this topic at the negotiating table during the short-lived TAFTA discussions between 2013 and 2016.

That said, does the absence of a screen quota provision in the KOREU FTA represent a risk for EU film industries in the future? As Korea could not reinforce a screen quota on US films without being forced to pay significant amount of compensation, it might be tempted to impose one on EU films if the Korean domestic film industry was to face any future difficulty and the government faced a corresponding pressure to act.

In the late 2000s, this was a hypothetical question from both an economic and legal perspective. From an economic view, both countries did not see the partner's market as critical for their film (and broadcasting) industry. The European film industries were more focused on their traditional export markets in Europe, Latin America, and Africa—relying on public subsidies to stay present in these regions. For their part, the successful Korean film companies were only concerned about the domestic and Asian markets, although this environment may be changing. Over the past few years, there has been an ongoing debate in Korea on the "screen monopoly" which evokes the possibility of reintroducing a screen quota as a way to limit the dominance of a few blockbusters over Korea's screens, hence make room for other small-budget films. This issue is examined in detail in Chapter 7.

From a legal point of view, this issue should be examined in light of the increasing internationalization of the film industry over the last decade and the dramatic changes in the global trade regime. Upon first glance, the absence of a screen quota provision in the KOREU FTA does not create any risk for the EU film industries. The screen quota cut was a stand-alone pre-condition agreed by Korea which was then integrated into the KORUS FTA: as a result, Korea shall apply it to all its trading partners because if GATT Article IV allows screen quotas—a rare exception to the usual ban on quotas—it specifies that such measures should be applied on a non-discriminatory basis to all GATT members. Indeed, the Korean law that cut the screen quota does not make any difference between the origins of foreign films: it makes only a distinction between Korean films and non-Korean films. As long as 73 days per screen are allocated uniquely to Korean films, other days should be available for any non-Korean films. To sum up, EU films seem protected against any possible future discriminatory action that would attempt to strengthen the quota system against them. However, the political and legal context today is very different than the late 2000s. Agreements based on WTO rules have been significantly undermined by a vast number of unilateral protectionist initiatives. Given these changes, a specific KOREU FTA provision on the screen quota would have been a welcome addition to WTO general rules for protecting more effectively the interests of the EU film industries.

3.2 *The Protocol of International Co-production: What Is Its Purpose?*

While the KOREU FTA has no provision on market access for films, it has a full protocol in the annex devoted to cultural cooperation—meaning international co-productions in filmmaking including the appropriate provisions on freedom of movement for cultural and artistic activities. When addressing such a goal, negotiators have taken into consideration a much wider set of restrictive measures than those strictly related to market access issues (such as the screen quota). These measures consist of all the laws and regulations of a country that restrict the access of filmmakers to some domestic or foreign "factors of production" or "inputs" that are needed for producing films such as financing, hiring local talent, shooting locations, and subsidies.

In the current age, a good is almost always produced with parts made in many other countries and assembled in factories located across several international locations. These "international value chains" raise the question on the "nationality" of the goods produced. This is crucial because nationality defines the conditions that will be imposed on this product when imported into a given country, such as which tariff to apply or which norms to enforce. These conditions are broadly referred to as "rules of origin" in international trade law and can be defined by the importing country or by international agreements.

The film business is no different in this regard. International value chains exist in the filmmaking process: shooting can be undertaken in several countries, actors can have different nationalities, and funding can come from various sources. Countries impose detailed conditions on the use of foreign or domestic factors of production by the domestic film industry and the respect of these conditions define the nationality of the films: some aspects may include—how many national actors should be hired for a film, which language should be used for the script and/or in the shooting locations, and what are the permissible level for the inflow of foreign capital or on imports of special equipment.[4] These criteria are listed in regulations referred to as "cultural test" in the UK or as the "agrément" in France. All these conditions are equivalent to the rules of origin in the case of goods. Only films that abide by these conditions are considered "national" with all the benefits that may be attached to this status in terms of regulations to be enforced, such as whether they will be subjected to an existing import quota, screen quota, or TV quota. Last but not least, such regulations determine whether the films are entitled to receive domestic subsidies.

As all these criteria vary substantially from country to country, they make life complicated for film producers when they want their film to be recognized as a "national" production in another country, in addition to their own country, if dual nationality is what they seek. Filmmakers have to navigate among all the national regulations when seeking the best package of factors for production in the world which will be compatible with all these different criteria. Large film companies—especially the Hollywood studios—are well-known for having developed vast capacities for "regulation shopping" over the past few decades.

[4] Sometimes, these rules may have comical consequences. For instance, UK actors are barred for being auditioned to play the role of Prince William, the son of Princess Diana, in a forthcoming biopic on her life. This is due to the fact that while in pre-production, the film casting notice stipulated that only European passport holders can apply (Shoard 2020). At the time of this notice, UK citizens were still technically European passport holders, but since the end of the Brexit transition period in 2021, UK passport are no longer classified as European.

From the film industry's perspective, trade agreements can be seen as a way to make "compatible" the different rules of origin among the signatories—hence facilitating the creation of international value chains in the film industry. This role is not easy to fulfill in the case of goods. It is even more difficult in the case of the film industry because it intensively uses services which are often activities heavily regulated. For instance, making compatible the detailed skills of film crews required by the two countries is a more complicated task than simply exchanging concessions on tariffs or even harmonizing technical norms. Trying to solve these problems on a case-by-case basis is rarely an option if only because there are often too many regulations to consider. Moreover, the impact of each regulation is likely to be appraised differently by the negotiating countries—making it difficult to reach a mutually satisfactory agreement. For instance, to what extent could the elimination of some provisions on qualification of the film crew imposed by Korea be seen as the equivalent to the elimination of restrictions on dubbing activities that are enforced by France? Answering this question is essential because two parties will only conclude an agreement if they feel they have a satisfactory balance of concessions—the situation where a country feels it receives from its partner roughly the same amount of concessions as what it gives up.

This question has been debated at length since the 1990s in the context of the negotiations in the WTO, with PTAs, and within the EU (Messerlin 2012, 2015). The most promising option would be that the two countries agree on the minimum "core" requirements that the producers—the filmmakers as it happens—should fulfill in order to consider a film as a national production by the two parties. The treatment of the requirements outside the core would then be left to the discretion of each party, but automatically recognized as legitimate by the partner. Clearly, the smaller the core requirement, the easier the access of the production to the film market of the partner country. Interestingly, the first illustration of such an innovative approach has been in the broadcast sector with the first EU Directive on Television without Frontiers in 1989. However, the fact that this approach has been de facto abandoned in the 2018 version of this Directive underlines how this ideal framework has a hard time to resist pressures for adopting new protectionist measures.

3.3 The KOREU FTA Protocol of Cultural Cooperation: Is It Up to the Task?

How close is the KOREU FTA Protocol to such an ideal agreement? Without doubt, it shares the intent of an ideal agreement, as expressed in general terms by its Articles 5.4 (EU commitments) and 5.5 (Korean commitments) which state "co-produced audio-visual works shall be entitled to benefit from the schemes of both Parties for the promotion of local cultural content." However, a brief review of the main provisions suggests that in practice, the KOREU FTA Protocol is still far from ideal, hence does not contribute greatly toward more efficient filmmaking.

The conditions imposed on co-production partners are revealed in a separate "leaflet" published by the EU Commission (undated[5]) which can be summarized as follows: (i) each potential co-producer should satisfy the conditions for being eligible as producing a national work in its own country; moreover for the EU, there should be producers of two Member States (three in case of animation audiovisual works); (ii) there should not be permanent relations (in terms of management, ownership, and control) between co-production partners; (iii) each co-producer should bring financial, technical, and artistic contributions to the film production, which should abide by given thresholds and ceilings; (iv) the status of co-production has to be granted to the film in question by the competent authorities of the two countries; (v) producers from third countries can participate if their countries have ratified the 2005 UNESCO Convention on the protection and promotion of the diversity of cultural expression. All combined, this makes up for a tight net of conditions. Condition (i) seems to keep the integrality of the existing provisions in both countries: in other words, there is no attempt to define the provisions which would be part of the minimum "core" requirements that a film has to fulfill in order to be considered as a national production by the two parties, and what to do with them. For their part, conditions (ii) and (iii) add new constraints. Condition (iv) continues to provide the existing national governments with full independent authority while condition (v) excludes US audio-visual firms since the US is not a Party to the UNESCO Convention.

[5] EU-Korea: Audio-Visual Co-production, https://ec.europa.eu/assets/eac/culture/policy/international-cooperation/documents/leaflet-eu-korea-coproductions_en.pdf.

As a result, the benefits to be expected from the Protocol seem limited, and many opportunities have been missed. The first potential benefit would be access among film producers to the subsidies given by one partner or possibly two. The KOREU FTA Protocol Article 5.2 states that: "The Parties reaffirm that the Member States of the European Union and Korea *may* (emphasis added) grant financial benefits to co-produced audio-visual works [...]. Any subsidies, tax incentives or other financial incentives which may be granted by either Party [...] *shall* (emphasis added) accrue to the co-producer who is permitted to claim those benefits in accordance with the existence measures of that Party." This provision is unlikely to be attractive for Korean or EU film producers to the extent that subsidies remain attached to each subsidizing country. This is due to the fact that Korean filmmakers are trained to produce films with few subsidies while EU producers are likely to find Korean subsidies too limited for their taste, as shown in Chapter 4.

The second potential benefit of the Protocol consists of facilitating the entry and temporary stay in their territories of artists and other cultural professionals (Article 4) which also goes on to cover temporary importation of material and equipment (Article 7). Yet, it contains no commitment other than "encouraging" or "facilitating" these importations in the old-fashioned approach of promoting a territory as a location for shooting films. For instance, Article 7 reads: "Each Party shall encourage as appropriate the promotion of its territory as a location for the purpose of shooting cinematographic films and television programmes." In short, there is a lot of uncertainty on how the national authorities would implement this supporting feature.

The Protocol could have made a real difference if it would have addressed in a pragmatic manner the two most critical issues in terms of market access—the Korean screen quota and the EU TV quotas. Indeed, if these two issues were coupled together, they could have made a quid pro quo package, with both Korea and the EU Member States opening more their film markets. First, by refining the definition of the nationality of the films, the Protocol could have defined by the same token the enforcement perimeter of the Korean screen quota on a film-by-film basis. A coproduced film fulfilling the core requirements set up by the Protocol would be deemed to have dual nationality—hence eliminating the potential threat of the Korean screen quota for EU-Korean co-produced films. In other words, such a co-production agreement could have opened a new dimension to market integration: a better utilization of resources for film production in addition to better market access.

Second, a less narrow Protocol could have provided better access for Korean co-productions to the TV markets of EU Member States. This benefit is related to the so-called EU "TV quotas" which limit the broadcasting of non-EU films by European TV networks (Parc and Messerlin 2020). The EU Television without Frontiers Directive specifies that 60% of the transmission time among European TV networks reserved for exhibiting films or similar works should be allocated to European films. Access to the EU TV markets for Korea-EU film co-productions in the 1990s and 2000s would thus have been an attractive source of revenues for Korean films, either directly—by being broadcasted—or indirectly by making Korean productions more known among a larger European audience. However, the existing Protocol does not allow for such opportunities to be exploited. It should be noted though that since the mid-2010s, the multiplication of public and private platforms in Europe offering alternatives to the exhibition of Korean films on TV channels has eroded these opportunities for benefits.

To sum up, the above analysis of the detailed provisions of the KOREU Protocol and of their potential benefits suggests that the Protocol is too restrictive and/or outdated to have a significant positive impact on the cultural cooperation between Korea and the EU. Available information on the thirty films coproduced under KOFIC aegis is limited (Kobiz 2017). It shows no strong correlation between the coproduced films and the existence of a Protocol for cultural cooperation signed in the context of Korea's "deep and comprehensive" PTAs. The vast majority of Korean coproduced films involve countries that do not pertain to these PTAs: fifteen co-productions with China, six with Japan, and one with Malaysia. These numbers outweigh by far the six Korean co-productions with countries that are part of Korea's network of PTAs (five with France and one with Spain which have benefited from the bilateral cultural cooperation agreements with these two countries). Budgets are very limited; less than USD 6 million, except for one case. Box office revenues are available for only two of the 30 films recorded, are very small (less than USD 170,000), and they seem to have been earned entirely in Korea (Box Office Mojo).

4 Has a Korean Agenda Emerged with Its International Film Agreements?

The agendas on the film industry included in the KORUS FTA and the KOREU FTA were both defined by the US and the EU. On paper, it would appear that the KOREU FTA agenda is more in line with Korean views toward the film industry but this is not actually how it emerged. It was in fact driven mainly by the EU's own political interests—the need to counterbalance its rigid and costly "no negotiation on access to film markets" stance by showing other ways to negotiate on the politically sensitive but economically important film industry. The EU could present the culture-related contents of the KOREU FTA as a "UNESCO-consistent and culture-friendly alternative" to the narrow approach pushed by the US (allegedly) based on "free trade." Indeed, such an initiative could have had a powerful appeal among many film industries in the world. Barriers on the access to the markets of the inputs for films—shooting locations, freedom to move people across borders, access to foreign capital—are among the most prominent obstacles for film producers, especially those from developing countries which are limited by the small size of their domestic markets.

Although Korea did not set the agenda for the film provisions in the KORUS FTA and the KOREU FTA, can it still be argued that it acquired with these two PTAs any knowledge on how to design its own agenda for future agreements? This section explores this question across several steps. First, when and how has Korea adopted a trade-based approach toward bilateral PTAs? Second, has Korea signed many PTAs with provisions on the film industry beyond the KORUS FTA and the KOREU FTAs? Third, what have been the key challenges from the KORUS FTA and the KOREU FTAs that could have helped Korea with the design of the agendas for its other PTAs? Finally, what is the main content of the PTAs that Korea has concluded after the KORUS FTA and the KOREU FTA? All these questions are likely to become important in the future as and when the Korean film industry will continue to grow and become more dependent upon international factors.

4.1 Korea: The Last Country to Swing to Bilateral PTAs

Since the early 2000s, Korea's new trade strategy based on PTAs has had two main objectives. First, it sought to take further advantage of the benefits from globalization, which led it to conclude the so-called deep and comprehensive bilateral trade agreements covering a wide array of issues, sectors, and trade barriers. This explains why Korea began to negotiate with like-minded countries, such as Chile (October 2003), Singapore (November 2004), and the members of the European Free Trade Agreement (July 2005). These negotiations provided an opportunity to train Korean officials for negotiating future deals with more difficult trade partners and to further liberalize the economy without having to wait for an increasingly improbable agreement at the WTO forum. Second, the failure of the WTO Hong Kong 2005 Ministerial Conference and the increasing shift of the US and then the EU toward bilateral agreements added a new rationale: Korean PTAs were increasingly conceived as an "insurance" against being discriminated in foreign markets where goods exported by rival countries were already enjoying preferential access thanks to the PTAs they had already forged.

Today, Korea has a network of seventeen PTAs covering forty-six countries as of September 2020 to which one should add the recent conclusion of the Regional Comprehensive Economic Partnership (RCEP) signed by fifteen Asian-Pacific countries in November 2020.[6] This list does not include the many agreements concluded with developing countries under the General System of Preferences which is a multilateral framework of tariff preferences granted by developed countries to developing countries. Korea's PTA network is one of the densest in the world and one of the very few that includes agreements with the three major economies of China, the EU, and the US. Korea's PTA partners have a global GDP fifty times larger than Korea and account for two-thirds of the world's GDP. These figures illustrate the two major achievements of Korea's PTA policy within the space of less than two decades: it has expanded vastly the size of the markets accessible to Korean goods and has acted as an insurance against any disruption to the WTO system.

Negotiating such a network has been a much more demanding exercise than the talks at the WTO forum because PTAs cover not only goods, but also services, public procurement, and investment—all topics only lightly touched in the context of the WTO negotiations. In other words, they deal with a broader range of barriers to trade and investment: the so-called behind-the-border barriers created—voluntarily or not—by domestic laws

[6] Some RCEP signatories have already a PTA with Korea. RCEP has no specific provision on audio-visuals.

and regulations that happen to be so critical in protecting domestic industries like the film industry. Negotiating such topics requires each partner to thoroughly scrutinize the other's laws and regulations in each sector as a way to assess their potentially protective or restrictive impact—hence the benefits that can be expected from their reduction or elimination.

4.2 Korea: A Major Signatory of PTAs with Provisions on the Film Industry

Table 2 focuses on the main PTAs that have specific provisions on the film industry. At first glance, the sheer number of such PTAs is quite surprising. Both the tense Korea-US bilateral negotiations on the import and screen quotas and the disastrous outcome of the film negotiations during the Uruguay Round, which almost brought down the whole process, have generated the widespread view among trade officials and observers that this sector is a non-starter for international negotiations. The dramatic collapse of negotiations for the "Multilateral Investment Agreement" at the OECD in 1998 due to intense lobbying by European film industries joined by the Korean Coalition for Cultural Diversity in Moving Images—seemed to be the final knockout blow toward such initiatives.

Another unexpected result with Table 2 is the fact that the EU has many PTAs with provisions on audio-visuals despite the official claim that

Table 2 Preferential trade agreements with provisions in audio-visual sectors (2021)

Signatory	*No. FTAs*	*Other signatories or pairs of FTAs*
US	15	Israel, Canada (CUSFTA), Mexico (NAFTA), Jordan, Chile, Singapore, CAFTA (Central America), Australia, Morocco, Bahrein, Colombia, Oman, Peru, Korea, Panama
EU	13	Israel, South Africa, Mexico, Macedonia, Chile, Egypt, Albania, Korea, Central America, Georgia, Moldova, Ukraine
Korea	10	Australia, Canada, China, EU, U.S., India, New Zealand, Peru, Singapore, United Kingdom
Other FTAs	4	Chile-El Salvador; China-Costa Rica; India-Singapore; Peru-Mexico

Source WTO

it will never negotiate on this sector in the context of trade agreements. This contradiction is circumvented through a trick in the presentation of these FTAs. On the one hand, the main text in all of the EU's PTAs contains provisions which explicitly exclude negotiations on access to film markets. Yet on the other hand, the "cultural cooperation" protocols that are located in the annexes of these agreements—hence distinct from the main text—are specifically designed to overcome the regulatory barriers in the film industry by promoting separate coproduction agreements.

The last and most surprising result from Table 2 is that Korea is one of the most active countries in negotiating PTAs with provisions on the film industry. As shown above, Korea has been able to conclude such agreements with both the US and the EU, despite the very opposite views held by these two partners on what should be included in the provisions of an international film agreement. Moreover, Korea's partners for its PTAs are countries with large audiences (Australia, Canada) and/or notable capacities for film production or co-productions (Australia, Canada, New Zealand). The only exception would be China as its PTA with Korea cannot be qualified as a deep and comprehensive agreement. Such a network is in sharp contrast with most of the US and EU whose PTA partners have negligible audiences and production capacities. These features suggest that Korea is now in an advantageous position to set the agenda in this sector.

4.3 Korea Builds Its Expertise in Negotiating Film Agreements

Pursuing the KORUS and the KOREU FTAs negotiations simultaneously was for Korea a unique opportunity to build its expertise on international negotiations in the film industry. In particular, Korea's negotiators had to be careful not to give concessions to the US that would be inconsistent with those it granted to the EU and vice-versa.[7] Table 3 presents the key differences and similarities between the two PTAs in the film industry and shows the main challenges that Korea was faced with.

First, interactions between negotiations on market access and on regulatory issues among the various PTAs are hard to spot and can be costly.

[7] This issue was considered so important by Korea that it appointed Ambassador Hye Min Lee as its chief negotiator with the EU the same person who was its deputy chief negotiator with the US—hence ensuring the maximum level of consistency and continuity in its approaches to both countries.

Table 3 The major differences between the KOREU FTA and the KORUS FTA

	KOREU FTA	*KORUS FTA*
Market access	Excluded (Article 7.4.1 (a))	Cut of screen quota (Annex I, Schedule of Korea) Many "reservations" in the broadcasting sector
Copyrights Fighting piracy	Extended duration to 70 years (Article 10.6) Less stringent than KORUS FTA	Extended duration to 70 years (Article 18.4.4) More stringent than KOREU FTA
Subsidies	Protocol on Cultural Cooperation	(no provision)
Ratchet effect	No	Yes (Article 12.6)

Source Authors' summary based on the KOREU FTA and KORUS FTA

For instance, as mentioned above, Korea agreed to a screen quota cut through the KORUS FTA alone, but this commitment is enforceable with respect to all other WTO Members. In the same vein, the duration of copyrights was extended from 50 to 70 years after the death of the author in the KORUS FTA. This made it hard for Korea not to do the same with the KOREU FTA as well as its other PTAs. However, extending an economically questionable provision such as a longer duration to other PTAs can only amplify its initial economic costs. Many economists have doubts on the benefits of a longer copyright duration for the audience as well as for the authors themselves (Parc and Messerlin 2020). Indeed, Korea offers a good example of a cultural industry which has been successful without relying upon stringent copyrights (Parc 2021; Parc and Kawashima 2018; Parc and Kim 2020; Parc et al. 2016). Introducing a US copyright regime into Korean law is very likely to have a positive impact for US studios or publishers, but its capacity to improve the welfare of Korean producers, authors, and consumers of cultural goods—hence to increase the country's cultural creativity—is highly debatable. Granting the same provision in the KOREU FTA only serves to amplify these doubts.

Second, one of the most intractable issues in international trade agreements concerns the restraints—the "disciplines" in the jargon of international trade negotiations—on the use of subsidies. Subsidies create major distortions on competition in global film markets, and they have caused a number of disputes because a few film industries benefit from larger subsidies, hence enjoy "unfair advantages." This issue is particularly important for Korea which grants limited subsidies to its own film industry, noticeably when compared to other large film producers, such as France, the UK, or even the US. As a result, Korea has an intrinsic interest in disciplining the subsidies provided around the world—as explained in Chapter 4—since eliminating them would be excessive because there are some economic reasons justifying the appropriate use of subsidies in cultural industries.

A multilateral forum such as the WTO is the only approach available toward generating effective disciplines on subsidies. From an economic perspective, bilateral PTAs cannot compel the partner country to stop subsidizing its film production altogether: they can only make them stop exporting subsidized films to its PTA partner. Simply, the subsidizing country can still export its subsidized films to the rest of the world, which could then still end up in the market of the PTA partner that thought it was protected by the bilateral deal—hence it displaces the competition among the films available in the partner's market. Furthermore, from a political point of view, the WTO is the only forum that provides medium-sized economies like Korea with the opportunity to mobilize support from other countries who are also interested in disciplining film subsidies. Such a wide political support is needed in the film industry as the US—once a strong supporter of restricting subsidies in international trade deals—has shifted its stance since the late 1980s. This came about when Hollywood studios began to increasingly pursue "runaway productions" in Ontario or the UK, which were considered as attractive business prospects (a process explained further in Chapter 4). Given that the WTO option is de facto out of reach today, building a network of PTAs which possess common rules on subsidies in their protocols toward co-productions appears to be the only alternative for Korea to introduce some disciplines, albeit a limited one as shown below.

Lastly, there are provisions which initially look appealing during the negotiating phase of a PTA but ultimately end up working against further liberalization in the future. This was certainly the case with the "ratchet clause" in the KORUS FTA. Such a clause ensures that if Korea wishes to open a domestic market—say its film market—when concluding an agreement with a new partner, it shall automatically extend the corresponding liberalization measures to the partner(s) of its other existing

PTAs. This creates a dilemma for Korea: negotiating future PTAs that offer better access to the Korean film market than the one included in the KORUS PTA would then automatically trigger the "ratchet clause," hence granting by the same token to Hollywood films better access to the Korean domestic market.

4.4 *The Basis for a Korean Agenda for the Future?*

All these limits and difficulties raise one final question: Why then has Korea undertaken negotiations on film provisions through so many PTAs? One potential answer is that it could have been a manifestation of mere diplomatic routine: Korea and its major partners have trained their negotiators on these specific film issues in the early PTAs (with the US and the EU in the case of Korea), making them ready to duplicate film provisions in subsequent PTAs. Another potential answer is that, as mentioned above, it reflects the recent view that PTAs are a form of "insurance" against an increasingly weakened multilateral regime. Australia, Canada, and New Zealand have PTAs with the US and have all experienced difficulties when negotiating "cultural" issues with the US as Korea has had. Finally, Korea may increasingly realize that after a growth largely centered on its domestic market, its film industry had to go up a gear by expanding overseas, hence it has interests in consolidating the existing access to foreign film markets or opening them further.

That said, examining the content of the major PTAs concluded by Korea after the KOREU and KORUS FTAs shows that Korea has indeed made use of its experience. First, none of the subsequent PTAs have included a ratchet clause. Second, they do not focus on freer access to movie theaters. Third, by contrast, the FTAs with Australia and New Zealand have a protocol on cultural cooperation, both located in a special annex, while the FTA between Canada and Korea is expected to have such a protocol in the future.[8] Finally, the text on "co-production on film" with China may have the same headings as the other protocols, but the many domestic regulations of the Chinese film market raise doubts about the positive impact of these provisions.

Overall, these protocols may well come to foreshadow a future Korean agenda on international provisions in the film industry. In particular, the

[8] Annex 7B in the KAFTA was concluded in 2014 and Annex III in the Korea-New Zealand Free Trade Agreement (KNZFTA) was concluded in 2015.

texts of the two protocols with Australia and New Zealand are similar to the KOREU FTA text but have a more open tone. If one looks at Article 5.1 of the Korea–Australia FTA (KAFTA), it refers to the "full enjoyment of all the benefits which are accorded to national audio-visual works of either Party." The annex has similar provisions on the import of equipment and on immigration facilitations that are more comprehensive than those included in the KOREU FTA. Furthermore, they are written in more legally binding terms regarding the opening of markets and have a wider coverage in terms of professions. To conclude, as these PTAs involve countries in the Asia–Pacific region, they could eventually constitute a basis of a Korea-led network of international treaties dealing with film issues in the region.

5 Conclusion

This chapter has focused on Korea's international film agreements that were negotiated between the mid-2000s and the mid-2010s, two decades after the elimination of the Korean import quota in 1986. It has first analyzed the profound changes in the global film industry since the 1990s at a time when the US film industry has taken on an increasingly pugnacious approach toward opening further overseas markets. Such pressure from the US has emerged out of the rising economic challenges the US film industry has faced—the relative shrinking of its domestic market compared to its international sales and the skyrocketing growth of China's market. As a result, there has been a profound transformation of the international legal framework—namely, a rapid shift from the multilateral WTO forum to more confrontational bilateral preferential trade agreements. Consequently, this has made the international environment less predictable for middle-sized countries like Korea, and more difficult for them to develop their future strategies, especially in regards to the sensitive topics of the film industry.

The rest of the chapter has examined how Korea has been able to respond and manage these new realities. First of all, Korea has had to face repeated requests from the US to eliminate or reduce its screen quota as a pre-condition for negotiating a "deep and comprehensive" bilateral FTA. The economic rationale of the US request on the screen quota has been shown to be largely groundless, explaining why cutting the screen quota by two has not been a big cost for the Korean film industry—simply because it had already come to challenge the dominance of the US film industry at home. This chapter has also shown that the brief dip in the Korean film market during the period of 2007–2009 has not been due to this quota cut—contrary to popular belief in Korea at the time—but has actually been due to deep structural changes coupled with a temporary decrease of investment in this sector.

Next, the negotiations for the KOREU FTA have induced Korea to concentrate on a completely different set of barriers in the film industry: those embedded in domestic laws and regulations which restrict the access of inputs—shooting locations, freedom to move people across borders, access to foreign capital—needed by film producers. The KOREU FTA Protocol for Cultural Cooperation has intended to provide a framework capable of reducing as much as possible these barriers, hence offering huge growth potentials. However, this Protocol has had little if any impact because the drafting of its provisions has been far too modest, limiting the opportunities to make it easier for the film companies to pursue ambitious co-productions.

Finally, the mid-2010s have witnessed Korea forge a number of "deep and comprehensive" bilateral trade agreements with Australia, New Zealand, and Canada. The PTAs with Australia and New Zealand have a Protocol for cultural cooperation which reflects the lessons learnt from the KOREU FTA by having provisions more conducive to market opening. Still, it is questionable whether enough progress has been made in this respect.

The policy implications of this chapter are twofold. First, preferential trade agreements with countries large enough to impose their views on the film industry have revealed serious limitations. This is due to the fact that the large countries tend to impose their own narrow agenda and have either targeted the wrong objectives (Korea-US) or they have been too timid (Korea-EU and Korea-China). By contrast, PTAs among mid-size economies (Australia, New Zealand, and possibly Canada in the future) have seemed to be more promising. They include more open protocols for cultural cooperation, which could serve as a basis for building a network of coproduction agreements among Pacific countries and beyond. If successful, these efforts will offer to Korea options for expanding and/or consolidating the reach of its film industry to foreign markets—an attractive counterbalance to an excessive focus on the Chinese market which is subjected to unpredictable regulations and *ad hoc* policy decisions.

Second, this chapter has stressed that all these international agreements have largely ignored subsidies and domestic regulations which have become the main "barriers" in the film industry since the 2000s. What approach can be taken toward reducing or eliminating these barriers in a globalized film industry? The next chapter explores the issues raised by subsidies. In particular, it compares Korea with its major competitors and highlights a remarkable feature of the Korean film industry—its ability to outperform these competitors with fewer subsidies. Regulatory issues are left for Chapter 5.

References

Acheson, K., and C. Maule. 1999. *Much ado About Culture: North American Trade Disputes, Studies in International Economics*. The University of Michigan Press, Ann Arbor.

Bernier, I. 2004. The Recent Free Trade Agreements of the United States as Illustration of their New Strategy Regarding the Audiovisual Sector. Chaire UNESCO sur la diversité des expressions culturelles. http://www.unescodec.chaire.ulaval.ca/sites/unescodec.chaire.ulaval.ca/files/conf_seoul_ang_2004.pdf.

Bhagwati, J. 1993. The Diminished Giant Syndrome: How Declinism Drives Trade Policy. *Foreign Affairs* 72 (2): 22–26.

Box Office Mojo. https://www.boxofficemojo.com/year/2019/?ref_=bo_yl_table_3.

Buchsbaume, J. 2017. *Exception Taken: How France Has Defied Hollywood's New World Order*. New York: Columbia University Press.

Chase, K.A. 2018. Audiovisual Goods and Services in Preferential Trade Agreements. In *Trade Cooperation: The Purpose Design and Effects of Preferential Trade Agreements*, ed. Andreas Dür and Manfred Elsig, 218–245. Cambridge, UK: Cambridge University Press.

Chang, A.R. 2014. The Effect of Foreign Pressure on Liberal Policy Autonomy: The Case of South Korea's Screen Quota System. *International Review of Public Administration* 19 (1): 1–22.

Centre national du cinéma et de l'image animée (CNC). Various issues. *Bilan*. https://www.cnc.fr/cinema/etudes-et-rapports/bilans/.

Epstein, E.J. 2012. *The Hollywood Economist: The Hidden Financial Reality Behind the Movies, Release 2.0*. Brooklyn, New York: Melville House.

Fong, J. 1997. The Cultural Industries Exemption from NAFTA: Another Canadian Perspective. *Canada-United States Law Journal* 23: 201–210. https://heinonline.org/HOL/LandingPage?handle=hein.journals/canusa23&div=26&id=&page=.

Gagné, G. 2016. *The Trade and Culture Debate: Evidence from US Trade Agreements*. Lanham, Boulder, New York and London: Lexington Books.

Grantham, B. 2003. *Some Big Bourgeois Brothels', Contexts for France's Culture Wars with Hollywood*. Luton, UK: University of Luton Press.
Korean Film Council (KOFIC). Various issues. *Korean Cinema Yearbook*. Busan: KOFIC (in Korean).
Kobiz. 2017. Ko-Production Projects. http://www.koreanfilm.or.kr/eng/coProduction/projects.jsp?pageIndex=3.
Lee, H.M. 2013. *FTA Economic Policy of Korea*. Thesis (PhD), Université Paris I.
Lee, H.S. 2005. An Economic Analysis of Protective Film Policies: A Case Study of the Korean Screen Quota System. Paper presented at the annual meeting for the International Communication Association, New York. http://citation.allacademic.com/meta/p_mla_apa_research_citation/0/1/4/9/6/pages14967/p14967-1.php.
Lee, B., and H.S. Bae. 2004. The Effect of Screen Quotas on the Self-Sufficiency Ratio in Recent Domestic Film Markets. *Journal of Media Economics* 17 (3): 163–176.
Messerlin, P.A. 2012. The Influence of the EU in the World Trade System. In *The Oxford Handbook on the World Trade Organization*, ed. Amrita Narlikar, Martin Daunton, and Robert M. Stern, 213–233. Oxford, UK: Oxford University Press.
Messerlin, P.A. 2015. TTIP: The Services Dimension. In *Rule makers or rule takers, Exploring the Transatlantic Trade and Investment Partnership*, ed. Daniel S. Hamilton and Jacques Pelkmans, 341–369. London, UK: Rowman and Littlefield International.
Moon, S.Y. 2006. Trade Minister Denies Deal on Screen Quotas. *Korea JoongAng Daily*, January 20. https://koreajoongangdaily.joins.com/news/article/article.aspx?aid=2674982.
Motion Picture Association (MPA). Various issues. *THEME Report*. https://www.motionpictures.org/.
Motion Pictures Association of Japan (MPPAJ). Various issues. Statistics of Film Industry in Japan. http://eiren.org/statistics_e/index.html.
Parc, J. 2014. *An Eclectic Approach to Enhancing the Competitive Advantage of Nations: Analyzing the Success Factors of East Asian Economies with a Focus on the Development of South Korea*. Thesis (PhD), Seoul National University and Université Paris Sorbonne.
Parc, J. 2017. The Effects of Protection in Cultural Industries: The Case of the Korean Film Policies. *International Journal of Cultural Policy* 23 (5): 618–633.
Parc, J. 2018. Evaluating the Effects of Protectionism on the Film Industry: A Case Study Analysis of Korea. In *Handbook of State Aid for Film*, ed. Paul Murschetz, Roland Teichmann, and Matthias Karmasin, 349–366. Cham, Switzerland: Springer.

Parc, J. 2021. Business Integration and its Impact on Film Industry: The Case of Korean Film Policies from the 1960s until the Present. *Business History* 63 (5): 850–867.

Parc, J., and N. Kawashima. 2018. Wrestling with or Embracing Digitization in the Music Industry: The Contrasting Business Strategies of J-pop and K-pop. *Kritika Kultura* 30 (31): 23–48.

Parc, J., and S.D. Kim. 2020. The Digital Transformation of the Korean Music Industry and the Global Emergence of K-pop. *Sustainability* 12 (18): 7790–7805.

Parc, J., and P.A. Messerlin. 2020. The True Impact of Shorter and Longer Copyright Durations: From Authors' Earnings to Cultural Creativity and Diversity. *International Journal of Cultural Policy* 27: 607–620.

Parc, J., P. Messerlin, and H.C. Moon. 2016. The Secret to the Success of K-pop: The Benefits of Well-Balanced Copyrights. In *Corporate Espionage, Geopolitics, and Diplomacy Issues in International Business*, ed. Bryan Christiansen and Fatmanur Kasarci, 130–148. Hershey, PA: IGI Global.

Pauwels, C., and J. Loisen. 2003. The WTO and the Audiovisual Sector: Economic Free Trade vs Cultural Horse Trading. *European Journal of Communications* 18 (3): 291–313.

Roy, M., J. Marchetti, and H. Lim. 2007. Services Liberalization in the New Generation of Preferential Trade Agreements (PTAs): How Much Further than the GATS. *World Trade Review* 6 (2): 155–192.

Roy, M. 2008. Beyond the Main Screen: Audiovisual Services in PTAs. In *Opening Markets for Trade in Services: Countries and Sectors in Bilateral and WTO Negotiations*, ed. Juan A. Marchetti and Martin Roy. Cambridge, UK: Cambridge University Press.

Shoard, C. 2020. British-Only Passport Holders Barred from Playing Prince William. *The Guardian*, November 26. https://www.theguardian.com/film/2020/nov/26/british-actors-barred-from-playing-prince-william-in-diana-film-kristen-stewart.

Valenti, J. 2007. *This Time, This Place. My Life in War, the White House, and Hollywood*. New York: Three Rivers Press.

Yeceis, B.M. 2007. Parleying Culture Against Trade: Hollywood's Affairs with Korea's Screen Quotas. *Korea Observer* 38 (1): 1–33.

Yecies, B.M., and A. Shim. 2016. *The Changing Face of Korean Cinema: 1960 to 2015*. Oxon, UK: Routledge, Asia's Transformations Series.

World Trade Organization (WTO). https://www.wto.org/.

CHAPTER 4

Subsidies: The Korean Exception

Throughout the period from the early 1980s to the late 1990s, the Korean film business has overseen its remarkably successful industrial rejuvenation with very few financial public incentives—the subsidy scheme in place since 1963 was very modest. In fact, during these years, subsidies in Korea were cantoned toward what were regarded as "real" industries, such as shipbuilding, steel, or chemicals. The perception of the film sector as an industry only came about following the roaring success of the 1993 Hollywood film *Jurassic Park*, which proved to be a waking up moment for the Korean government. In fact, it has been said that President Kim Young-Sam was amazed by the fact reported to him that the box office revenues of this blockbuster amounted to the annual sales for 1.5 million Sonatas, Hyundai's leading car produced at that time (Leong 2014; Song 2012). This comparison reveals an interesting approach in Korea toward the film industry: it has both cultural and economic value. In a nutshell, economic aspects were not perceived in Seoul as irremediably "antagonistic" to the cultural dimension as is so often the case in Europe. In this new context, film subsidies increased in the late 1990s but remained modest until 2006 (Parc 2017, pp. 627–629).

J. Parc and P. A. Messerlin, *The Untold Story of the Korean Film Industry*, Cultural Economics & the Creative Economy,
https://doi.org/10.1007/978-3-030-80342-1_4

In July 2006, the Korean government agreed to cut its screen quota by half as a pre-condition for the negotiations of the Korea-US Free Trade Agreement (see Chapter 3). This cut came as a great shock to the Korean film industry who inspired by France then sought out a similar subsidy policy as a way to soften this blow. Strangely enough, none of those who called for such a policy instrument paid attention to the fact that since 2003 box office revenues per capita of Korean films were larger—and increasingly so—than those of the heavily subsidized French films (see Chapter 1). In 2007, the Korean government introduced a seat tax which has been de facto used for funding subsidies—a mechanism which borrowed its main legal and institutional features from the French scheme—making this scheme the main instrument of Korean film policy since.

Knowing that the emergence of the Korean film industry began in the late 1990s with few subsidies, how was Korea able to achieve such a successful outcome that the heavily subsidized European film industries failed to generate? The answer can be provided by dividing this question in four components.

Are there general economic arguments justifying the use of subsidies to the film industry in general, and to the Korean film industry in particular? Indeed, there are: different market sizes among countries as well as cultural diversity. That said, are these arguments supportive of an "unlimited license to subsidize"? Or should they respect the golden principle that "there is no such a thing as a free lunch" in an economy? Put simply, this principle sees an economy as a huge machinery in which every part is dependent upon each other: as a result, any public action—such as a subsidy—on one part of the economy has an impact—possibly negative—on some others. This is a powerful call for caution in the use of subsidies, including from the perspective of the film industry itself.

The last three decades have witnessed many countries in the world that have shifted away from imposing quotas toward providing financial support under two main forms: subsidies and tax relief schemes. What have been the economic and political forces behind this common evolution? Has the Korean subsidy policy followed the same growth pattern with the policies of the other countries, or has it shown any significant difference?

Next, who are the ultimate beneficiaries of the financial support granted to the film industries? It used to be the domestic film companies, but is this still the case or has the worldwide boom in national subsidy policies generated an "internationalization" of the beneficiaries in favor of large multinational film companies? To what extent is this evolution sustainable for the long run? Does Korea's film subsidy policy share the same pattern?

Finally, are subsidies truly helpful to the film industries they target? The answer to this question is all the more important because, over the last two decades, the Korean government has faced constant pressure from some segments in the domestic film industry to increase subsidies in the long run. As the Korean domestic debate often makes, explicitly or implicitly, reference to the French case and its experience over the past fifty years, this example should be scrutinized in order to test the robustness of the main claims behind this pressure.

1 An Economic Analysis of Subsidies

The literature on the desirability of film subsidies rests on two main arguments (Doyle 2014; Grant 1994; Horowitz and Davey 1996; Karpe 1995; Kim 2000; Peltier 2003; Prowda 1996).[1] First, subsidies are needed to compensate the advantages that "economies of scale" associated to the size of the market provide to films released in the world's largest markets. In a nutshell, this argument contends that the wider the audience, the more profitable the film will become. Thus, film industries with a large domestic market benefit from an advantage over those based in smaller domestic markets. This advantage is amplified if the exhibition of the films released in the largest market is extended by a release across national borders. Compensating this disadvantage can be done by granting subsidies to films that are initially limited to small markets. The second justification for subsidies addresses a completely different issue. Markets do not deliver necessarily the level of variety in cultural productions which is socially desirable, be it in terms of genres, inspirations, and aesthetic choices. In this case, subsidies are needed for promoting "artistic" or "non-commercial" films and encourage further "cultural diversity."

[1] For simplicity sake, this first section uses the term subsidies as a generic term covering the subsidies strictly speaking and the other financial incentives evoked in the following sections.

1.1 An Unlimited "License to Subsidize"?

Expressed in such general terms, these two arguments could give the false impression that each of them constitutes an unlimited "license to subsidize." This section examines the interactions between these two arguments. This is a perspective that is rarely adopted but that is crucial because it reflects the strong global constraint on any subsidy policy. In a nutshell, the use of subsidies is greatly limited by the basic principle of "there is no such thing as a free lunch in an economy." Subsidizing a film allows its producer to hire more and/or better resources—screenwriters, directors, actors, and crew. As all these inputs are available in limited quantities, a subsidy granted to produce one film prevents other films produced in the country to have access to these resources. In short, a subsidy creates an advantage for one domestic beneficiary while inevitably imposing a disadvantage on its fellow local competitors—be they producers of commercial or artistic films. Granting more subsidies to all films does not solve this problem: what is at stake is not the level of subsidies per se granted to films, but how much each film receives compared to the others. It is a question of the "relative"—not absolute—level of subsidies granted to each film.

This key result sheds new light on the cultural diversity argument. It suggests that—paradoxically at first glance—reducing subsidies granted to potential blockbusters could be actually the best way to promote indirectly cultural diversity. This is because blockbusters consume vast resources but are often characterized by limited cultural diversity as they seek to please the broadest audience possible. A cut to the provision of subsidies to these films would make a lot of more resources available to the filmmakers producing diversified films. This is a question on which type of films the film policy of the country intends to favor or disfavor. This is a fundamental question that each nation should reflect upon.

These arguments are further strengthened if one scrutinizes the two—not one—assumptions behind the diversity argument: markets fail to provide a socially desirable level of diversity—this seems a plausible assumption; and public subsidies do ensure diversity—this is an assumption far from assured. Indeed, the literature on film subsidies recognizes this limitation when it suggests that public subsidies may mirror a failing private sector unwilling to take risks and invest (Benghozi and Delage

2000; Hayward 2005). The business community is also well aware of this aspect, as stressed by the leading French producer Jérôme Seydoux who stated that "the film business is a risky business, but in France we are too timorous" (Vulser 2019). This statement suggests a link between the level of subsidies and the lack of innovation. Finally, the procedures for granting subsidies can be biased against promoting diversity. If films aim to be cultural goods and seek to share widely their unique artistic and cultural values with the public, then these values should be enjoyed by the largest audience possible, not just by specific groups who have a limited range of cultural interests. In this regard, the commercial success—either big or modest—of artistic films emerges as a welcome counterforce to avoid producing works that are too self-centered. If commercial success is not forthcoming, the provision of regular subsidies can quickly generate a vicious circle that can erode cultural diversity.

To sum up, ideally the gains and benefits of each subsidy should be carefully assessed. This is the opposite of the argument "may the best win," which is too often used as an excuse for providing a lot of subsidies to a film industry characterized by highly unpredictable successes. Moreover, such a prudent approach would reduce enormously the risks of costly inconsistencies among unbridled incentives. As all these subsidies granted by the country's film policy are competing among each other, they are to some extent cancelling each other out. Such a policy is harmful for the film industry it intends to protect. And it represents a collective cost for the whole country.

1.2 *The Best Instrument, in Theory*

The above discussion has stressed that scale economies and diversity are not an unlimited "license to subsidize." However, what follows shows that, if action has to be taken on the basis of one of these two arguments, then subsidies are a much better measure of protection than others used in the film industry, in particular quotas. By its sheer nature, a quota has an impact on both the supply and demand of the good. This impact is "excessive" if the problem to be addressed resides in only one side of the market—either the supply side or the demand side. For instance, if a government wants to help the local producers of a certain good in a small market, imposing a quota to protect the local producers allows them to increase the price of their product. But by the same token, the price also rises for local consumers; as this is harmful, for which the government should not wish to happen.

Subsidies help to avoid such "excessive" protection because they can be tailor-made toward achieving precisely the desired goal—in this respect, they are the best instrument. The government which wants to help domestic filmmakers avoid high production costs can grant them a specific subsidy to compensate for these higher costs while the ticket price remains the same. As a result, moviegoers are not hurt. Therefore, compared to a quota, a production subsidy achieves the same goal (protecting the producers to be protected and only those) at a lower cost (no harm for the consumers). The major benefit from using subsidies is thus to "target" the exact market participant that the government wants to support—the producers in the film case—without creating costs for other market participants—the moviegoers for instance. If the product in question is internationally traded, the same scenario works; simply the price prevailing on the domestic market is the global price, if one assumes for simplicity sake that this country has no other trade barrier.

Identifying the exact market participants to be supported appears thus as an essential task from a good governance perspective. In fact, it is the basic first step of any well-designed cost–benefit analysis of public policy (see, for instance, Australian Government [2020]). For instance, let us consider the case where domestic film producers suffer not because of too high production costs but because of a lack of workers having some specific skills.

In this case, subsidies should aim to develop the skills that are lacking—this is the target. Granted directly to the filmmakers, subsidies will almost certainly be used for other purposes than to improve the desired skills. This is because fostering skilled labor (technicians and experts) takes much time and does not have a guaranteed outcome in producing competent trainees given the fact that filmmaking usually takes 3–5 years. In this case, why then would a film producer use a portion of the subsidies (s)he receives for a given film to fund a study program if there is the great risk that the trainees will be unsatisfactory or—if competent—hired by other film producers? Hence, filmmakers would rather utilize well-trained and/or well-experienced workers from other countries. The key lesson to be drawn from this case is that the level of subsidies is only one aspect of the problem—not the most important. More crucial is the adequacy of the subsidies to the desirable targets for developing the national film industry.

Box 1 A More Detailed Economic Analysis of a Production Subsidy
This box presents the simplest case of a subsidy to producers in a market where it is assumed that all films have the same level of attractiveness. Price refers to the ticket price, quantity to the number of films. The supply curve SS for domestic films has an increasing slope because domestic film producers who deliver this supply are lined up by their capacity to keep costs low when they produce one film. The demand curve DD for all films has a decreasing slope because it is assumed that the consumers who are behind this demand have a limited capacity to watch movies. Finally, there are foreign film producers. Again, for simplicity sake, they are assumed to be so numerous that it is always possible to find a filmmaker in the world creating a movie at a cost OP: the supply curve of the foreign filmmakers is thus a flat curve, PP. In such a market, domestic filmmakers can produce and "sell" in the movie theaters OK films, and the foreign film producers can sell KN films. The domestic moviegoers watch a total of ON films for a ticket price OP.

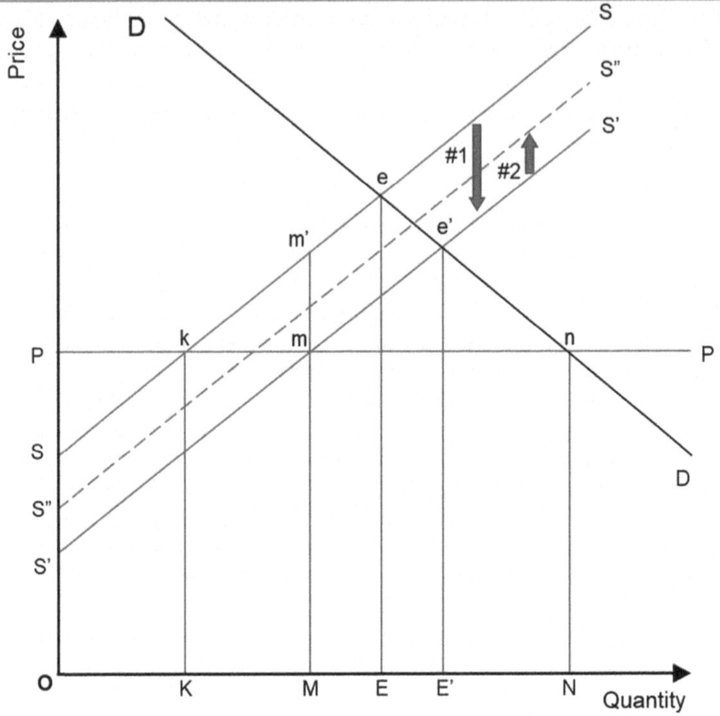

In what follows, one assumes that the subsidy SS' is the same for each domestic movie. Granting this subsidy to domestic filmmakers is thus illustrated by a shift downward (arrow #1) of their supply curve—from SS to S'S'. In other words, domestic producers "earn" for each film the ticket price (which is still OP because there is no tariff or quota restricting the entry of foreign filmmakers) plus the subsidy per film SS'. They can then produce and sell OM films despite the fact that their production costs are m'M because the subsidy "pays" the difference m'm. Note that moviegoers continue to watch the same amount of films (ON) but that they watch more domestic films (OM instead of OK) and less foreign films (MN instead of KN).

This standard presentation of the impact of a subsidy allows to rectify two mistakes that are routinely made when discussing the film policy. First, the fact that more domestic films are produced when subsidies are granted should not be seen as two independent results: the increase in the number of movies—from OE to OE'—is a purely mechanical effect of the subsidy granted SS'. It is easy to see that granting a subsidy SS' and having the same number of films produced OE would mean that something has gone very wrong in the way the subsidy has been enforced. Second, a similar remark could be said about the share of domestic films in the total film market: the fact that the post-subsidy market share (OM/ON) is greater than the pre-subsidy market share (OK/ON) is a mirror image of the subsidy SS'.

So far, granting subsidies has been assumed to be costless. In fact, running a subsidization process costs money, and that changes the expected result of subsidies: it shifts upwards the supply curve reached by subsidy S'S' to a position shown by S"S" in the figure above. In other words, the "net" subsidy (the subsidy received minus the cost it generates for being requested and granted) is smaller than the "gross" subsidy granted by the government (the subsidy generally considered in the policy debate). The impact of the subsidy—the reduction of the production costs to the firms—is thus smaller than the one expected in the case of a cost-free subsidy scenario. One cannot even exclude the case where the implementation costs are so large that the costs of producing domestic films is larger when subsidies are granted than when they are not provided.

1.3 *Confronting Reality: Four Warnings on the True Costs of Subsidies*

The analysis in the previous section has an important limitation: it assumes that granting subsidies has no costs because public funds used in the subsidization process are freely available. In reality, providing subsidies does require sizable resources. What follows presents the four main costs that should be taken into consideration, all the more because they can end up ultimately harming the film industry itself (see the last paragraph of Box 1).

First, getting public funds is costly. Conditions for requesting subsidies in the real world are generally complicated, and this is particularly the case in the film industry. As has been mentioned when examining the KOREU FTA Protocol for Cultural Protection (see Chapter 3), filmmakers have to comply to "cultural tests" that list the many conditions that they have to fulfill if they want to be eligible for domestic subsidies. That may force film producers to change their initial production plan in order to fit the mold imposed by these cultural tests, such as hiring more national actors and crews than initially required, changing the shooting location, or some elements of the script. All these changes result in additional costs of all kinds.

Second, subsidies are also costly from the perspective of those who grant subsidies—the state and ultimately the taxpayers. For instance, granting a subsidy to another activity than to the film industry could deliver a larger benefit for society as a whole. From a "good governance" perspective, this "opportunity cost" argument should be pushed one step further. Before granting a subsidy, a government should always consider the possibility that not granting the subsidy—hence not levying the tax needed for funding the subsidy—may be the best option with respect to the national interest. This is because taxpayers may have a better use of their money than any alternative use envisaged by the government or a collective body. Opportunity costs deserve one important remark: the larger the subsidies granted to the film industry, the bigger the likely size of the opportunity costs of these subsidies. This argument should induce the subsidizing countries to circumscribe and carefully define their subsidy policies—a principle that resurface often throughout the rest of the book.

Third, subsidies are costly because they are based on a decision process that is not disciplined by the many forces present in the market (Kornai 1986). There is no other way to grant subsidies than to allocate them through committees who can easily ignore or misread market needs. It is important to stress that these market needs exist for "commercial" as well as "artistic" films. The audience for artistic films has preferences and tastes for films that may not well be taken into consideration by the committees that are in charge of artistic films. In all these cases, subsidies distort the film market because production companies are more induced to follow the committees' decisions than to behave in an entrepreneurial manner for the benefit of the moviegoers who are willing to watch interesting films regardless of whether they are commercial or artistic productions. In other words, there is a high risk that beneficiaries produce films that please a few members of the committees in charge of granting the subsidies rather than the wider public. Such a situation also helps create a form of "collective censorship" that ends up filtering films that can be subsidized (Parc 2020, p. 462).

Last but not least, subsidies are hard to monitor. A subsidy can be granted to a film producer, but its ultimate beneficiaries are the owners of the resources that subsidies have been made available. A parallel can be made with agricultural subsidies: they are generally paid to the farmers, but the farmers buy land, equipment, or fertilizer with these subsidies. As a result, the final recipients of the subsidies are likely to be the owners of these inputs, not the farmers who were supposed to be aided. Needless to say, monitoring the ultimate recipients of the subsidies in these conditions is an almost impossible task—as illustrated by the last sixty years of agricultural subsidies. The final part of this chapter will come back on this essential issue.

1.4 The Case of the Other Financial Incentives

Until the late 1990s, the countries that implemented significant film subsidy policies over a long period of time—such as France—relied mostly on granting direct subsidies to film producers or distributors. In more recent times, other financial incentives have increasingly emerged as the dominant type of public financial support, as shown in detail later in this chapter. They consist of a wide range of measures—tax waivers, tax exemptions, credits, grants, cash rebates, and among others—generally based on the expenses that producers pay to produce their films. The range of the eligible expenses is also very wide. They vary from very film-specific expenses, such as renting a studio, filming, or special IT skills for visual effects, to expenses related to basic needs, such as hotel accommodation and meals for cast and crew.

From the film industry perspective, the most robust argument in favor of such "tax relief schemes" compared to direct subsidies for production is the lower level of constraints they generally impose on the production choices of the film companies. Direct subsidies for productions tend to be very intrusive on the basic choices of the film producers with their numerous requirements and constraints listed in the "cultural test." Tax relief schemes also possess such constraints, although they tend to be expressed in less precise and restrictive terms.

Furthermore, tax relief schemes are often justified on the basis that they generate localized activities and income—more jobs or value added in the region or country. Yet there is much doubt on whether these goals can really be achieved. Most of the existing studies that estimate the increases in terms of jobs or value added generated by tax reliefs are based on accounting methods which almost invariably find net benefits—more jobs or value added than in the absence of support.[2] However, this result answers the wrong question: it is not whether these tax relief schemes bring more jobs or value added—indeed, it would be quite astonishing if they did not. Rather, the question is whether the same amount of funds allocated to a tax relief scheme for the film industry would have generated more jobs and/or value added than if they were used in another activity outside of the film industry. Answering this question requires a fully-fledged cost–benefit analyses. The few cost–benefit studies that have addressed this question show that the costs of tax relief schemes tend to be larger than their benefits.[3] And the few econometric studies testing the relations between the goal(s) officially targeted, such as jobs or value added, and the magnitude of tax relief schemes have found no statistically significant relationship between the goal(s) and tax relief schemes.[4]

Up until the early 1990s, tax relief schemes were primarily devoted toward supporting domestic companies. Since then, there has been an increasing number of tax relief schemes available to foreign film companies, channeling an ever-growing amount of funds. The surge of such schemes has been driven by different reasons for the beneficiary companies and the host countries.

From the perspective of the beneficiaries, the main rationale for film producers is to gain access to cheaper inputs for producing their films. This movement began in North America, with the delocalization of Hollywood film productions from their usual filming locations (California) to less expensive places (other US states, Canada, or the

[2] For the UK, see Oxford Economics. (2007). *The Economic Impact of the UK Film Industry*. https://www2.bfi.org.uk/sites/bfi.org.uk/files/downloads/economic-impact-of-the-uk-film-industry-2007.pdf; For the US, see MNP LPP (2013), *Economic and Social Impacts of the Florida Film and Entertainment Industry Financial Incentive Program*, https://www.motionpictures.org/wp-content/uploads/2014/01/Economic-and-Social-Impacts-of-the-Florida-Film-and-Entertainment-Industry-Financial-Incentive-Program.pdf.

[3] See Zin, D. (2010). *Film Incentives in Michigan*. https://www.senate.michigan.gov/SFA/Publications/Issues/FilmIncentives/FilmIncentives.pdf; New England Public Policy Center, *Cost–benefit Analysis of Connecticut's Film Tax Credit*. https://www.bostonfed.org/-/media/Documents/neppc/weiner011609.pdf.

[4] See Thom, M. (2018). Lights, Camera, but No Action? Tax and Economic Development. Lessons from State Motion Picture Incentive Programs. *American Review of Public Administration* 48 (1): 33–51; Thom, M., and B. An (2017). Fade to Black? Exploring Policy Enactment and Termination through the Rise and Fall of State Tax Incentives for the Motion Picture Industry. *American Politics Research* 45 (1): 85–108.

UK). Interestingly, this move has triggered the first significant anti-globalization movement in the US as seen with the candidacy of the billionaire Ross Perot for the presidential elections of 1992 and 1996. His famous campaign slogan during this time was the "giant sucking sound going south," which he used in reference to the negative effects brought on by NAFTA.

From the host (donor) countries, the rationale is more varied. First, a number of governments believe that tax relief schemes can attract foreign filmmakers to a host country and let local filmmakers and workers enjoy the spill-over effects by collaborating together. Second, there is also the hope that idle local filmmaking facilities will be used by foreign producers. Finally, hosting a blockbuster filmmaking project which mobilizes a large number of various inputs such as accommodation, alimentation, and transportation as well as other additional equipment can boost the reputation of the donor country—revealing, for instance, the beauty of its national landscape, the richness of its monuments, or the quality of its tourism industry (Parc and Messerlin 2020, p. 35).

The truth is less rosy. Very often, it can be perceived that at best foreign filmmakers enter a country to create shared value with the local producers but not to improve them, or at worst only to benefit from their local advantages. This means that if there is a positive effect from hosting foreign filmmakers, it is only within the limited time when they shoot their films. This relatively short-term horizon implies that foreign filmmakers have more incentives to bring in their own workers than to foster local labor or technician pool for specific skills which are not available locally. In short, they have few chances to generate significant spill-over effects. Another aspect of this time dimension is that if a country does not continuously attract foreign films, the benefits of its whole policy are unsustainable. The important question then becomes: is frequently attracting a number of foreign film projects an easy task or not? Finally, all these arguments raise a crucial question which is largely ignored by the decision makers of the subsidizing country—but not by its domestic film companies: to what extent do tax relief schemes targeting foreign filmmakers ultimately discriminate against the domestic filmmakers of the host country, a crucial issue examined in Chapter 5.

From the perspective of governments, an important difference between tax relief schemes and subsidies is that these other financial incentives impose additional fiscal burdens for them. The final expenses of these schemes are often known with less certainty and longer delays than in the case of direct subsidies to the film producers. The best illustration of such problems has been the UK schemes known as "Section 42" and "Section 48" introduced in 1992 and 1997, respectively. They were abruptly terminated without warning in 2006 after the UK government concluded that the system was being abused (Stephen Follows 2016).

When attracting foreign filmmakers, there is thus a great danger that the host country is ready to give "excessively" generous offers. For instance, preliminary studies undertaken for preparing the new UK tax relief schemes in 2008 have suggested that production costs in the UK "should" be roughly 30% lower than those in Los Angeles, and 5 to 15% lower than those in countries such as Australia or Canada (Olsberg|SPI 2008). In this case, foreign studios reap the benefits from the inflated advantages built-in with the tax relief or subsidy schemes. In passing, the fact that these cost differentials are so large raises serious questions not only on their economic justification but also on the true economic value derived from the competition among countries granting such fiscal benefits.

2 What Explains the Irresistible Rise of Film Subsidies in the World?

It is remarkable that all the countries covered in this book have followed broadly the same historical pattern in terms of instruments of protection. After a period of almost exclusive reliance on import or screen quotas to protect their domestic industry, they have shifted to an almost exclusive recourse to subsidies or tax relief schemes—the quotas which remain still on the rule books for most countries concerned have often a limited impact (MPA 1994).

The countries covered in this book are diverse enough to cast doubt that such a common shift has been a series of fortuitous events. Rather, this general evolution suggests that the same economic and political forces have been at work in all of these countries. If this is the case, the emergence of subsidies as the key instrument of protection during the last twenty or thirty years is unlikely to be challenged soon. It is thus important to understand the motives behind this widespread shift.

2.1 Implementing Quotas: Embroiled in Endless Feuds

The first reason for a shift to subsidies is that the use of quotas has created an endless source of domestic and international conflicts among a number of vested interests. First, in the domestic context, a quota benefits mostly one segment of the film industry which is to the detriment of the other segments. In the Korean import quota case, the importers have reaped almost all its benefits to the detriment of the film producers, and above all moviegoers. Expressed in general terms, this means that a quota regime divides a film industry into segments with opposite interests. Those who are in the losing camp have strong incentives to fight for a change in the domestic regulations to suit their favor.

Korea offers a good illustration of this divide. Table 1 presents a brief overview of the evolution of the Korean Motion Picture Law (MPL). It has been amended no less than six times between 1962 and 1986 as the government believed that these changes would contribute toward boosting the Korean film industry.

From the international context, implementing quotas has also generated a number of endless feuds. This has been studied at length with the thirty years of the Korea-US saga on the import and screen quotas (see Chapters 2 and 3). However, the Korean case appears as a simple one. Table 1 presents a brief history of the more complicated Franco-US disputes. The long list of French quotas suggests an interesting remark: US pressure to eliminate them has not been as powerful as is often believed. They have not prevented successive French governments from imposing new barriers on US films as soon as the previous ones were eliminated—the main result being a vicious circle of ever costlier distortions.

The most famous case in this respect is the Blum-Byrnes agreement. Signed in May 1946, it sought to eliminate France's huge existing debt to the US and obtain new US credit in exchange for opening the French market to a number of cultural products, mostly Hollywood films. Although France's international negotiating position was weak at the time due to its poor economic condition, US pressure was not sufficient enough to prevent France to renege on its film commitment a few years later. In September 1948, the French Parliament passed a law requiring French movie theaters to reserve five weeks out of every thirteen for domestic films (a screen quota) and re-introducing import quotas on dubbed US films.

Table 1 The main instruments of the French and Korean film policies

Instrument	*France*		*Korea*	
Import quotas	1928–1930	Import licenses only to exporters of French films	1958–1966	Import quota granted on a reward basis
	1932–today	Dubbing of US films to be made in France	1963–1970	Import licenses granted to integrated firms (producer and importer)
	1936–1952	Quotas on dubbed US films (150, then 110 in 1952)	1966–1986	Import quota: Three Korean films to be produced for importing one foreign film
	1960–today	Agreement with Motion Picture Export Association of America (MPEAA) to limit imports of US films to 110 per year	1970 to 1984	Frequent amendments for import and screen quotas
Screen quotas	1946–1948	French films to be screened at least 4 weeks per quarter (31%)	1986–2006	Korean films to be screened at least 146 days per year (40%)
	2010–today	Private *programming commitments* covering 70% of the French film market	2006–today	Korean films to be screened at least 73 days per year (20%)
Subsidies	1948–1959	Temporary Assistance Law renewed in 1953	1990s–2007	Subsidies funded by a general budget
	1959–today	A permanent subsidy policy funded (initially) on a 10.72% tax per ticket	2007–today	More subsidies funded on a 3% tax per ticket

Sources Parc (2014) and Messerlin and Parc (2017)

A particularly interesting aspect of the international conflicts generated by quotas is that their main beneficiaries can be foreign film companies not the domestic ones that they are meant to help. For instance, the French import quota adopted in 1928 was scrapped not because of US pressure but there were too few French films produced and too many movie theaters that only Hollywood studios could feed—unintended negative results of the trade barriers (Hayward 2005, p. 26).

Another illustration is the 1960 French agreement with the MPEA which has limited the imports of US films to 110 per year. From a political aspect, this looks like a French diplomatic success but from an economic perspective, such an agreement is an "export quota" similar to the so-called voluntary export restraints. These measures were imposed between the 1960s and the 1990s by developed countries on the industrial products that emerging Asian industrial economies like Korea exported at that time. The key feature of export quotas is that they grant to foreign exporters—the US studios in the case of the 1960 film agreement with France—the prime responsibility to enforce the quota agreed, meaning a privileged access to the rents generated by the quota.

2.2 *Implementing Subsidies: The Sweet Sound of Cooperative Behavior*

These permanent conflicts were a strong incentive for policymakers and the film business alike to find an alternative measure of protection which would eliminate, or at least reduce drastically, these feuds. To achieve this goal, such alternative measures should rely on and develop a more "cooperative" behavior among the various segments of the industry that would facilitate the creation of a "coalition" among all these players. The film interests would then be in the best position to collectively extract from the government the highest level of protection for the whole domestic industry. The solution to this situation is public financial support—subsidies and tax relief schemes, which explains the irresistible rise of public support and the inevitable decline of quotas over the last seventy years.

The "magic formula" ensuring such a cooperative behavior is based on a two-step process guaranteeing cooperation among the various segments of the industry. The first step is to make sure that all the segments of the film industry are included in the coalition in order to extract collectively the largest possible financial support from the government. No key segment of the industry should remain outside the coalition because its absence would weaken the coalition and/or make it less stable. This explains why, after some debate, the exhibition segment was finally included in the French film industry in 1967—making it eligible to an important share of the total amount of French subsidies (see Chapter 5). The second step of the magic formula is to devise a mechanism acceptable by all segments on how to share public funds among them in a sustainable manner—that is, in a manner that would ensure that the situation of every segment cannot be improved without deteriorating the situation of another segment.

This magic formula has been put into a workable legal and institutional framework by the 1948 French Temporary Assistance Law which has inspired many of the film subsidy schemes, including in Asia—notably China and Korea. This frame relies on two pillars. First, the financial resources of the subsidy scheme are under the direct control of the film industry itself. For instance, in the earlier years, the funds for the subsidy scheme have relied on a tax on ticket sales (hereafter the "seat tax"): this tax is levied by the movie theaters, and its revenues do not transit through the general budget procedure but are directly collected and disbursed by a specific body acting on behalf of the whole film industry. As a result, these funds do not run the risk of being re-allocated to economic activities other than the film industry—as if they were transiting through the general parliamentary process of adopting the nation's budget. Second, the allocation of subsidies among the various segments of the film industry is decided, implemented, and monitored by the same crucial institution which is run by the representatives of all segments of the film industry. This institution is the *Centre national du cinéma et de l'image animée* (CNC) in France and the Korean Film Council (KOFIC) in Korea (see Chapter 5 for more details).

2.3 The Flip Side of Financial Support: Easily Out of Control

It took time for the magic formula to reveal its flip side. It has largely "insulated" the film industry from the rest of the economy, with the government progressively losing control of "national" film policies to the benefit of private vested interests. This crucial result can be best illustrated by the French subsidy policy which is often seen by many in the global film industry as the example to follow and which has the huge advantage of having been in place for over seventy years—basically since 1948—making it the perfect test case for checking whether a loss of control has occurred or not in the long run, and how serious it has been. For comparison sake, the same information is shown for Korea which has introduced a subsidy scheme apparently similar to the French one in 2007.

Figure 1 reports only the subsidies *stricto* sensu granted from 1970 to 2018 for France and from 1999 to 2018 for Korea since Korean subsidies were very small before 1999. This ensures the fairest comparison possible between the two countries since, until 2017, Korea did not use

Fig. 1 French and Korean film subsidies in the long run (1970–2018) (*Sources* CNC [various issues] and Cour des Comptes [2012, 2014] for France, Kim [2013], Parc [2014, 2017, 2018], and Messering and Parc [2017] for Korea)

the other forms of financial support that have been progressively introduced in France, such as subsidies to the TV industry for producing films and tax relief schemes. Figure 1 deserves a preliminary remark which sheds an interesting light on the risk of losing control in the French case: the exact level of the annual subsidies in France is surprisingly hard to know. For instance, the years 2008–2012 show notable discrepancies in the amounts of French subsidies granted for these years published by the CNC and those published by the Cour des Comptes (2012, 2014), the most independent and informed French institution on public funding or by the *Inspections Générales des Finances et des Affaires Culturelles* (2013).[5] These discrepancies reveal how much freedom the "managing arm" of the film industry—the CNC—has for collecting and interpreting data. By the same token, it reveals how difficult it can be for a government to reform and to regain control of their support scheme. This is a

[5] The main mission of the "Cour des Comptes" (Court of Auditors) is to ensure the proper use of public money and to inform citizens thereof. In practice, wherever public money is committed, the Court ensures the regularity, efficiency and effectiveness of management. It is an independent jurisdiction, "equidistant from the Parliament and the Government" for which it assists both.

recurrent observation from the Cour des Comptes (2012, 2014) or, in more felted terms, from the latest budgetary discussions at the National Assembly (Giraud 2018).

Figure 1 shows two essential features of the "flip side of financial support." First, the growth trajectory of the French subsidy scheme exhibits almost no-reversal after the early 1980s, but rather a relentless increase. In 2018, the level of French film subsidies is almost three times—in constant USD—their level in 1970. Interestingly, its level in 1970 was already higher than the peak of Korean subsidies reached in 2014. In fact, this constant growth has existed since its origin: in 1948, the French seat tax was initially supposed to last for only four years, but it was renewed in 1953 for another four years, and it was definitively included in the French legal system in 1959 (Vézyroglou and Péton 2014). This evolution is all the more remarkable because it has required not only increases of the seat tax but also the adoption by the French Parliament of a number of new taxes to expand always further funding for subsidies over the last thirty years: taxes on TV channels (1986), videos (1993 and 2003), video-on-demand services (VoD) (2007), Internet subscriptions (2013), and streaming platforms (2018). All these new taxes (except the tax on videos) benefit from the same special fiscal status as the seat tax: they are levied by the film industry, and their revenues do not transit through the general budget.

This general impression of a process that has been out of control for the last thirty years becomes even stronger if one carries out a more detailed examination. Key peaks of the growth trajectory for French subsidies can be easily related to important events in the French political history. For instance, Fig. 1 shows two particularly visible peaks in 1977 and 1983, which both correlate with national (presidential and parliamentary) elections, revealing the ambiguous relationship between top politicians and the media. These cases are not unique, and there are other more recent examples.[6] They all reveal the strong leverage of the film industry's vested interests on French political life.

[6] These cases involve all the French political parties: the 1977 peak involved the conservative party, the 1983 peak the socialist party. The latest case dates from May 2019 with the creation of an investment fund of EUR 225 million for the creative and cultural industries in accordance with a commitment taken by President Macron during his presidential campaign. https://www.lemonde.fr/economie/article/2019/05/13/un-financement-plus-large-pour-le-cinema_5461609_3234.html.

The second result of Fig. 1 concerns Korea which shows a different picture. Until the late 1990s, Korean subsidies have been insignificant. Once again, this point is important to stress because, as shown in Chapter 2, during the period from the late 1980s to the 1990s there have been the most decisive efforts of industrial restructuring in the Korean film industry. In other words, these major industrial efforts have been undertaken without public support. This significantly challenges the usual argument that public intervention in film industries to counter the dominance from Hollywood films is necessary during the take-off phase of the domestic film industry at stake. As already mentioned, it is fair to note that this low level of public support has not always been a conscious choice among successive Korean governments and also reflects the fact that in the past they simply did not consider the film industry as important for the country's economic development.

While Korean film subsidies may have become more substantial since 2007, they have followed a very different trajectory than the French ones. Between 2007 and 2014, the Korean scheme has shown an ever-increasing pattern similar to France during the period 1950s–1960s: the creation of a 3% seat tax was initially expected to last for only four years when it was renewed in 2014 (Parc 2021). However, since 2014, Fig. 1 shows a sharp fall of 40% in Korean subsidies between 2014 and 2018—an evolution radically different from what happened in Korea, as examined further below.

3 Public Financial Support: The Panacea for the World Film Industries?

The previous analysis can be extended further into two directions. First, the growth of public support is not just limited to France and Korea as other major film producing countries, in particular the UK and the US, have followed a similar route. There is thus a need to look at these additional countries in order to see whether they confirm the evolution observed in France and Korea. Second, simply examining the total level of public financial support is not enough. One should also pay attention to the distribution of this support among the two main forms of public support—subsidies and tax relief schemes—because these two instruments differ sharply in the respective role that they give to governments and companies.

3.1 A Worldwide Boom

Table 2 presents the first attempt ever made to collect information available on the overall size of the financial support granted by four countries—Korea, France, the UK, and the US—and its distribution by the main type of financial support. The limited coverage in terms of countries is due to the difficulty to find trustworthy and time-consistent data in this regard. However, this limitation is not such a handicap for this study because these four countries represent roughly 55% of the world's box office revenues in the early 2000s, and 40% in the late 2010s—a fall

Table 2 Financial support: overall size and structure (selected countries, constant 2018 USD)

	Subsidies				*Tax relief schemes*			*Investment funds*
	Korea	*France*		*UK*	*France*	*UK*	*US*	*Korea*
		Film	*TV*					
	[1]	*[2]*	*[3]*	*[4]*	*[5]*	*[6]*	*[7]*	*[8]*
2005	n.a	364.2	105.7	n.a	34.8	n.a	141.2	n.a
2006	40.7	336.0	109.0	219.2	49.4	241.0	274.6	9.7
2007	80.6	334.5	102.2	233.2	59.9	202.6	638.9	11.1
2008	95.8	339.3	111.4	237.8	71.9	169.4	894.2	32.5
2009	90.3	289.9	93.4	245.6	72.5	159.0	870.0	62.7
2010	79.5	296.0	87.5	251.0	71.5	225.3	1,033.8	106.4
2011	113.1	385.6	95.9	232.2	68.5	310.2	1,282.4	148.0
2012	115.4	398.2	90.0	229.6	84.1	309.6	1,621.8	191.8
2013	116.5	394.0	99.0	239.2	75.5	316.8	1,638.8	109.4
2014	124.1	425.0	87.4	237.6	99.6	344.1	1,769.4	151.0
2015	110.8	399.5	81.7	246.2	100.9	418.2	1,528.4	126.4
2016	90.8	425.3	99.8	244.1	104.0	523.3	1,651.8	57.1
2017	80.3	441.6	95.2	226.6	192.1	564.0	n.a	n.a
2018	71.8	423.2	102.7	n.a	211.5	n.a	n.a	n.a

Notes Korea-subsidies schemes (General and Special Accounts, Movie Pictures Development Fund in column [1]) and investment scheme (Fund of the Funds in column [8]); France-subsidies granted by CNC to the film industry (column [2]) and to the broadcasting industry as film producers (column [3]); UK-subsidies mostly granted to domestic production (column [4]) and granted in the tax relief regime (column [6]). Data on fiscal years have been recalculated on the basis of calendar year; US-tax relief scheme of states (column [7])

Sources: Based on Parc and Messerlin (2018); originally from The Ministry of Culture, Sport and Tourism of the Republic of Korea (various issues), *Centre national du cinéma et de l'image animée* (various issues), British Film Institute (various issues), Thom (personal contact in 2018).

due to the rise of the Chinese film market, which is now close to being the largest in the world. Interestingly, each of these four countries is a representative case. The US is the dominant power and considered as the most successful in terms of commercial films. France and the UK are the leading film producers in Europe while their approach to their respective industry is rather different: France claims to insist on cultural and artistic aspects while the UK adopts both a commercial and cultural approach. For its part, Korea illustrates the case of a film industry starting from scratch and having grown without relying upon subsidies until 2007.

A clear picture of the boom for the total financial support can be seen in Table 2. In 2016, after ten years of continuous growth, the total support granted by France, the UK, and the US or more precisely the individual states in the US is 2.5 times bigger than in 2006, a much higher growth than the one observed (1.5 times) for the box office revenues of these film industries over the same period (the box office revenues of the US films are those earned in the ten countries selected in Fig. 1 in Chapter 3). The most important force behind this surge is the support granted by the individual states of the US: almost non-existent in the late 1990s, it is six times larger in 2016 than in 2006. However, French and UK support have also grown by more than the corresponding box office revenues of their own industries: 1.6 times between 2006 and 2017 compared to 1.4 times, respectively.

3.2 *The Korean Exception*

Korea emerges as a remarkable exception with respect to public support. It has a much lower level of total public support than France and the UK while having a larger film industry than these two countries in terms of production and market size. This is the case even if one adds subsidies (column [1] of Table 2) to the private–public investment funds which is called as the Fund of the Funds (column [8]). These funds need to be interpreted correctly: they are generally operated on a private profit basis, receiving the same rate of return as films that were entirely produced on a commercial basis. However, these funds also go to films that can have a promising potential without government intervention. This seems a sound approach for promoting cultural creativity. However, if such films have a too systematically low rate of return, these funds should be interpreted as de facto subsidizing bodies.

Yet even if one assumes that the whole Fund of the Funds behaves as a group of purely subsidizing agencies, Korea remains an exception. First, since 2014, both the subsidies and the Fund of the Funds have markedly declined (see Table 2). This parallel evolution has left the composition of the overall Korean public support broadly unchanged since the late 2000s, with subsidies and the Fund's funds being almost on par. Second, recently, Korea has begun to implement financial incentives devoted to domestic film companies (tax deductions in 2017) and foreign firms (cash rebates on qualified spending in 2019) for a period of five years. The ceiling of the budget available for to the first scheme is estimated to be USD 26 million, but that does not mean that such a budget will be entirely spent. That said, it is worth noting that even if entirely spent, these USD 26 million will not be enough to compensate the decline in subsidies.[7] Together, all these features confirm that Korea's outperformance has little to do with its public support policy, as highlighted in Chapter 1.

3.3 *Changes in the Composition of the Financial Support*

Another crucial point observed in Table 2 is the profound change in distribution between subsidies and tax relief in France, the UK, and the US. There has been a continuous increase in the provision of tax relief compared to subsidies. In 2006, more than half of the public support granted by the three countries consisted of subsidies, that is, transfers from taxes levied directly by the domestic film industries (seat taxes) or from the public budget. In 2016, this share was only 24%. However, this global evolution masks vastly different evolutions in each of these three countries.

French support is probably the most complex. It consists of three main categories: subsidies to the film industry per se (column [2], also illustrated in Fig. 1), subsidies granted to the TV industry for their contribution to the film production (column [3]), and tax relief schemes (column [5]). It has further witnessed substantial reforms of the tax relief schemes at the end of the period covered—in particular a U-turn on their beneficiaries. Up until the mid-2010s, they used to be reserved for French films, but have since then undergone reforms largely driven by

[7] This result remains true even if one takes into consideration the available information on the increase of Korean subsidies in 2019. Data on French subsidies available for 2019 shows stagnation when compared to the previous year.

the desire of the French government to "compete" with the tax relief programs provided in other countries by granting more generous subsidies to foreign films. The idea was that this effort will attract "back" foreign filmmakers to shoot films in France and cooperate with French studios (see Chapter 5). As a result, France which granted exclusively subsidies (90%) in 2006 has now a sizable share of its support in the form of tax relief that represents roughly 30% of France's total support in 2018.

The UK subsidy policy has always relied mostly on tax relief schemes (53% in 2006, 73% in 2017). Since its reform in 2007, the new tax relief scheme (column [6]) targets films produced by Hollywood studios, either alone or in close cooperation with UK companies. It is estimated that two-thirds of this group of tax relief go to US film companies (interview at the British Film Institute 2018). The UK also grants subsidies under the heading of "total public sector selective investment" (column [4]) mostly for supporting the so-called UK independent films—that is, films with little or no involvement from the US studios. These funds involve roughly twenty institutions: various government "departments" (Ministries), the National Lottery, Channel 4, and the BBC among other institutions.

The US federal government does not run a notable subsidy program. However, no less than 31 individual states of the US (alongside Washington, D.C., Puerto Rico, and the US Virgin Islands) are operating their own support schemes—predominantly under the form of tax relief schemes (Messerlin and Parc 2020; NCSL 2018). When Canada introduced various forms of subsidy programs in an attempt to gain the economic benefits from runaway productions of the US filmmaking business, these runaway productions to Canada have come at the center of political scene. Local states of the US have set up subsidy programs in order to hold back this filmmaking business and to enjoy their economic benefits while preventing departs of this business for other destinations (Messerlin and Parc 2020). That said, since the 2010s, some individual states of the US have concluded that the benefits were not as great as expected, leading them to abandon these schemes.

Each individual US state has a different coverage of the expenses eligible for tax relief. Most of these schemes do not require a specific nationality for the film producers in order to be eligible. Yet there are some conditions that can be seen as close to the notion of nationality, for instance, the company should have been based in the state for a minimum number of years. Indeed, the US studios seem to have been de facto the largest beneficiaries. Finally, it is noteworthy that the annual amount of tax relief provided by a few individual US states are larger than the support granted by individual EU Member States. For instance, California alone has a film credit program of at least USD 330 million operating since 2015.

3.4 *Is There an Ongoing Worldwide Competition for Granting Subsidies?*

It is hard not to perceive this simultaneous growth of the national financial supports as a form of competition among the countries in providing public support. Such competition has two dimensions: each country grants support in order to help its own domestic firms and as a way to attract foreign film companies—an evolution increasingly visible since the 1990s. Anecdotal evidence from the press suggests that such a competition is ongoing and that its "foreign" dimension is amplifying. Official statements candidly justify the increase of a country's public support—especially tax credits—by pointing to the increasing amount of support provided by other countries. Such a "matching up" behavior is not new. As already mentioned above, a study for the British Film Institute has evaluated the level of tax relief schemes where UK support would be systematically more attractive than the public support provided by other countries (Olsberg|SPI 2008). That said, such a behavior is more widespread and frequent since the mid-2010s and the level of support involved is higher. For example, France and Germany have increased the funds that they make available for tax relief schemes which are seeking to attract foreign studios: between 2016 and 2018, these funds have risen from USD 60 million to USD 150 million in Germany and from USD 14 million to USD 66 million in France. Both countries have openly justified their decisions by the need to match each other's tax relief schemes—as well as that of the UK.[8]

[8] Laborde, F. (2018). *Projet de loi de finances pour 2018: Médias, livre et industries culturelles: Livre et industries culturelles.* http://www.senat.fr/rap/a17-112-43/a17-112-430.html; Bomnüter, U. (2018). State Aid for Film in Germany: Analyzing Institutions and Discussing Efficacy. In *Handbook of State Aid for Film*, ed. Paul Murschetz,

Understanding the exact process of competition among subsidizing countries requires specific attention on the increasing share of tax relief schemes in most countries. Tax relief schemes are measures made available by the governments that film companies use if they fit their needs. In fact, film companies compile information on the various schemes available in the world, compare their benefits and costs in order to use the best ones from their point of view. In this context, the rising competition among subsidizing countries results more as the complex outcome of a dynamic set of interactions between film companies and governments than as an outcome of governments' policies alone. In such an environment, no government is really capable to fully appraise the benefits and costs of its "supply" of tax relief schemes compared to those from other governments. Ultimately this situation gives the clear impression that national financial support schemes have become increasingly "out of control" at both the national and international level.

In this context, the increasing share of tax relief schemes in total support and the multiplication of the available types of support that goes with this increasing share becomes a source of concern in itself. Implementing more types of support is likely to increase the risk of inconsistencies among them—both within the national film policies and these policies—hence the global costs of the subsidy policies for the whole economy and for the film industries themselves since one type of support can undermine another type. The proposition that the more varied the instruments are, the higher the risks that they interact in a complicated and unforeseen way is a key point examined in detail in Chapter 5.

3.5 Film Support: Increasingly "Internationalized"

A corollary of this international competition in public support is that it has greatly amplified the "internationalization" of the beneficiaries of national film policies. Until the early or mid-1990s, a country provided financial support mostly to its domestic industry. The main exceptions

Roland Teichmann, and Matthias Karmasin, 297–310. Cham, Switzerland: Springer; Lodderhose, D. (2017). Germany to Court Hollywood with New $80 M Film Fund. *Deadline*, March 16. https://deadline.com/2017/03/german-courting-hollywood-with-new-big-budget-film-fund-dfff2-1202042923/; It is noteworthy that, ten years before the same argument was used in the UK for justifying an increase in UK film support; see UK Parliament. (2010). Chapter 2 : A better future for UK films, https://publications.parliament.uk/pa/ld200910/ldselect/ldcomuni/37/3706.htm.

were co-productions. In this case however, each government typically only subsidizes its national filmmaker that is involved in co-production (Parc 2020). That said, US-EU co-produced films in the 1970s have widely benefited from the financial support provided by some European countries, such as France, Italy, and the UK (Guback 1974). Today, the situation is different. Film companies, notably from Hollywood, "shop" systematically for tax reliefs that are available all over the world while increasing their bargaining power. There are fascinating anecdotes on these "hunts for subsidy." For instance, US filmmakers routinely began their quest for public support by selling the copyrights of their films to German insurance companies before leasing them back with an option to repurchase them later—all this due to German financial regulations of the insurance sector (Epstein 2010, p. 88). Since the late 1990s, this situation has become more frequent as a number of countries have openly designed their support schemes for foreign companies—with tax relief based on the expenditures of foreign film companies made in the subsidizing country, as illustrated by the above-mentioned press reports on the competition between France and Germany over funds for foreign firms.

This increasing "internationalization" of the recipients of national film policies deserves close attention. After all, presumably the film companies which are best placed to use these opportunities are the large film companies—especially the Hollywood studios—that have the staff with the necessary skills to follow the regulations all over the world and to "shop" for the most profitable ones. This creates a contradictory situation: on the one hand many countries claim to fight Hollywood's expansion; yet on the other hand, they contribute to its dominance.

At this stage it is worth exploring the magnitude of this internationalization. This can be done by reversing the perspective adopted so far: rather than to document the level of support from the point of view of the subsidizing countries—as was done until now—one can calculate the level of support from the receiving end—the film companies. Figure 2 illustrates the difference between providers and recipients of public support. It focuses on the UK and the US tax relief schemes for two reasons. The French scheme targeting foreign producers has been subjected to many revisions that make hard any stable or rigorous comparison. The Korean scheme is too small for allowing meaningful comparisons. Curves US-c and UK-c show the tax relief schemes spent by the subsidizing countries. Meanwhile the curves US-f and UK-f show those received by the film

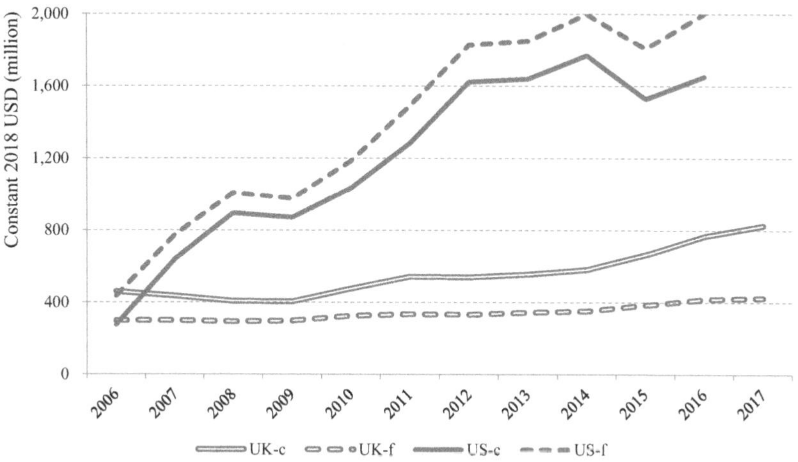

Fig. 2 Financial support: a view from the beneficiaries (*Note* UK-c and US-c stand for tax relief schemes spent by the subsidizing countries; UK-f and US-f stand for the same tax relief schemes as received by the film companies. *Sources* Based on Parc and Messerlin [2018]; originally from British Film Institute [various issues], Thom [personal contact in 2018])

companies according to the following working hypothesis: roughly two-thirds of the UK tax relief schemes have been allocated to films produced by the US majors or the so-called UK-US films. These are films co-produced by Hollywood studios and UK film companies that specialize in special effects.

Figure 2 reveals two interesting results. First, the UK-based support for US studios represented a substantial share—about half in 2006—of the support received by these studios from the individual states of the US. This share sharply declined until the mid-2010s due to the huge increase of schemes run by the individual states of the US. Since then, this share has been growing again. In other words, this UK public support emerges as a substantial "buffer" for the US studios in the volatile world of the contributions from individual states of the US. Second, the gap between UK-c and UK-f has been increasing. This evolution raises the question on which is the true objective of the UK support policy—which are its main beneficiaries. This question is recurrent, as shown in the last section of this chapter and in the next chapter.

3.6 *The Addiction to Public Support: Dependence and Fragility*

Such a glut of financial support at the international level raises several systemic questions for the future of the film industries. First, what can be the impact in the long run on the quality of the films produced with increasingly abundant public support? From what has been revealed in this chapter, severe competition among subsidizing countries is a worrisome development. It can be costly for each subsidizing country, and ultimately collectively for all the countries involved. This is all the more the case because the large film companies can shift rapidly from one subsidizing country to another one, creating adjustment stress for the film industries they abandon and for those that they enter.

Second, what are the consequences of an "addiction" among film industries to the ever-increasing subsidies from domestic and foreign countries? How would these film companies handle a sudden drop in public support which could be due to simultaneous budget cuts all over the world? Until recently, depending upon support provided by different countries would have been seen as an insurance against a sudden change in one specific country. The COVID-19 crisis offers the counter-example, with the budgetary constraints imposed in almost every country on highly subsidized sectors outside the health sector.

4 Film Subsidies: Unexpectedly Harmful to the Film Industry in the Long Term

So far, Korea has been able to keep under control its financial support to its film industry. Yet there have been repeated calls to increase the level of public support with often special reference to the French subsidy policy which is considered by proponents as the model to follow. Indeed, what is particularly interesting in the French case is that it shows an ever-increasing level of subsidies over the past seventy years—in short a remarkably stable policy over a very long period. It offers thus a unique opportunity to gather real-life evidence on whether a subsidy policy can be beneficial in the long run to a film industry—or on the contrary whether it has turned out to be ultimately detrimental after a possibly positive impact during the first years of the implementation of the subsidy schemes.

Such an analysis deserves a preliminary remark. It is important to stress that pursuing an ever-growing film subsidy policy relies on the implicit assumption that such an approach cannot generate an increasing negative impact after some time. There are good reasons to have doubts about this premise for two reasons. It assumes that the subsidies are allocated every year in the most efficient way possible—a static condition. And it assumes that the inefficiencies of the subsidies granted in the past period(s) have no impact on the efficiency of the subsidies granted in the current and future periods—a dynamic condition.

4.1 *The "Negative Impact" of Subsidies as They Grow Over Time*

There are several possible criteria for defining a "successful" subsidy policy. The most common ones used in the analyses of the film industry are the number of films produced or released and the number of box office revenues or admissions. For instance, the French box office revenues per capita of the domestic films have been larger in France than in Korea from 1980 until 2002, and have been consistently smaller since 2002 (see Fig. 2 in Chapter 1)—supporting the view that subsidies are only a "quick-fix" solution (Tannenwald 2010).

However, these criteria have a limit: they do not make visible the link between box office revenues and subsidies. The "visualization" of this link can be done by calculating the annual "impact ratio" of subsidies. This ratio is defined by the average box office revenue earned by—say French—films associated to one dollar of—say French—subsidy spent for each year. Naturally, the long-run evolution of such a ratio is influenced by other variables than subsidies, such as macroeconomic environment, technical progress in the film industry, and the tastes of moviegoers among the most important ones. In order to control for these external factors, one has calculated the impact ratio for the US films exhibited in the French movie theaters which have shared with the French films roughly the same background in terms of macroeconomic environment, technology and tastes in France.

The impact ratio for French films exhibited in France is presented in Fig. 3 (left vertical axis). The French impact ratio has rapidly and substantially declined over the whole period. This first result is not surprising when one knows that French subsidies have increased roughly threefold over the whole period (see Fig. 1) while the box office revenues for French films have slightly decreased (in constant 2018 USD) over the same period.

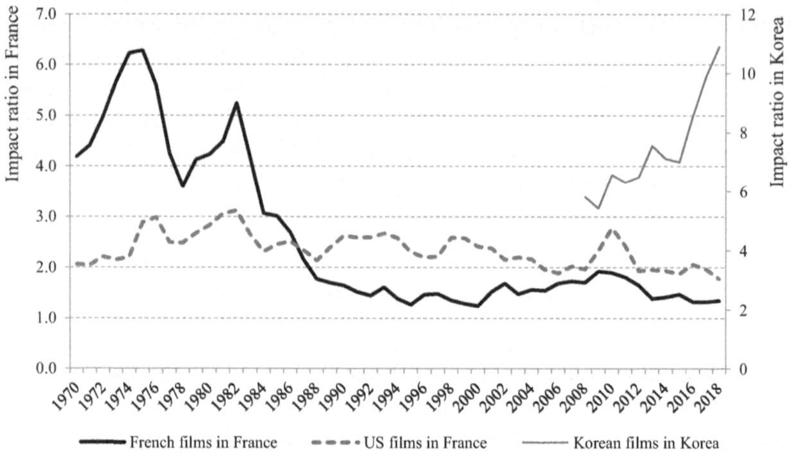

Fig. 3 The "impact ratios" of French and Korean subsidies (1970–2018) (*Source* Messerlin and Parc [2017])

Figure 3 provides another result much less predictable and much more interesting because it answers the question on the possible rising cost of granting an increasing amount of subsidies over the long term. The French impact ratio went through three clearly different sub-periods which reflect the distinction between "short" and "long" terms. It has been relatively high from the 1970s to the early-1980s (short term); it sharply declined in the 1980s; then, it was crawling at a very low level from the early 1990s until today (long term). In 2018, one dollar of subsidies is associated with less than 1.3 dollar of revenues. In other words, the French box office revenues today are barely larger than the amount of public funds injected in the French film industry. This result supports the working hypothesis of a "risk of negative long-term impact" of subsidies on the growth path of the film industry, which is not a desirable outcome of the film subsidy policy. It suggests that the value added generated by the French film industry itself is low: subsidies amount to 40% of the sum of the box office revenues and the subsidies.

This result is confirmed by a radically different approach which estimates the true contribution of subsidies to the French film industry by calculating the "subsidy rate" defined as the share of subsidies in the value added of the film industry (Parc and Messerlin 2020). Since these calculations require highly detailed data on the film industry and on the subsidies, they can be done for only one year, in fact 2012, which pertains to the last (long run) portion of the period. The estimated subsidy rate is 39% for the film industry alone—a figure consistent with the impact ratio for the year 2012. This rate is huge: it means that more than one-third of the activity done by the film industry exists because of transfers from public funds (which could have been used in more productive activities).

This result is reinforced when one compares the impact ratio for French films with that for US films exhibited in French movie theaters. Calculating an impact ratio for US films has been justified above as a way to control for external factors. It can also be justified on its own ground because the exhibition of US films in France benefits from French public support granted to movie theaters. French public support to the exhibition segment is a little known fact. It is granted for upgrading the movie theaters' facilities—this illustrates the point made in the first section of this chapter according to which enrolling the exhibition segment in the film coalition has been rewarded by a share of the total subsidies to this segment (Messerlin 2019). Indeed, subsidies to French movie theaters are considerable: no less than a third of all the French film subsidies (EUR 167 million, see Chapter 5). At first glance, these subsidies are granted in a manner that is independent from whether movie theaters exhibit foreign or French films. However, the reality is that these subsidies discriminate de facto in favor of US films simply because a large portion of this subsidies have been utilized for modernization of movie theaters, such as 3D and 4D equipment. On average, it is US films that are released in the enhanced format when compared with others; thus, they are the ones who take advantage of this modernization with the latest hi-tech equipment more than French films.

Figure 3 reveals only a modest declining trend of the impact ratio from US films screened in France, in sharp contrast with the sharp fall of French films. There is another difference: since the late 1980s, one dollar of French subsidies is associated to higher box office revenues of US films exhibited in France than on the box office revenues of French films. These two results—especially the second one—suggest that the French subsidy policy has had a substantially less positive impact in the long term on French films than on those from Hollywood. Such an undesirable result from the French film industry perspective has two causes. On the one hand, US films did not have access to French subsidies for production during this period. Simply, they had enough funds for their own production—especially with their wide access to the tax relief schemes in the UK or the individual states of the US. These schemes are much less intrusive in the key production decisions than the French production subsidies subjected to the cultural test. On the other hand, US films benefited from French subsidies that are given to movies theaters. The returns from these subsidies have presumably been higher at the beginning of the period when French movie theaters were in an urgent need to be upgraded. The declining trend at the end of the period is likely to reflect the overall lower productivity of these subsidies after decades of pouring public money into this segment.

Finally, it is interesting to calculate the impact ratio of Korean films in Korea (left vertical axis) and to compare it with the impact ratio of French films domestically (right vertical axis). Figure 3 shows two major differences: the Korean ratio is much higher and it is increasing. The first result is not surprising since it reflects the smaller subsidies in Korea compared to those in France and their recent sharp decline. This increasing impact ratio deserves though a careful interpretation. Following the economic analysis at the beginning of this chapter, it should not be understood as a "license to subsidize more." Rather, the correct question it raises is: how much potential room is left in Korea for granting more subsidies without risking a diminishing impact comparable to what has happened in France?

Again, this question can benefit from the French experience. Figure 3 shows that the fall of the French impact ratio began in 1982 and has become a permanent feature since. In the same year, the French government launched a program to provide massive subsidies with only one short pause during the period 1986–1991 (see Fig. 1). In other words, as soon as it became clear that the French film subsidy policy was running on an ever-growing path, the film industry has had lower incentives to become more efficient and/or creative. This suggests that as long as the Korean subsidy policy does not take a clear path of ever growing subsidies, the negative effects of the current Korean policy in the long term are likely to be limited.

4.2 *Distorting the Domestic Film Markets*

The decision to watch films in movie theaters depends on a large bundle of factors: the intrinsic attractiveness of the film, the marketing and advertising policies of the filmmaker and distributor, etc. Although the ticket price is almost the same from the consumers' perspective regardless of whether a film is domestic or foreign, it can be a different view for the companies as the "ticket price" itself is the result of several components. For instance, since the 1970s, French movie theaters offer a wide range of de facto different prices based on criteria, such as the hours of the (peak and off-peak) sessions for watching the films, the frequency at which the moviegoers go to theaters with yearly passes, or the fact that moviegoers form a specific group (e.g., students) or subscribe to special programs. These criteria have made the French movie theaters capable to charge de facto widely different prices for French and US films that they screen. For instance, prices in 2018 range from zero euro (2.4% of the admissions) to EUR 10 or more (11.4% of the admissions) (CNC 2018). For simplicity sake, the below analysis assumes that moviegoers make their choice based on the two criteria that seem the most important: the intrinsic attractiveness of the film and the "price" to be paid for watching the film.

The following analysis relies on the notion of "relative price"—that is, the price for watching French films compared to the price for watching US or foreign non-US films. These relative prices which should be expected to vary over time are key in the consumers decision-making process. For instance, if the moviegoers feel that the expected attractiveness of the two films is the same, they will watch the French film if its price is lower than for the US one. If the expected quality of the French film is higher than the expected quality of the US film, then moviegoers may be ready to pay a "premium" for watching the French film. The existence of such "premia" is an interesting information because it reflects indirectly the relative expected attractiveness of the two films. Comparing over half a century the evolution of the relative ticket prices for French and US films in the French film market can thus shed some light on the influence of subsidies.

There is no direct data on the relative prices for French and US films in France. But they can be estimated by dividing the box office revenues by the number of admissions for French, US, and non-US films. These "average box office revenue per admission" are acceptable proxies for the prices of each of these three groups of films. Figure 4 shows the two ratios of average box office revenue per admission which can be generated by these three prices: the first ratio corresponds to the price paid by moviegoers when watching French films relative to the price paid for watching those from the US, and the second ratio corresponds to the price paid

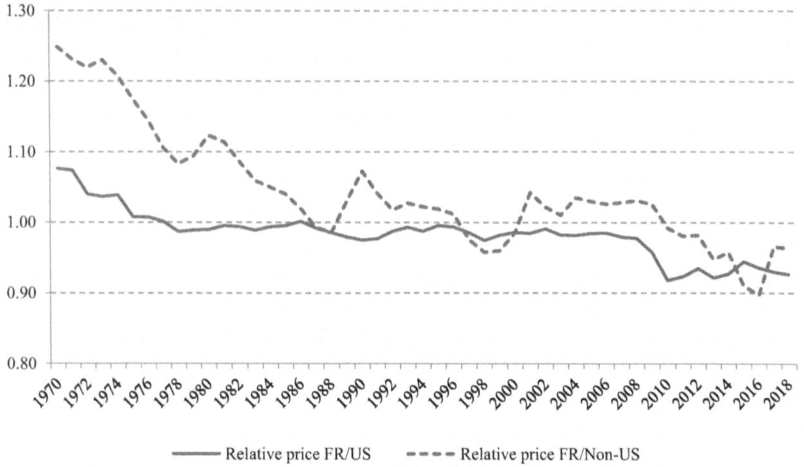

Fig. 4 Relative prices: French, US, and non-US films (1970–2014) (*Note* For making easier the visibility of the broad evolutions, the impact ratios presented are based on two-year moving averages. *Source* CNC [various issues])

by moviegoers when watching French films relative to the price paid for watching foreign non-US films. In Fig. 4, the horizontal line at 1 illustrates the case where French moviegoers do not show any preference for one type of film at the prevailing price.

In the early 1970s, prices paid for watching French films were, on average, eight percent higher than those paid for watching US films and 30% higher than those paid for watching non-US films. However, these relative prices have fallen rapidly. By the late 1970s, the relative price for French films compared to US ones was almost on par, and this situation has continued to deteriorate until the late 2000s. Finally, the 2010s have witnessed the emergence of a sharp and continuous negative gap: the prices for watching French films have been on average eight percent lower than that for US films during the 2010s. There is a similar evolution for the non-US films, though with a time lag.

This evolution mirrors two interacting forces. The first one is related to the demand side: the relative price then reflects the evolution of the comparative quality of these three types of films as perceived by French moviegoers. From this perspective, throughout the twenty one years of the period, French audiences expected that domestic films were on average "better" than US films, but the converse perception has been prevailing in more recent years. The second force is related to the supply side: the reversal of the relative price may also mirror the marketing and advertising policies of the French distributors and movie theaters as a response to the perception of the French moviegoers on the relative quality of French and US films. In other words, distributors and/or movie theaters may have been induced to find new ways to charge lower prices for French films losing attractiveness in order to attract a larger audience.

4.3 Cost Inflation Effects

Once granted, subsidies are likely to generate "cost inflation." As mentioned at the beginning of this chapter, this phenomenon has been well-documented in the case of agricultural subsidies by a host of studies from the World Bank, the OECD, or other research institutes on agriculture. When subsidized farmers buy more land, farm equipment or fertilizers because they receive subsidies, they necessarily push up their prices—triggering a cost inflation of widely different magnitude depending on the inputs. Land prices often skyrocket while the price for farm equipment or fertilizer increases more modestly. These differences are due to the fact that arable land is available in an almost fixed quantity—or needs very costly investments to be expanded. In contrast, increasing the available supply of equipment or fertilizer faces lower constraints and can be done with lower additional costs, hence requires smaller price increases to cope with a growth in demand due to subsidies.

There is no reason that similar forces do not work in the film industry. Some parts of this sector are particularly sensitive to cost inflation because they rely on crucial inputs—directors, script-writers, lead actors and actresses, and producers. These inputs are, from an economic point of view, similar to land because they tend to be very "specific": few actors can play a given role; few scriptwriters can write a given type of production—like few land plots are available for growing a specific type of grape for wine production. Because they are unique yet essential, such inputs have a particularly strong capacity to inflate their costs for the activities that use them. This is particularly the case of the film industry because of their influence on the media and their strong political clout. The other inputs used by the film industry—film locations, film crews, and studios facilities—are closer to the case of farm equipment or fertilizers, with more moderate cost increases in the case of subsidies due to the existence of substitutes among production processes or among varieties of the products.

Subsidized film companies which can buy or hire the inputs they need above what might have initially been planned are thus doomed to generate cost inflation. This is difficult to measure as it can be channeled by a myriad of complicated and/or opaque accounting and legal practices. For instance, a producer can artificially inflate the provisional accounts he/she will show when applying for subsidies by presenting actors' costs as fees paid for "image rights." Such a practice has been widely used in France, resulting in a huge increase of the fees paid for "image rights."

That said, there are some limited information on cost inflation. For instance, the *Cour des Comptes* noted that the median and average costs of French films produced between 2002 and 2012 have increased by five percent which is significantly above the inflation rates of this period (Cour des Comptes 2014).[9] Information on individual cases provides a less systematic view but gives a better idea of the magnitude of cost inflation—and especially on the range of these costs depending on the level of specificity of the inputs. For instance, a major French film producer has reported that the fees for French performers have ranged from EUR 500,000 to EUR 2 million when performing in French films, whereas they have ranged from EUR 50,000 to EUR 200,000 when the same actors have performed in foreign films (Maraval 2012). However, the most important aspect of this cost inflation is that it tends to discriminate against the domestic film industry. Local film producers have to pay inflated prices when purchasing the domestic inputs while foreign film producers benefit from tax relief schemes when purchasing the same inputs. Knowing that shooting films in European countries is generally cheaper than in the US, tax relief schemes offer more to foreign producers than what the scheme should allow, especially when compared with domestic film producers.

Though anecdotal, this information suggests several results that are essential for a correct assessment of the capacity of subsidies to inflate

[9] The main mission of the "*Cour des Comptes*" (Court of Auditors) is to ensure the proper use of public money and to inform citizens thereof. In practice, wherever public money is committed, the Court ensures the regularity, efficiency and effectiveness of management. It is an independent jurisdiction, "equidistant from the Parliament and the Government" which it assists both. See Chapter 5.

costs. First, it shows the importance of the "specificity" of inputs used by the film industry. A rough estimate suggests that specific inputs (artistic rights, producers' fees, and cast) represent at least 20% of the production costs for French films (CNC, various issues). Second, the above information suggests that cost inflation is linked to the source of subsidies. French subsidies generate cost inflation for French actors, but they have no or little impact on the costs of these actors in the rest of the word. In other words, national subsidies seem to have a much higher capacity to generate cost inflation with national inputs than with the foreign ones. All these aspects suggest the following plausible proposition: generally, the larger the public financial support to the domestic film industry, the higher the probability of cost inflation.

5 Conclusion

This chapter has begun by presenting the broad economic rationale—relative size of the film markets and cultural diversity—that seeks to justify the use of financial support as a key instrument of a film policy. At the same time, it has also highlighted the many limits of what financial support can achieve in the real world, and at what cost. Next, this chapter has focused on why so many countries have shifted from quotas to financial support over the last two decades: the cooperative behavior made possible by financial support has been very welcome after decades of never-ending bitter feuds associated with implementing quotas. However, this cooperative behavior has turned out to have a "dark side": the loss of control over film policies by the government and its increasing capture by domestic or international film companies.

The chapter has provided empirical evidence of the two key aspects of this dark side: the unprecedented boom of the total financial support granted in each country, hence at the international level; the shift in the composition of total support—away from subsidies toward tax relief schemes. This boom and this composition shift have deeply undermined the control of the national policy by governments in two ways: they have favored "competition" among subsidizing countries fueling a dangerous addiction among film companies to public funds at the national and international level; they have amplified the "internationalization" of public support given by every country—an evolution at the opposite of the official discourse on cultural diversity. Finally, this chapter has explored three brief case studies on the unexpected effects of long-term support for the industry that it intends to help.

These analyses have provided four general policy guidelines which, combined, set the core principles of what would be an "ideal" pragmatic film policy. First, a subsidy policy is preferable to a quota policy. Second, however, it runs the permanent risk to become uncontrolled and harmful to the film industry it is supposed to help—hence it requires a constant effort from governments to keep public support on sound economic objectives and at a desirable size. Third, the cases of France, the UK, and the US as the largest providers of subsidies illustrate a key problem that needs to be addressed: the emergence of a damaging competition among countries which have provided public funds to foreign as well as domestic films. Lastly, the duration of financial support schemes has been a crucial parameter of its costs: the longer the duration of a scheme, the bigger its size, the larger its likely negative effects on the film industry it is supposed to help.

At each step, this chapter has underlined how much the Korean subsidy policy is an exception: it has been relatively modest in size, has shown recent substantial decreases, has relied mostly on subsidies easier to control than tax relief schemes, and did not participate much in competition with other subsidizing countries. All these features show that the rapid growth trajectory of the Korean film industry highlighted in Chapter 1 has been achieved with a low level of public support. This is a key justification for using the term "outperforming" when qualifying the growth of the Korean film industry. The Korean policy emerges thus as an appealing benchmark case for other countries who are willing to support their film industry.

Before becoming final, this conclusion needs to be confirmed by a careful investigation of the second pillar of public support to the film industry: the regulations that shape the way domestic film markets operate and the institutions that are in charge of writing and monitoring these regulations. This forms the topic for the next chapter.

References

Australian Government. 2020. *The Australian Government Guide to Regulatory Impact Analysis* (2nd ed.). https://pmc.gov.au/sites/default/files/publications/australian-government-guide-to-regulatory-impact-analysis.pdf.

Benghozi, P.J., and C. Delage. 2000. *Une histoire économique du cinéma français: 1895–1995: Regards croisés franco-américains*. Paris: Editions L'Harmattan.

British Film Institute (BFI). Various issues. *Statistical Yearbook*. http://www.bfi.org.uk/education-research/film-industry-statistics-research/statistical-yearbook.

Centre national du cinéma et de l'image animée (CNC). Various issues. *Bilan*. https://www.cnc.fr/cinema/etudes-et-rapports/bilans/.

Cour des Comptes. 2012. *La gestion et le financement du Centre national du cinéma et de l'image animée (CNC): Exercices 2007 à 2011*. Paris: Cour des Comptes. https://www.ccomptes.fr/fr/publications/gestion-et-financement-du-centre-national-du-cinema-et-de-limage-animee-cnc.

Cour des Comptes. 2014. *Les soutiens à la production cinématographique et audiovisuelle: des changements nécessaires*. Paris: Cour des Comptes. https://www.ccomptes.fr/fr/publications/les-soutiens-la-production-cinematographique-et-audiovisuelle-des-changements.

Doyle, G. 2014. Audiovisual Services: International Trade and Cultural Policy. In *Trade Policy in Asia: Higher Education and Media Services*, ed. OECD and Asian Development Bank, 301–335. Singapore: Asian Development Bank Institute.

Epstein, E.J. 2010. *The Hollywood Economist: The Hidden Financial Reality behind the Movies. Release 2.0*. Brooklyn, New York: Melville House Publishing.

Giraud, J. 2018. Niches fiscales: «Les crédits d'impôt liés à la culture ont explosé». *Le Parisien*, November 26. https://www.leparisien.fr/economie/niches-fiscales-les-credits-d-impot-lies-a-la-culture-ont-explose-26-11-2018-7954188.php.

Grant, J. 1994. Jurassic Trade Dispute: The Exclusion of the Audiovisual Sector from the GATT. *Indiana Law Journal* 70 (4): 1333–1365.

Guback, T.H. 1974. Film as International Business. *Journal of Communication* 24 (1): 90–101.

Hayward, S. 2005. *French National Cinema*. London and New York: Routledge.

Horowitz, D.H., and P.J. Davey. 1996. Financing American Films at Home and Abroad. *Columbia-VLS Journal of Law & the Art* 20: 461–487.

Inspection Générale des Finances et Inspection Générale des Affaires Culturelles. 2013. *L'apport de la culture à l'économie en France*. Décembre, Ministère de l'Economie. https://www.economie.gouv.fr/files/03-rapport-igf-igac-culture-economie.pdf.

Karpe, C.R. 1995. European Cultural Protectionism and the Socioeconomic Forces That Will Defeat It. *Indiana International & Comparative Law Review* 5 (2): 425–459.

Kim, C.H. 2000. Building the Korean Film Industry's Competitiveness: Abolish the Screen Quota and Subsidize the Film Industry. *Pacific Rim Law & Policy Journal* 9 (2): 353–378.

Kim, K. 2013. Hanguk munhwakontenchŭsanŏp chinhŭngchŏngchaekŭ naey-onggwa sŏnggwa: 1974–2011 munhwayesan bunsŏkŭl tonghan tongsichŏk gochal [The Characteristics and Achievements of Korean Government's Content Industry Policy: A Longitudinal Study on the Cultural Budget Between 1974 and 2011]. *Journal of Communication Research* 50 (1): 276–317.

Kornai, J. 1986. The Soft Budget Constraint. *Kyklos* 39: 3–30.

Leong, M. 2014. How Korea became the world's coolest brand. Financial Post, August 2. https://business.financialpost.com/news/retail-marketing/how-korea-became-the-worlds-coolest-brand.

Maraval, V. 2012. Les acteurs français sont trop payés! *Le Monde*, December 28. Available at http://www.lemonde.fr/a-la-une/article/2012/12/28/les-acteurs-francais-sont-trop-payes_1811151_3208.html.

Messerlin, P.A. 2019. Building Consistent Policies on Subsidies in the Film Industry. *Kritika Kultura* 32: 375–396.

Messerlin, P.A., and J. Parc. 2017. The Real Impact of Subsidies on the Film Industry (1970s–Present): Lessons from France and Korea. *Pacific Affairs* 90 (1): 51–75.

Messerlin, P.A., and J. Parc. 2020. The Myth of Subsidies in the Film Industry: A Comparative Analysis of European and US Approaches. *Innovation: The European Journal of Social Science Research* 33 (4): 474–489.

Ministry of Culture, Sports and Tourism. Various issues. *Munhwa sanup backsuh* [Cultural Contents Industry Whitepaper], Ministry of Culture, Sports and Tourism, Seoul.

Motion Picture Association (MPA). 1994. *Trade Barriers to Exports of US Filmed Entertainment*. Washington, DC: MPA.

National Conference of State Legislatures (NCSL). 2018. State Film Production Incentives & Programs, January 30, *NCSL*.http://www.ncsl.org/research/fiscal-policy/state-film-production-incentives-and-programs.aspx.

Olsberg|SPI. 2008. A Comparison of the Production Costs of Feature Films Shot in Ten Locations Around the World. A Report for the Office of the British Film Commissioner, September. UK Film Council. London.

Parc, J. 2014. *An Eclectic Approach to Enhancing the Competitive Advantage of Nations: Analyzing the Success Factors of East Asian Economies with a Focus on the Development of South Korea*. Thesis (PhD), Seoul National University and Université Paris Sorbonne.

Parc, J. 2017. The Effects of Protection in Cultural Industries: The Case of the Korean Film Policies. *International Journal of Cultural Policy* 23 (5): 618–633.

Parc, J. 2018. Evaluating the Effects of Protectionism on the Film Industry: A Case Study Analysis of Korea. In *Handbook of State Aid for Film*, ed. Paul Murschetz, Roland Teichmann, and Matthias Karmasin, 349–366. Cham, Switzerland: Springer.

Parc, J. 2020. Between State-Led and Corporation-led Co-Productions: How Has Film Co-Production Been Exploited by States in Europe. *Innovation: The European Journal of Social Science Research* 33 (4): 442–458.

Parc, J. 2021. Business Integration and its Impact on Film Industry: The Case of Korean Film Policies from the 1960s until the Present. *Business History* 63 (5): 850–867.

Parc, J., and P.A. Messerlin. 2018. In Search of an Effective Trade Policy for the Film Industry: Lessons from Korea. *Journal of World Trade* 52 (5): 745–764.

Parc, J., and P.A. Messerlin. 2020. Overcoming the Incoherent *'Grand Maneuver'* in the French Film and TV Markets: Lessons from the Experiences in France and Korea. *Global Policy* 11 (S2): 31–39.

Peltier, S. 2003. Les Industries Culturelles: Une exception économique ? *Culture, Etqt Et Marché, Cahiers Français* 312: 31–36.

Song, Y. 2012. Audiovisual Services in Korea: Market Development and Policies. ADBI Working Paper Series 354, Asian Development Bank Institute, Tokyo. http://www.adbi.org/working-paper/2012/04/16/5048.audiovisual.services.korea.

Prowda, J.B. 1996. US Dominance in the Marketplace of Culture and the French Cultural Exception. *New York University Journal of International Law and Politics* 29: 193–210.

Stephen Follows. 2016. *How Much Has the UK Government Paid in Film Tax Breaks*? Story of the Subsidies Scheme. https://stephenfollows.com/film-tax-breaks-by-the-numbers/.

Tannenwald, R. 2010. State Film Subsidies: Not Much Bang for too Many Bucks. *Center on Budget and Policy Priorities*, November 9. http://www.cbpp.org/research/state-film-subsidies-notmuch-bang-for-too-many-bucks.

Thom, M. 2018. Lights, Camera, but No Action? Tax and Economic Development. Lessons from State Motion Picture Incentive Programs. *American Review of Public Administration* 48 (1): 33–51.

Vézyroglou, D., and G. Péton. 2014. La politique française du cinéma au moment du rattachement du Centre national de la cinématographie au ministère des affaires culturelles (1957–1962). In *Le cinéma: Une affaire d'état (1945–1970)*, ed. Dimitri Vézyrouglou. Paris: La Documentation Française.

Vulser, N. 2019. Jérôme Seydoux: «Le cinéma est un métier à risques, mais en France on est trop frileux». *Le Monde*, May 13. https://www.lemonde.fr/cinema/article/2019/05/13/jerome-seydoux-le-cinema-est-un-metier-a-risques-mais-en-france-on-est-trop-frileux_5461202_3476.html#:~:text=d%C3%A9fensif%20qu'offensif.-,Le%20cin%C3%A9ma%20est%20un%20m%C3%A9tier%20%C3%A0%20risques%2C%20mais%20en%20France,s'il%20cartonne%20en%20salle.

CHAPTER 5

Governance: Regulations and Institutions

The previous chapters have focused on the important policies that have been very often used to protect a film industry—import quota, screen quota, and subsidies. This chapter expands the scope of these investigations to "regulations," specifically domestic laws or decrees, which may have an effect on the film industry of a country and the institutions in charge of enforcing these regulations. This global approach allows us to tackle an issue that has rarely been touched upon by the studies devoted to the film industry: the "quality" of these regulations and institutions, that is, the soundness of their objectives and their effectiveness to fulfill these goals. In fact, it is often argued that institutions and regulations are established and implemented in order to achieve cultural creativity and diversity. However, the achievement of this goal cannot be verified by simply describing or even analyzing documents: it also requires a thorough assessment of the various outcomes brought about by these regulations and institutions.

The regulations to be reviewed are of two types: those that have been specifically designed for the film industry, and those which have been written for other business and economic activities but have an impact on the various segments of the film industry such as production, distribution, and exhibition. These regulations can have good or bad as well as

J. Parc and P. A. Messerlin, *The Untold Story of the Korean Film Industry*, Cultural Economics & the Creative Economy,
https://doi.org/10.1007/978-3-030-80342-1_5

intended or unintended effects on the way the domestic film market functions. This chapter thus explores the extent to which local moviegoers and film producers get the highest benefits from the whole domestic regulatory environment—while ensuring the ultimate objectives of cultural creativity and diversity.

The effectiveness of the public institutions in charge of enforcing regulations is as important as the quality of their regulations. These institutions are often described in their respective country as "autonomous" (France) or "self-administered" (Korea) organizations. In order to reflect this crucial aspect, the generic terms of "autonomous agency" or "agency" are used in this chapter. Such wording reflects more than a mere legal feature: it conveys a sense of influence and power as best illustrated by the French *Centre national du cinéma et de l'image animée* (CNC) whose mandate describes that it "leads the policy of the State in film and audiovisual production, under the direct authority of the Culture Minister. It proposes and enforces regulations, grants authorizations, and classifies films..." (CNC 2013). So far, a large number of existing studies on the film industry generally view film policy as a mere set of legal texts, and the agencies as obedient and costless enforcers of these laws. In other words, they do not pay attention to the real functioning and operating mode of these agencies.

These issues are critical in an industry where there is so little room for standardization and so much freedom for designing and implementing tailor-made regulations. This aspect is all the more essential because, from a political point of view, the film industry is very attractive but also formidable. It is attractive because a successful film industry can help a government to promote its country's brand and to enhance its reputation domestically and internationally. At the same time, it is formidable because its capacity to produce the images that play such a crucial role in modern societies gives filmmakers a powerful influence. Indeed, it can be hard for governments to overrule the narrow vested interests among filmmakers and impose decisions on behalf of the "general interest" of the country as a whole.

This chapter explores these issues across four steps by using a comparative approach. Firstly, it presents an overview of the Korean regulations and seeks to gain a sense of their potential "restrictive" impact on its film industry. It then compares them with those implemented by China, France, Japan, the UK, and the US.

Secondly, this chapter focuses on the agencies in charge of the film industry in Korea and in France—the Korean Film Council (KOFIC) and CNC, respectively. Such a comparison is very much pertinent given that these two agencies are polar opposite cases. Thus to which extent do their institutional differences (for example size or mandate) have an impact on the evolution of public support?

Thirdly, close attention is then devoted to a comparison of how financial incentives have been implemented over the years by these two agencies. The way the agencies have been created and the degree of autonomy they enjoy in defining or implementing the film policy of their country have naturally led them to generate a different array of incentives, and even more importantly to use them in different proportions and perspectives. Have these differences been instrumental in the success of Korea's film policy?

The last section comes back to the core question of this book: what could be the best governance possible for designing and implementing a film policy? Answering such a question naturally raises the dilemma that has been mentioned before: beyond its immediate goal, any incentive—financial or regulatory—is doomed to have positive and negative effects on the other segments of the film industry. The "art of good governance" is therefore to assess these costs and benefits in the most comprehensive way and to balance them in order to reach the best solution. This chapter illustrates this point by briefly analyzing two concrete case studies, each involving financial incentives worth hundreds of million US dollars. In doing so, it allows us to suggest some useful guidelines toward designing the best governance possible in the film industry which combines economic efficiency and cultural creativity.

1 Korea's Regulations: Protectionist or Restrictive?

The film industry combines a multitude of inputs—scriptwriters, directors, actors, shooting locations, crews with a wide range of technical skills, equipment, studios, movie theaters, bankers, insurers, lawyers, and many other professionals—which are traded on numerous markets. As a result, in every country, a host of domestic regulations have an impact on how easily domestic and foreign films can be produced and screened in the country. If some of these regulations are clearly aimed at protecting some market participants (not necessarily domestic) from their competitors, at least the intention for most of them is to make the domestic market operate as efficiently as possible. However, intention and goodwill are not enough: the concrete way in which these measures are designed and enforced can make them—possibly unintentionally—restrictive to the point of becoming costly for their alleged beneficiaries.

1.1 The STRI Database

Having a sense of the restrictiveness of the regulations in a film industry is a key factor toward understanding the relative competitiveness of this industry in a country. What follows is based on the information on the "restrictive measures" listed by the Services Trade Restrictiveness Index (STRI). This large database of all the measures in services industries is compiled by the Organisation of Economic Cooperation and Development (OECD), and it has a special section devoted to the film industry—"movie pictures" in the official OECD language (OECD 2019). A key feature of this database is that it has been done with the full cooperation of the countries covered—hence ensuring that it is the most comprehensive information available.

The STRI database covers forty-five countries and deals with eighty-five different potentially restrictive measures among them. For each individual measure, OECD has assigned a "weight" ranging between zero and one—zero means no restrictive effect on the market in the country at stake while one means a closed market. Measures can be aggregated into groups: then the weight of a group of measures is obtained by adding the weights of the individual measures pertaining to this group. As a result, the lower the weight of a measure or a group of measures adopted by a country, the less restrictive this measure or this group of measures.

This chapter aggregates the STRI measures into four "categories" which have been specially designed to suit adequately the purpose of this chapter: market access, movement of capital, movement of labor, and "other measures." The measures related to market access concern the restrictions imposed on films already produced and ready to be screened—import, distribution, and exhibition activities. Those dealing with the movements of capital and of labor are imposed on these two inputs that are needed for producing and distributing films in the country at stake. The domain of the "other measures" deals with the wide range of remaining measures that are not specific to the film industry but can have an impact on this industry—such as rules on state-controlled companies or general restrictions on cross-border data flows.

1.2 An Overview of the Korean Measures

Table 1 shows that Korea enforces only fourteen potentially restrictive measures (out of a possible eighty-five) and names the countries that implement similar measures to Korea. It is important to have a sense of the extent to which these measures are restrictive in Korea specifically. This is because the STRI database records all the "potentially" restrictive measures included in the laws and decrees of a country. In other words, a given measure can be effectively restrictive in a country and not in others. This is a point particularly important to have in mind when one examines the cross-sectoral measures, such as those classified as related to movement of capital and labor and to other measures. Moreover, a certain number of measures may stay legally on the books but be practically inactive because they were designed for a different context or may have had a purpose that is today irrelevant. Still, as long as these "sleeping" measures have not been removed from the country's body of laws and decrees, one could not exclude the possibility that they could be reactivated as restrictive at some point in the future.

All the measures dealing with market access are specific to the film and audio-visual industries. Screen quota (measure #1) has been discussed at length in Chapter 3: its conclusion strongly suggests that the Korean film industry is prosperous enough to make this measure de facto irrelevant. A similar remark can be made for TV quota (measure #2), which requires national TV channels to broadcast domestic movies at least 25% or more of the total annual time dedicated for films while cable/satellite TV channels must commit 20%.

Article 4 of the law that established KOFIC (measure #3) has been classified as a measure related to the movement of capital since it deals with international aspects other than pure trade activities. KOFIC assists with the creation and production for Korean films and the subsequent export and international exchange of these titles. The Ministry of Culture, Sports and Tourism (MCST) may also provide support to movie theaters that screen "independent art" films. However, as many of the titles screened in art house theaters are foreign films from Europe and other

Table 1 The Korean potentially restrictive measures in the film industry (2018)

Group		*Individual measures*	*Weight*[a]	*Countries with similar measures*
Market access				
	#1	Screen quotas are in place	0.014	France, China
	#2	Broadcast or airtime quotas are in place for motion pictures	0.014	France, China
Movement of capital				
	#3	Foreign suppliers are treated less favorably regarding eligibility to subsidies	0.010	France, UK, US
	#4	Acquisition and use of land and real estate by foreigners is restricted	0.014	China
	#5	Local presence is required for cross-border supply	0.014	France, Japan
Movement of labor				
	#6	Laws or regulations establish a process for recognizing qualifications gained abroad	0.012	-
	#7	Labor market tests: intra-corporate transferees	0.012	France, UK, Japan, China
	#8	Limitation on duration of stay for contractual services suppliers (months)	0.012	France
	#9	Limitation on duration of stay for independent services suppliers (months)	0.012	France
	#10	Visas on arrival or visa exemption are available for temporary entry/transit of crew	0.010	France, UK, China, US

(continued)

Table 1 (continued)

Group		*Individual measures*	*Weight*[a]	*Countries with similar measures*
Others				
	#11	Total cost to complete official procedures required to register a company (% income per capita)	0.010	Japan, China
	#12	Cross-border data flows: certain data must be stored locally	0.014	China
	#13	Public procurement: regulation explicitly prohibits discrimination of foreign suppliers	0.010	France, UK, Japan, China, US
	#14	Vertical integration is monitored and regulated	0.007	-

Note [a]weights are from OECD (2019)
Source Authors' recalculations based on OECD (2019)

countries, this Korean support can be seen as indirect support for overseas film distribution in Korea. Finally, Korean financial support is further provided to famous overseas film companies that produce films in Korea through the "Overseas Location Support Project," such as *The Avengers: The Age of Ultron* and *Black Panther*—a case of direct support for overseas film production. The two other measures on capital movements (measures #4 and #5) are not specific to the film industry, and their impact on the Korean film industry is likely to be negligible.

Shifting to measures related to labor movements, they can be divided into two main groups. There are those which have an explicit reference to the film industry, such as Article 44 of the Film Act on the recognition by Korea of "qualified projectionists" (measure #6) and specific visas for people working in the cultural industries (measure #10). The first measure has a limited restrictiveness to the extent that it does not consider the potential equivalence of the qualification procedures granted by some other countries. Concerning visas, cultural artists are able to use short-term tourist visas on the condition that no additional revenue is generated—in this case, they should obtain the relevant forms for income tax purposes. However, they could benefit from specific long-term residence visas (E6). The other measures in this category are entirely defined from an economy-wide perspective, such as the condition imposed on intra-corporate transferees to work at least one year in the company (measure #7) and the duration of the stay in Korea and associated visas (measures #8 and #9). That said, it is worth noting that Korean regulations related to the stay of foreigners changes regularly and often haphazardly—therefore their assessment needs to be revised frequently, an impediment to setting in place long-term business plans.

Finally, the "other measures" are all economy-wide. Measure #11 refers to the World Bank database on the costs of "Doing Business" in the world and it has little impact in the vast majority of cases related to the film industry. The obligation to store locally some data (measure #12) seeks to prevent leakage of personal information abroad and to ensure national security—a marginal topic from the film industry perspective. The sensitive topic on the regulations of mandatory domestic server installations has long been the subject of debate in Korea, as in many other countries. These discussions have not led to any definitive decision given their debatable consistency with commitments taken in the context of preferential trade agreements and their risks in terms of over-regulation. Lastly, the last two measures—on public procurement (measure #13) and on the monitoring of vertical integration (measure #14)—are not discriminatory in the case of the film industry.

2 Comparing Korea to the Other Selected Countries

Table 2 lists a total of sixty-seven restrictive measures for the film industry among the countries covered. Some of these measures are enforced in most of these countries, for instance, restrictions on access to public procurement (six countries) or labor market tests and visas (five countries). What follows seeks to provide a more systematic and detailed analysis of these measures by exploring three key questions. Which countries have the lowest and highest level of overall restrictiveness? Which categories in its film industry does Korea protect the most, compared to the same categories in other countries? And finally, which categories does Korea protect the most when compared to the other categories in its own film industry?

Table 2 Level of regulatory measures in selected countries

	Overall	Measures and barriers in the film industry [1] = [2] + [3] + [4] + [5]			
	[1]	Market access [2]	Capital [3]	Labor [4]	Others [5]
A: No. of measures					
China	44	6	15	11	12
France	22	3	3	7	9
UK	16	0	3	9	4
Korea	14	2	3	5	4
US	14	0	2	7	5
Japan	9	0	1	3	5
B: Weights					
China	0.615	0.082	0.260	0.142	0.130
France	0.235	0.039	0.032	0.077	0.087
UK	0.179	0.000	0.039	0.098	0.042
Korea	0.165	0.029	0.039	0.056	0.041
US	0.155	0.000	0.025	0.080	0.050
Japan	0.103	0.000	0.014	0.035	0.054
C: Percentages					
China	100.0	13.3	42.4	23.1	21.2
France	100.0	16.6	13.5	32.9	37.0
UK	100.0	0.0	21.8	54.9	23.4
Korea	100.0	17.5	23.6	33.9	25.1
US	100.0	0.0	15.9	51.6	32.5
Japan	100.0	0.0	14.0	33.8	52.2

Source Authors' recalculations based on OECD (2019)

2.1 An Overview

While Block A of Table 2 compares the total number of restrictive measures, these numbers should be interpreted with caution. If a country has twice more measures than its counterpart, this does not automatically mean that it is twice more protected. It would therefore be far more accurate to compare the level of restrictiveness among these measures. For this, Block B presents the overall weights (Column [1]) and the individual weights by category (Columns [2] to [5]). Column [1] of Block B shows that the Japanese film industry is on the whole the least restrictive, with the lowest overall weight (0.103). It is followed by the US, Korea, and the UK, which are relatively close to each other in terms of weight. France exhibits a more marked pattern of protection. Finally, the Chinese film industry is by far the most protected in the sample, with the highest overall weight (0.615).

At this stage, it is important to point out one key observation regarding the high level of China's protection combined with the huge size of the country's market in terms of audience and revenues. These two features will shape the future of the global film market in a way that has never occurred throughout the history of the film industry. Up until the 2000s, protectionist measures imposed on the world's largest exporter—the US—have had a limited impact on Hollywood given the relatively small market size of these countries. The Hollywood studios could always find ways to compensate for their losses in these protected markets by making gains in other more open markets—including the US domestic market. Moreover, as these restrictive measures on imports had a strong negative impact on moviegoers in the importing markets, these countries were often induced to soften the level of restrictiveness of their barriers, as shown by the Korean import quota in Chapter 2 or by the French subsidies in Chapter 4. But the emergence of one huge importer—China—changes dramatically this situation. Import restrictions imposed by China alone on US films can have a significant impact on Hollywood's film exports that cannot be easily compensated by US gains in other export markets. The only remaining brake to Chinese protectionist measures is the costs it imposes on the country's moviegoers—a fragile and volatile constraint.

2.2 International Comparisons of the Most Protected Categories for Each Film Industry

With Block B of Table 2, we can compare the detailed weights by category, which shows the areas that the Korean film industry is seeking to protect the most. This information is important because a high level of protection in one category is likely to send the wrong signal to foreign film companies who are willing to enter the market in question: it induces them to "jump the barrier" by looking at alternative entry doors to the country that is being targeted. For instance, if a foreign company does not have easy access to the exhibition market of a country, it will then have strong incentives to enter through other channels, such as movements of capital or labor for instance. However, this strategy of "barrier jumping" or "barrier circumventing" can be costly for the importing country in question as well as for the foreign companies involved.

Focusing on Korea, Column [2] of Table 2 demonstrates that the Korean barriers to market access (exhibition market) are relatively low. Korea appears more restrictive—in relative terms—in the other measures, especially those on labor movements, which induces foreign companies to enter directly through its exhibition market. It should be added though that these incentives remain modest because Korean regulatory restrictions on labor or capital movements are not that high. In this respect, it is at the opposite end of China where all four domains are highly protected: as a result, entering China through the exhibition market is (by far) the least difficult, even if it is challenging to undertake.

Given that US films are the main competitor for Korean films domestically, it is interesting to compare the Korean and US measures on capital movements, labor movements, and "other measures." It should be noted that these categories are not covered by the Korea-US FTA. Table 3 reveals the key reason for this: Korea and the US use different kinds of measures for protecting each of these three categories. That creates systemic difficulties for Korean and US negotiators who have to agree on concessions that they find equivalent in order to get a "balanced" package of reciprocal concessions toward reaching an agreement. This is difficult: for instance, how could US negotiators consider the lifting of Korean restrictions related to labor market tests (intra-corporate transferees) as being a concession equivalent to the elimination of the US screening on capital movements by Korea? In other words, Table 3 reveals the major structural reason that explains why the Korea-US Free Trade Agreement was unable to include a meaningful outcome for the film industry across these three categories (see Chapter 3).

From a broad policy perspective, this result sends a crucial message: it stresses how much the reduction or elimination of restrictive measures depends on the willingness of the country to make unilateral domestic reforms (much) more than on negotiating "balanced" international deals. This then raises the following question that is at the center of the decision-making process: how could one generate or facilitate such a willingness to undertake unilateral domestic reforms—which could then be backed up by international agreements? This question will be addressed in this chapter.

2.3 Analyzing the Domestic Distortions Created by the Regulations: The Korean Case

At this stage, it is crucial to apply the golden rule regarding "no free lunch" as set out in Chapter 4: any restrictive measure creates almost inevitably counter-effects, often unintended, in the other categories of

Table 3 Korean and US restrictive regulations (2018)

Topic of the regulations	*Korea*	*US*
Capital movements		
Acquisition and use of land and real estate by foreigners is restricted	0.014	
Screening exists without exclusion of economic interests		0.014
Local presence is required for cross-border supply	0.014	
Foreign suppliers are treated less favorably regarding eligibility to subsidies	0.010	0.010
Labor movements		
Cross-border transfer of personal data is possible when certain private sector safeguards are in place		
Cost to obtain a business visa (USD)		0.014
Labor market tests: independent services suppliers		0.010
Labor market tests: intra-corporate transferees		0.012
Labor market tests: contractual services suppliers	0.012	
Visas on arrival or visa exemption are available for temporary entry/transit of crew		0.012
Laws or regulations establish a process for recognizing qualifications gained abroad	0.010	0.010
Quotas: contractual services suppliers	0.012	
Quotas: independent services suppliers		0.012
Limitation on duration of stay for contractual services suppliers (months)		0.012
Limitation on duration of stay for independent services suppliers (months)	0.012	
"Other" regulations		
Cross-border data flows: certain data must be stored locally	0.014	
Total cost to complete all official procedures required to register a company (in % of income per capita)	0.010	
Number of mandatory procedures to register a company		0.010
Public procurement: Explicit preferences for local suppliers		0.010
Public procurement: The procurement process affects the conditions of competition in favor of local firms		0.010
Public procurement: Procurement regulation explicitly prohibits discrimination of foreign suppliers	0.010	0.010
Vertical integration is monitored and regulated	0.007	
Collective copyright managers apply a non-discriminatory and equal treatment policy		0.010
Total	0.136	0.155

Note This table excludes measures restricting access to movie theaters
Source Authors' recalculations based on OECD (2019)

the industry in question. A good illustration of this outcome is the French and Italian film policies after World War II where they sought to restrict US film companies and their subsidiaries from repatriating the profits they had made in Europe back to the US. In raising such barriers, French and Italian policymakers believed that these profits would then have to be reinvested into European film companies (Johnson-Yale 2017). Instead what transpired is that these profits became "frozen funds" and were used by US filmmakers to produce a large number of films in Europe—benefitting in passing from the subsidies granted to their European subsidiaries. In this respect, the US filmmakers were de facto using Europe as runaway production site for producing films and dramas that were ultimately intended for the US market (Guback 1974; Parc 2020a).

Looking then at Korea, which category in its film industry is it seeking to protect the most—hence which one benefits the most from this structure of protection? A rough answer is given by the percentage of the weight of each category from the overall number which is shown in rows of Columns [2] to [4] in Block C of Table 2: the higher the percentage of a category, the greater its advantage will hold. These rows provide a remarkable answer: Korea emerges as the country with the narrowest range—slightly below 2—between the highest percentage (labor movement: 33.9%) and the lowest one (market access: 17.5%). This figure is lower than those in France, China, Japan, and the US.

In general, when foreign film companies enter a market, they tend to choose the most favorable—with the lowest restrictions—category by considering all the possible business and economic risks. The level of restrictions among Korean measures being relatively even among all the categories, the distortions that Korean regulations could generate in its film industry are likely to be limited; hence less prone toward generating substantial unintended negative effects. This is quite different from the situation in China or in the US where the range between the highest and lowest contributions is large.

This observation happens to be an extremely useful guide in deciding which reform to pursue first in order to improve governance in the Korean film industry or any other film industry. Box 1 explains that a major result of the cost–benefit analysis of a tax or any protectionist measure is that cutting the tax "peaks" in an industry should be done first because it is the largest source of potential gains for consumers' welfare. Alternatively, this result can be expressed as follows: if one—say—triples the rate of a tax, the losses imposed by this tax increase on the well-being of the consumer can be multiplied by up to nine times (3 times 3)—not three times.

Box 1 Good Governance and Taxes: Golden Rules

What should be the "right" level of a tax? As shown in the final section of this chapter, a complete answer to this question depends on the precise objectives—economic and cultural—justifying the tax. However, there is a "golden rule" that every government should follow if it wants to avoid the "excessive" burden of a tax. This rule deserves a lot of attention because of its wide range of applications: it can be applied to tariffs (which are taxes on foreign goods), quotas (which raise the price of the products, these price increases being equivalent to tariffs), and all types of regulations (which increases the prices of products, hence have a tariff-equivalent impact).

The figure below shows the quantity demanded OA for a product when the price free of tax is OP. If one imposes a tax Pt1, the price increases to Ot1, and the demand shrinks to OQ. The area PEBt1 can be broken down into two components. The area PFBt1 is the tax revenue (Pt1 times OQ), which is paid ("lost") by the consumers and received ("gained") by the government. The area FBE is radically different: it is lost by everybody because it is based on the quantity QA of the good that the consumers do not buy anymore—and the government does not pocket any money either. As a result, it is lost for the country as a whole and is referred to as the consumers' deadweight loss (there is a similar mechanism on the production side that we ignore for simplicity sake).

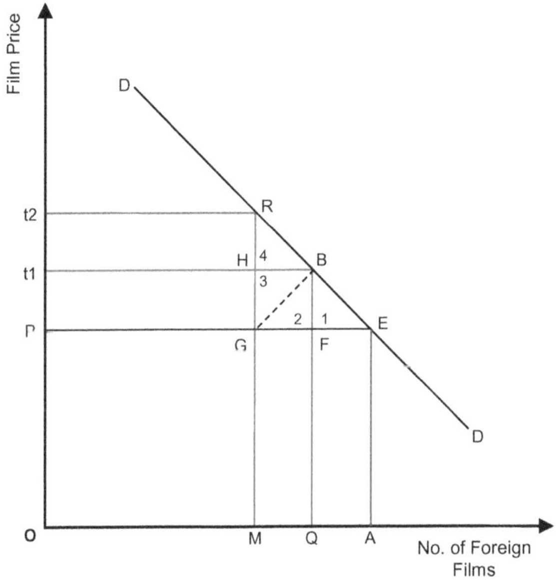

If the government doubles the tax to the level Pt2 (Pt1 = t1t2), the quantity demanded will be further reduced to an amount OM that we cannot estimate without more information. By contrast, we can have a more precise idea of the change in the consumer's deadweight loss. It will be quadrupled: the triangle RGE is four times the initial area BFE, as shown by the areas 1, 2, 3, and 4, all equal to area 1. Expressed in a general form, the consumer's loss is the square of the tax rate (Feenstra 2004, p. 217).

This result provides two golden rules for good governance in tax (tariff, quota, or regulation) policy. First, a government has to be extremely careful on the tax rate it chooses: any tax rate higher than the one strictly necessary creates rapidly increasing losses for consumers. Second, if a government wants to liberalize, cutting the highest tariffs first should thus be the most favored approach because it eliminates (much) larger deadweight losses than cutting the lowest tariffs. In other words, one gets the highest benefits from market opening.

These rules raise a final question: why are they so often ignored? The history of market liberalization shows that, over the last fifty years, the answer resides in the political dynamics of protection: the activities with

> the highest rates of protection are also the most powerful and aggressive vested interests, which are therefore capable of bullying governments.

As domestic reforms are politically difficult, it is thus crucial to pursue first those that will bring the largest benefits—a lesson that Korea could not escape because of the pressure of the Korea-US Film Agreements and that Mexico missed in the late 1980s and is still paying dearly for today (see Chapter 2). In the Korean case, that means looking first at how the "peak" protectionist regulations in the labor-intensive segment could be reduced—while still seeking out better ways to ensure the desired level of social protection for Korean workers in the film industry. The same approach should be undertaken in the capital-intensive and "other measures" categories. Interestingly, Table 2 shows that liberalizing market access in Korea (eliminating the screen quota) comes last in the ranking of reforms, reflecting the fact that the protection granted by this instrument is low, if any at all.

3 Comparing Agencies: Korea's KOFIC and France's CNC[1]

Most studies of the film industry tend to talk about the "government's policies" as if they were decided in detail by the country's policymakers and fully implemented by them without any bureaucratic interference or deviation. But such views ignore the existence of "autonomous agencies," such as CNC in France or KOFIC in Korea, who are in actual fact the real caretakers of their film industries.

Such an oversight is a great mistake. The economic literature on the "principal-agent dilemma" suggests that one should pay a great deal of attention to the extent to which an "agent" is an "obedient servant" of the "principal" (Shapiro 1983; Stiglitz 1989). In this chapter, the "principal" is the government and the "agent" is the agency in charge of the film policy. The principal-agent dilemma occurs when the motivations of the "agent" and those of the "principal" are not fully and securely aligned. This is likely to be the case with a country's film policy due to two mutually reinforcing reasons. First, this policy is not of prime

[1] This section relies on Messerlin (2019).

importance for many governments which have thus weak incentives to monitor tightly their autonomous agency. Second, for reasons that will be outlined below, agencies in charge of the film industry are likely to have strong connections with the industry's vested interests (film companies, producers, actors, and movie theaters) and these close links are likely to reduce their loyalty to the principal—the government and, beyond it, "we the people."

This loyalty is under even greater stress when, as documented below, the decisions about the types of financial support to grant, the timing of their introduction, and even their magnitude have been largely devolved to the agencies themselves, granting them a high "degree of autonomy" in their actions. It goes beyond this chapter to analyze the reasons that have induced governments to grant such a degree of autonomy. It could have been the noble desire to create some healthy distance between politics and culture. Or it could have been the less noble fear of the political power held by key vested interests in the film industry—for example, famous directors or actors who can heavily influence the career and/or reputation of policymakers through their media connections.

Although there are thus good theoretical and empirical reasons to scrutinize the agencies that run film policies, so far the existing film studies are limited to a description of the number and main features of the different incentives at the disposal of the agencies (Lange and Westcott 2004; Newman-Baudais 2011). These studies have not sought to connect these features to the success of the film industries concerned by using a rigorous economic analysis. They generally assume that the decisions of the agencies are inherently good, and the more actions they take the better. One other notable limitation among these studies is that most of them deal with cases in a close geographical proximity, either European countries or Québec. This undercuts the value of comparing these agencies: they are so similar in many respects that it is hard to draw any noteworthy lesson by comparing them. In sharp contrast, the development of the Korean and French film industries and policies offers a greater contrast that reveals clear lessons.

3.1 The French and Korean Agencies: Two Polar Cases

Table 4 provides the essential information on CNC and KOFIC, leaving aside the regional agencies which are less important for this analysis—although some of them (Seoul, Busan, or Paris) are notable. CNC's

Table 4 The agencies: mandate, funding sources, coverage, and budget (2016)

	CNC	*KOFIC*
Date of establishment	1946	1973 (1997)[a]
General mandate		
Devise domestic regulations	yes	some influence
Implement domestic regulations	yes	yes
Improve industry structure	yes	no
International relations	yes (since 1991)	no
Funding sources		
Tax on seat in movie theaters[b]	1948/ 10.72%/ 168	2007/ 3%/ 45
Tax on TV services[b]	1986/ 5.5%/ 564	no
Others[c]	1993 etc./ many/ 20	no
State budget[d]	small	small
Sectors covered	Film, TV, video, games	Film, video
Resources: budget and staff		
Annual budget for all sectors	868	62
Annual budget for film only[e]	495	62
Operating budget	41	9
Number of staff	471	130
Number of films supported		
Integrally domestic	209	[f]
Majority domestic	81	[g]
Minority domestic	74	[g]

Notes [a]The year 1997 is the year of the establishment of the Korean Film Promotion Fund, KOFIC's first financial arm; [b]respectively: year of introduction of the measure, current tax rate in %, amount of current revenues in 2016 (in USD million); [c]this entry covers a wide range of taxes (on videos, VoD, and streaming services); [d]does not take into consideration the losses of tax revenues due to tax relief schemes; [e]for France, includes support to horizontal actions (***dispostifs transversaux***) of interest for the film sector; [f]KOFIC supports only independent films and the budget is lower than USD 900,000; [g]irrelevant

Sources CNC (various issues) for France; MCST (2016) for Korea

dominance has been underlined by a recent report from the French Senate which does not hold back when it describes the agency as "omnipotent" (Laborde 2018, p. 91). Subsidies granted by the French Ministry of Culture are relatively small, and they are often handled by the CNC. By contrast, Korea's MCST is usually more involved, and its own subsidy budget for the film industry amounts to USD 22 million in 2016, one-third of KOFIC's budget.[2]

Forty years separate the establishment of these two institutions and the economic principles surrounding their creation could not be more different. KOFIC's last reorganization occurred at a time—from the late 1990s to the mid-2000s—when the belief in the positive role of competition and in the need to embrace markets in an increasingly globalized world was strong in Asia—it still is. By contrast, CNC is the heir of a private body (*Confédération Générale du Cinéma*) that was founded by French film companies in 1936 as part of an effort to preempt more direct state intervention in the film industry (Hayward 2005, p 34). The late 1930s were marked by general distrust in Europe, and to a lesser extent in the US, regarding the benefits of domestic and international competition. The dominant idea at that time was the notion of "organizing" national markets—facilitating collusion among the participants of the domestic market, with no or little international perspective.

This "corporatist" view was endorsed by the Vichy government during World War II and it was taken on board by the subsequent government when it created CNC in 1946 (CNC 2006; Farchy 1992; Hayward 2005). This economic heritage is still present, with both its positive and negative aspects. On the positive side, it has stimulated CNC to produce a remarkably rich set of data on the French film industry over decades that has been a source of its influence but that is also extremely valuable for independent research. On the negative side, it has considerably strengthened the influence of CNC vis-à-vis policymakers whose short political timespan limits their ability to grasp the complexities of film regulations, especially those schemes of public support created by CNC.

A second difference concerns the mandate of these agencies and their supervision. The CNC mandate includes all the essential tasks to prepare and implement the regulatory framework of the film industry as well as to advice on international issues, including on the international negotiations for trade agreements. The supervision of CNC by the French Ministry of Culture, the French National Assembly, and the Senate can be qualified at best as "notional."

This lack of oversight is made worse because very few French public agencies have the legal remit to make an independent review of CNC's

[2] Some recent changes have occurred, shifting funds from the central budget to regional budgets in both Korea and France.

policies. The only institution with enough legitimacy and clout is the French Auditing Court (*Cour des Comptes*) which indeed has devoted a fair amount of attention to the film policy over the last decade—strongly criticizing CNC for its "unorthodox" financial procedures (Cour des Comptes 2012, 2014). However, the Auditing Court does not conduct its monitoring process on an annual basis, and its recommendations have not led to any direct reform of the agency. For that to happen, the Court's recommendations would need to be translated into political measures and legal decisions from the government and then approved by the National Assembly and the Senate. As yet, few members of these three political bodies have been ready to fight the powerful French film lobby, although the critical tone of a recent report by the National Assembly and related debates may signal a change in this respect (Lebelle and Pelloli 2018; Magné 2019).

By contrast, the MCST of Korea maintains a tight grip on the country's regulatory framework, and its relationship with KOFIC is supervised by the government while its overall operations are supervised by the National Assembly. Yet, within this framework, KOFIC has been able to achieve influence in terms of policymaking and implementation, including by building a database comparable in quality and scope to what CNC has compiled. That said, tensions between the MCST and KOFIC have emerged on overlapping issues.

3.2 Differences in Funding Sources and Coverage

The second important difference between CNC and KOFIC is the source and level of their funds, and their evolution over time. As illustrated by Table 4, CNC funds have been based on an ever expanding array of sources: special taxes on theater seats (1948), on TV operators (1986), videos and Video-on-Demand (1993, 2003), and the audiovisual components of internet subscription services (2007). By contrast, KOFIC's Film Development Fund has been funded mostly by the seat tax since 2007. In this context, it is no surprise that CNC is a much richer organization as can be seen in Table 4 which shows that the overall budget for CNC is fourteen times larger than KOFIC's budget in the late 2010s. The large share of CNC's budget comes from the taxes imposed on TV operators which provide 65% of its total budget (*soutiens*). Its affluence has also allowed CNC to hire a large staff—three times larger than

KOFIC—which has been a key source toward creating and sustaining its influence in political circles and public opinion at large.

The major consequence of this ever expanding base of resources has been to make it possible for CNC to enforce a full-scale "micro-managed industrial policy" in the film industry. Table 4 shows that CNC is involved in the funding of virtually every French film—be it "integrally French" (French private funds represent 100% of private funds) or co-produced "majority French" (French private funds represent more than 50% of private funds) or "minority French" (French private funds represent less than 50% of private funds). In this context—somewhat ironically—being financed by CNC is often considered as a certificate of French nationality. By sharp contrast, the more limited resources held by KOFIC have prevented it from micro-managing the Korean film industry, inducing the agency to focus on independent art films with a small budget (less than 900,000 USD before marketing costs).

Finally, this larger base of resources has allowed CNC to relentlessly expand its mandate in terms of sectors covered, contrary to KOFIC. Not only is CNC in charge of the film industry, but it is also deeply involved in the production of films by TV channels and in the monitoring of their screening by TV channels; although it shares this latter role with the *Conseil Supérieur de l'Audiovisuel*. As a result, the economic fate of the whole French film production has been largely determined by CNC-driven regulations. The best illustration is the French regulations interpreting the TV quotas imposed by the 1989 European "Television without Frontiers" Directive and its successors, which have proven to be a net burden for both French sectors in the long run (Parc and Messerlin 2020). By contrast, KOFIC has no mandate beyond the film and video sector as it is very much independent of the TV industry. If these two sectors have increasing relations—as is the case with the production segment in recent years—it is essentially because of economically sound factors, especially with the competitive pressures of digitization. Furthermore, a large amount of recent foreign investment has promoted a number of Korean production companies to produce both drama series and films.

3.3 *Is "Fiscal Autonomy" a Blessing or a Curse?*

All the above information raises a crucial question: has CNC's broad "fiscal autonomy" been a blessing or a curse? At first glance, one is tempted to see it as a blessing: it gives the means needed by the agency toward fulfilling its mandate. However, this view assumes that the mandate is stable, and the associated means kept proportionate. The information gathered in Chapter 4 and the precedent sections strongly suggest that this has not been the case. Rather, increasing funds have offered the opportunity to enlarge the existing mandate for CNC, which conversely has been used as an argument to raise more funds for the agency—a two-way drift whose consequences have been amplified due to CNC's extraordinary privilege to collect taxes in place of the French fiscal authorities (Cour des Comptes 2014, p. 26). The last two years have provided further illustrations of this drift. For instance, in 2019, during the debate on the public budget at the National Assembly, the government has been unable to get from CNC a clear commitment to give back the revenues it has collected beyond and above those which were initially expected for the year in question—a systematic situation when the effective attendance is higher than the one forecasted by CNC (Magné 2019).

This continuous drift has created an ever-widening gap between the ever fast expanding agenda and resources of CNC and the relative stability of KOFIC. In other words, everything happens as if KOFIC's lower resources have prevented it to embark upon a CNC-type "grand scale" micro-managed industrial policy, forcing KOFIC to look for better alternatives than granting ever larger financial incentives—a point examined in detail in the next section.

4 Comparing the Measures Used by the Korean and French Agencies

This section goes one step further in the analysis of the financial support to the film industry. So far, our investigations have been limited to the global amount of this support—as most of the economic studies on film policies have done. However, the beginning of this chapter has stressed how important it is to go beyond such a global view and to scrutinize the structure of the protection—and in particular the "peaks" of protection. This section seeks to explore this aspect by making a distinction between the key types of financial incentives and by having a thorough examination of the respective pros and cons of each type as well as the positive or negative interactions among them. Such an approach is essential for revealing the most promising "net" effects of the subsidy policy from an economic and cultural perspective.

This analysis is needed all the more because, when agencies decide to react to a new request from some vested interests, they tend to do so by designing new *ad hoc* subsidies or regulations without examining their impact on the existing financial incentives and on the whole film industry in the long run. This lack of interest has led to an uncontrolled increase in the number of incentives. For instance, in France, there were sixty different types of so-called selective subsidies in 2011 (for the definition of "selective," see below) for an amount that was roughly USD 250 million (Cour des Comptes 2012, p. 46). Such an evolution is doomed to increase the risks and the costs of inconsistencies among the incentives.

4.1 A Fundamental Distinction: "Direct" vs. "indirect" Incentives

Parc (2017) was among the first authors to highlight the importance of the structure of protection and to apply it to the various types of financial incentives. He brought out the key distinction between "direct" and "indirect" incentives. The latter are those that fill the needs of the widest possible range of filmmakers in a country. They do so mostly by targeting "infrastructures" that generate potentially large benefits spread over many participants of the industry. For instance, subsidies for building the appropriate range of studio facilities or for acquiring the needed technical skills offers all filmmakers with good working conditions and a qualified work force at an affordable price.

In sharp contrast, "direct" incentives are granted to specific filmmaking projects—production of individual films, upgrading of individual movie theaters, and other such endeavors. Because they target individual projects, direct incentives are likely to be risky bets beneficial to only a small number of recipients. In short, they try to "select the winners," with the subsidizing agency "betting" on the capacity of the filmmakers in question to produce attractive films. Such incentives have two main flaws. First, the agencies are betting with taxpayers' money, not with their own. This is a fundamental difference which makes it virtually impossible for agencies to duplicate the behavior of genuine "patrons" with respect to cultural works. Second, the global budget of these agencies is still limited by the level of taxes raised. This is true even for a rich agency such as CNC: there will always be filmmakers who will not get subsidies for various reasons even if they have produced more attractive—commercially or artistically—works than those subsidized.

In this context, agencies tend to maximize the justification in their use of subsidies by showing off their effectiveness. In general, they are more likely to offer subsidies to big companies since they have a higher rate of commercial success and better visibility in the industry and society. What is then left over will be distributed to a large number of "artistic" films produced by the numerous small and medium sized companies (SMCs). However, such a large number implies that each film produced by these SMCs receives small amounts of subsidies. In this case, agencies justify their subsidy policy by arguing that they promote the largest possible number of films—an initiative they present as a "positive best practice" (CNC 2013; Parc 2020b, p. 463).

This argument has a downside: it increases the risk of selecting the wrong beneficiaries. Contrary to private investors, subsidizing agencies do not have to pay for their failures with their own money. They argue that they cope with this risk in two ways. One is by having recourse to the advice of a large number of "experts" organized in committees. For instance, in 2011, CNC had no less than 46 committees with 656 "professional experts" (Cour des Comptes 2012, p. 50). Still, this argument has serious limits as the "committee approach" favors the incumbents in the long run. It is all the more the case if it has been used for decades in a country, as has been the case in France. The vast majority of these professional experts, who are supposed to assess the project, are by definition working in the film industry and composed of friends and/or competitors of the film producers. Such a situation helps create a form of unspoken "collective censorship" that ends up guiding the choice of the films to be subsidized (Parc 2020b, p. 462). Such an outcome puts it on a collision course with one of the two key economic justifications for granting film subsidies—promoting cultural diversity (see Chapter 4).

The other argument presented by the agencies is almost at the opposite end of the previous one: there would be a need to fund as many films as possible "because a high number of domestic films allows a high market share, hence drives the exhibition market in a virtuous circle" (CNC 2013, p. 21). This point is challenged though by the available evidence on the domestic market share in France compared to Korea (see Chapters 1 and 2). Furthermore, between 2000 and 2019, only six French films have been mega hits—defined as films with more than 10 million admissions—out of a total of 5,634 films released in France during the same period which have benefited from an accumulated total of USD 7.5 billion in film subsidies. Only one of them—*Intouchables* (2011)—could be seen as not using the usual basic recipes for blockbuster commercial success.[3] This would appear to be far from what could be considered as a "virtuous circle" of cultural creativity.

That said, "indirect incentives" are not free from criticism either, but at the very least, they seem much more manageable by the agencies. The first criticism is that indirect public incentives are not always necessary: private operators do invest in the needed infrastructure, as best illustrated by the largest US film companies investing in the Hollywood "bricks and mortar" studios from the 1920s to the 1950s. This has also been the case with schools for actors or those for special visual effects engineers. However, it remains that private operators may not provide this fundamental infrastructure in the desirable amount, especially as today's infrastructure may require a large amount of funding. In such cases, indirect public subsidies may be needed to achieve the optimal scale of such fundamental infrastructure, for the same reason that public money is required for financing the optimal size of highways or internet networks.

The second criticism is that indirect public incentives could support ill-conceived or oversized infrastructure. Such misguided investments (for instance, the wrong kind of studio) are likely to always be a waste of public money that will be hard to reduce once made—an argument in favor of imposing limits on providing public support. Oversized infrastructure can be rectified if they are due to a conjectural fall or a structural decline in the domestic film industry: then costs could be covered—partly or fully—by renting the "excess capacity" of domestic studios to foreign filmmakers. But oversized infrastructure may also happen because the subsidizing governments or agencies have been willing to attract foreign filmmakers at any cost, as best illustrated by the famous case of the Cinecitta studios near Rome in the 1950s; although it is necessary to mention that the decline of Cinecitta is not only due to oversized infrastructure, but a number of other reasons as well. These risks may become serious if many countries decide to invest in their film infrastructure at the same time—leading to a global "excess supply" of studios. The period of 2000–2010

[3] These five films are: *Taxi 2* (10.24 million admissions in 2001), *Astérix et Obélix: Mission Cléopâtre* (14.56 million admissions in 2002), *Les Bronzés 3* (10.22 million admissions in 2006), *Bienvenue chez les Chtis* (20.36 million admissions in 2009), *Intouchables* (16.58 million of admissions in 2011), and *Qu'est-ce qu'on a fait au Bon Dieu* (12.3 million of admissions in 2014). Only *Intouchables* has received wide praise outside France for its quality.

witnessed such a situation where many governments all over the world were eager to invest in building new studios or rehabilitate old ones (as in Central or Eastern Europe) with the hope to attract foreign filmmakers. To sum up, all these criticisms stress the need for a carefully well-designed policy in terms of indirect subsidies—not for abandoning the principle of such a support.

4.2 *The Polar Opposite Cases of France and Korea*

The distinction between direct and indirect incentives offers a sound basis to present an empirical assessment of the fundamental differences between the French and Korean schemes. Table 5 presents the financial incentives granted in 2016 by CNC, KOFIC, and the General and Special Accounts of the MCST of Korea. It is based on the reasonable working hypothesis that incentives granted for the production, distribution, and exhibition segments are mostly "direct." The majority of subsidies granted to the production segment ranging from scriptwriting to special effects are for

Table 5 The structure of Korean and French financial incentives (2016)

Segments of the film industry	*CNC (France)*			*KOFIC[a] (Korea)*	
	All subsidies		*Automatic subs.[a] (%)*	*All subsidies*	
	(mil. USD)	*(%)*		*mil. USD*	*(%)*
Direct subsidies					
Production	139.2	28.1	64.1	6.6	10.6
Distribution	54.8	11.1	78.4	[b]	0.0
Exhibition	167.5	33.8	49.3	2.9	4.6
Indirect subsidies					
Promotion	64.2	13.0	n.a	13.5	21.6
Infrastructure[c]	69.2	14.0	n.a	39.5	63.2
Total direct subsidies	361.4	73.0	59.4	9.5	15.2
Total indirect subsidies	133.4	27.0	0.0	53.0	84.8
Total	491.8	100.0	43.4	62.5	100.0

Notes [a]Excluding USD 8.6 million allocated to the Fund of the Funds. [b]small amount. [c]indirect subsidies for infrastructure include support to horizontal actions (*dispostifs transversaux*) that involve both the film and TV sectors
Sources CNC (2016) and MCST (2016)

specific film productions, while those for the distribution (connecting film producers and exhibiting firms) and exhibition (movie theaters) sectors are also granted to individual projects. By contrast, most of the incentives granted for promoting the national film events (film festivals or fairs) or for building physical or human capital can be classified as "indirect" incentives because they rarely target specific projects.

Table 5 introduces an additional key distinction within the realm of the direct incentives by breaking them down into "automatic" and "selective" subsidies. Automatic subsidies consist of "drawing rights" made available to film producers based upon the pro-rating of their previous success at the box office. Such subsidies are particularly questionable since they tend to perpetuate the existing pool of human and physical factors of production (scriptwriters, producers, and distributors) when supporting new films. This is all the more the case when these subsidies are granted to a very small number of companies running these individual film projects. In this respect, a recent report by the National Assembly shows the stunning level of concentration among established companies who receive automatic subsidies in France.[4] In 2018, the top 5% of producers have received 48% of automatic subsidies, the top 10% of distributors have received 50%, while the top 2% of exhibitors have received 62% (Magné 2019, p. 32).

By contrast, selective subsidies seek to recognize promising film projects on the basis of a set of criteria set up by professional experts. To this extent, they are less toxic than automatic subsidies, though as seen before, they assume the agency's capacity to make the best choices in a very unpredictable industry and with an opaque maze of committees. The aura of this kind of subsidies in France emerged during the late 1950s where they were widely credited for the success of the French New Wave or *Nouvelle Vague* during the 1960s—although there is little evidence to support this belief (Buchsbaume 2017, p. 267, Gimello-Mesplomb 2003).[5]

[4] These results confirm those already observed two decades ago Lalevée and Lévy-Hartman (2007) suggesting an unhealthy permanence of this concentration; Lalevée, F. and Lévy-Hartman, F., (2007), "Le soutien à la production cinématographique française: A qui profite l'exception culturelle française ?" Groupe d'Economie Mondiale, Sciences Po, Working paper.

[5] Gimello-Mesplomb's study (2003, p. 117) provides two major results. It gives a thorough, fact-based analysis of what can be described as a politically correct "narrative"

Table 5 reveals the striking contrasts between the structure of the incentives in France (CNC) and in Korea (KOFIC and the MCST). In a nutshell, KOFIC's support consists largely of "indirect and selective" subsidies (84.8%) compared to 27% for CNC. In particular, subsidies provided to infrastructure represent 39.5% in the case of KOFIC—and almost all the subsidies granted by the MCST (not shown on Table 5)—compared to only 14% in France. By contrast, "direct and automatic" subsidies in France represent 59.4% of the total public support for the production, distribution, and exhibition segments and 43.4% of the total amount of public support for the film industry. Another puzzling result (as mentioned in Chapter 4) is the fact that the exhibition segment absorbs a third of the total amount of subsidies granted to the French film industry—a situation analyzed in detail in the final section of this chapter.

To sum up, CNC relies mostly on "direct and automatic" subsidies which have been shown to be less capable to provide benefits to the widest range of film companies and to promote cultural diversity. KOFIC is mostly based on a mix of "indirect and selective" support that has been shown to have a more positive impact on the whole film industry.

5 The Crucial Goal of Good Governance: Eliminating Inconsistent Incentives

How can agencies—or any other institution which could be specially mandated by the government (the principal agent)—spot the inconsistencies among the existing measures, evaluate the consequences, and suggest the necessary reforms? The answer is good governance practices—in a nutshell, appropriate cost–benefit analyses. This section illustrates this point with two case studies. As it is important to take into consideration the inter-actions among incentives, these cases look at the two "duos" of measures: the seat tax coupled with the subsidies to movie theaters and the tax relief for foreign filmmakers coupled with the older regime of tax relief for domestic filmmakers.

of the role of the subsidies in supporting the *Nouvelle Vague* films—quite different from what was happening in reality. It also shows how the subsidy mechanism was dominated by political factors: the need of the film crew to have a "card" (affiliated to trade unions), minimum number of technical staff, and "conform" budgetary and financing framework.

5.1 *The Duo "Seat Tax and Subsidies to Movie Theaters"*

Both Korea and France have adopted a seat tax to fund their respective film policies. Despite apparent similarities, there are two key differences. The first one is their rate: the French rate is substantially higher than the Korean one—roughly 3.5 times (10.72% in France vs. 3% in Korea). In other words, if one applied the analysis of Box 1, the French seat tax would generate losses for moviegoers up to 12 times (3.5 times 3.5) more than the Korean one.

The other crucial difference is the allocation of the subsidies. As previously noted, a large share of French support is granted to movie theaters: USD 167 million in 2016, which is one-third of all the subsidies to the film sector and twice the overall amount of all the Korean subsidies granted to the whole domestic film industry by KOFIC (see Table 5). The sheer size of the French subsidies to the screening sector implies that a big share is granted to movie theaters exhibiting commercial films—not only to theaters specialized in "artistic movies." Indeed, a recent report by the National Assembly reveals that, every year, the top thirty exhibitors receive roughly 62% (USD 49 million) of the automatic subsidies granted to the exhibition segment and that the top ten exhibitors receive 40% (USD 33 million) (Magné 2019, p. 32).

There is thus a need to scrutinize thoroughly the French subsidies granted to movie theaters exhibiting commercial films. In doing so, it is important to start by noting that the revenue of the current French tax seat (USD 168 million, Table 4) matches roughly the level of the subsidies granted to movie theaters (USD 167 million, Table 5), a remarkably stable situation that has prevailed every year since 2011. In other words, the whole seat tax is de facto, a tax imposed on moviegoers for supporting movie theaters.

At first glance, the duo "seat tax and subsidies to movie theaters" seems to be a "neutral" operation. It would be the case if one could be sure that such a tax provided the moviegoers with access to better seats made cheaper by the subsidies. However, many hidden factors make this theoretically "neutral approach" unworkable in practice. In particular, the phenomenon of "cost inflation" (see Chapter 4) may induce movie theaters to "overinvest" when they modernize or renovate their premises. As a result, they will then tend to charge seat prices higher than they would in the absence of subsidies. There is some evidence of such a cost inflation: if the average seat price for all the tickets has slightly declined in France over the last decade, there has been an increase for the most expensive tickets and their share (CNC 2019, p. 32).

There is a very concrete and powerful economic force fueling this cost inflation. Contrary to what one may believe at first glance, the major beneficiaries of subsidies to movie theaters are not their owners, but rather the suppliers of the equipment for these venues. In a simple fashion, the sequence of events is as follows. With these subsidies made available, the equipment suppliers are able to convince the exhibitors to buy equipment in larger quantity and/or with more features than they would really need. This artificial increase of the demand for equipment in quantity and quality pushes up the price of the equipment and the operating costs of movie theaters. The result is a level of seat prices above what would have been strictly necessary for compensating the seat tax.

This evolution hurts moviegoers and film producers because it reduces the size of the audience since the exhibition segment is more expensive than it should be. Moreover, it has two ripple-on effects which both discriminate against the French film industry. First, as already examined and documented in Chapter 4, the subsidies to movie theaters tend to discriminate in favor of US films and against French films because the former are more hi-tech intensive than the later. Second, by making seats more expensive than in the absence of subsidies, the exhibition segment makes the competition fiercer among filmmakers when attracting moviegoers. Films produced by large film companies are able to cope with this increased competition by advertising and marketing. However, the majority of French films are unlikely to have enough money and leverage to be in this favorable position: as a result, the duo "seat tax and subsidies to movie theaters" discriminates in favor of the most affluent film companies, presumably the US studios, hence it works against cultural diversity.

This cascade of costs and distortions does not spare the exhibition segment itself. As underlined above, some exhibitors—especially the larger ones—are better at getting subsidies than others. As a result, the current duo of the "seat tax and subsidies to movie theaters" favors the French exhibitors that are well equipped for hunting subsidies to the detriment of the others. As half of the subsidies granted to exhibitors are "automatic," they favor the concentration among incumbent companies.

How can this situation be improved? It is useful to look first at the most extreme solution: it is politically not likely, but it allows us to better understand the forces at play. This option would be to eliminate completely the seat tax and the subsidies to movies theaters altogether—that is, cutting CNC's budget by USD 167 million and cutting its subsidies to the exhibition sector by the same amount. Under such conditions, moviegoers will be better off because the tickets which are subjected to the cost inflation—such as the upper-end IMAX or 3D and 4D films—will be less expensive. This is simply down to the fact that in the absence of subsidies, theaters will be less subject to profligate behavior in terms of investments. Furthermore, the filmmakers and in particular French film producers will be better off to the extent that the audience will be larger. Even the exhibitors who are not as successful, the so-called subsidy-hunters, could still be better off in such an environment.

A more politically feasible option would consist of eliminating only a portion of the subsidies to movie theaters—raising the question of "by how much"? An interesting case to look at briefly as an illustration would be to cut—say by half—the automatic subsidies (roughly USD 83 million), which reinforce the position of large incumbents in the exhibition market for no justifiable reason. The remaining seat tax (USD 83 million) would correspond to roughly 5.5% of French box office revenues in 2016. Note that this would make the reduced French seat tax rate much closer to the Korean rate (3%). The success of the Korean film industry provides ample evidence that such a low tax rate is compatible with economic success (see Chapter 7). Last but not least, this reduced seat tax would be enough to fund the selective subsidies targeting movie theaters (*cinémas d'art et d'essai*) that promote cultural diversity—one of the two economic justifications for subsidies as explained in Chapter 4.

To sum up, even limited reform would improve the welfare of moviegoers and promote cultural diversity at the same time. This deserves a final remark. A progressive phasing out of the subsidies would always be preferable because it gives time to the exhibitors concerned to adjust smoothly to an increasingly less-subsidized environment. There is no strong reason to insist on a "big bang" operation—one brutal cut. Indeed, past cases of big bang reforms strongly suggest that they often lead to costly mistakes.

5.2 *The Duo "Tax Relief for Domestic Filmmakers and Tax Relief for Foreign Filmmakers"*

In 2004, CNC introduced a tax relief scheme—the *crédit d'impôt cinéma* (hereafter CIC)—to all French filmmakers using domestic studios services and having access to automatic subsidies. This scheme sought to reduce the increasing tendency among French filmmakers to "delocalize" their production to locations in Europe or other parts of the world. CNC justified its decision on two grounds. First, it felt that it was necessary to replace a previous support scheme which was scrapped because it was judged to be incompatible with the EU competition law on state aid. Second, CNC believed that French filmmakers were shifting their production to other countries because of the attractive financial incentives offered overseas. In 2009, CNC sets up another tax relief scheme targeting this time foreign filmmakers—the *crédit d'impôt international* (hereafter known under its acronym C2I). This scheme sought to induce foreign filmmakers to "delocalize" their filming to French studios—one of the many episodes of "subsidy competition" that was evoked in Chapter 4.

This section scrutinizes the combined impact of these two tax relief schemes. It reveals that the effects of these two measures tend to cancel each other out and that both measures are unable to solve the fundamental problem at stake—namely the lack of international competitiveness among the French studios. This example should spark interest in the many countries who enforce the same duo of tax relief schemes, such as Korea which has begun to do so since 2019.

The co-existence of the two French schemes became quickly problematic. It forced CNC to take almost every year "adjustment measures" expanding the coverage and composition of the eligible expenses under the two schemes in the hope of finding a more equal "balance" between them. These successive measures have had one clear end result: they made the two regimes increasingly generous for French filmmakers—hence more costly to the state budget. As illustrated by Table 2 in Chapter 4 Column [7], the duo CIC-C2I cost USD 211.5 million (in constant 2018 USD) in 2018, six times its amount in 2005 (USD 34.8 million) when CIC was first introduced. These skyrocketing costs have recently attracted a lot of criticism from politicians leading to an expected decrease in the amount provided (USD 170 million in 2020) (Laborde 2019).

Despite these problems, CNC continues to argue that the CIC has been a success since the share of spending in foreign studios by French filmmakers has declined from 27% in 2016 to 13% in 2018 (Bredin 2019). The increase in the business of the French studios business between these two years—estimated to be several hundreds of million US dollars—was also presented as justification for the existence of the duo CIC-C2I.

However, as stressed in previous chapters, the increase of business dependent upon public support is not the correct test for assessing the true economic impact of this support: from a country perspective, the accurate test is whether this amount of public money would have delivered more—or less—benefits if it would have been disbursed in a different sector of the economy for other purpose(s). Moreover, the 2016–2018 decrease in the share of French filmmakers' spending on foreign studios is only part of the full picture. It ignores a troubling evolution: the 13% share of foreign spending made by French filmmakers in 2018 is roughly the same as the share in 2004, that is, the year of the introduction of the CIC scheme.

These results thus call for a more thorough economic analysis of this duo of tax relief schemes. Such an approach involves a complex set of interacting forces that can be described by considering the following basic question: who have been the beneficiaries and the losers of these two schemes? French studios are unequivocally net beneficiaries: both schemes expand the demand of the quantity for their services, and possibly even push up the rental prices of their facilities. Foreign filmmakers are also unequivocally net beneficiaries: the C2I expands their access to the supply of French studios so long as they are by global standards sufficiently competitive—a key condition examined below. By contrast, French filmmakers are likely to be net losers: they have now to compete with foreign film producers for access to French studios—a situation they did not face before the introduction of the C2I. They have now thus access to a reduced supply of French studios at possibly higher rental prices. The only way for them to reduce or to eliminate these risks is to lobby for ever larger CIC funds from the French Treasury—or to run away and work with foreign studios.[6]

It should be stressed that the key problem at stake is not that French and foreign filmmakers compete for French studios. Indeed, this is a desirable situation in a market economy. The true problem created by the duo CIC-C2I is that the conditions regarding the competition for access to French studios among domestic and foreign filmmakers are decisively determined by the CNC's decisions on the amount of public support

[6] This negative impact would not have happened if French studios had an unused capacity of production in the first place. However, this condition is itself the sign of a problem: why do French filmmakers delocalize if there is idle capacity among domestic studios?

granted to each tax relief scheme. Every time CNC makes one tax relief scheme more attractive than the other, it tilts the balance of costs and benefits to the recipients of the more attractive scheme. In other words, each scheme is in a permanent position to "challenge" the other one—it "cancels out" at least partly the effects of the other one.

So far, our discussion has been limited to the official justifications for the two tax relief schemes. It does not evoke a more fundamental problem: possible inefficiency among the French studios compared to their competitors in other parts of the world. This performance issue has only been recently addressed in a report for the CNC which compared the main features of French and foreign studios (Siritzky 2019). Its findings led to a compelling picture of the "under-developed" nature among French studios: smaller total size of each studio, fewer "studio sets" (an impediment to shoot several scenes of the same film at the same time), no "backlots" (crucial for external film shooting), and no ownership of the land on which the studios are built (a feature that makes French studios poor in assets and makes the rents very costly for those that are close to large towns).

These are structural failures that none of these two tax relief schemes can address. These schemes merely make the consequences of this lack of competitiveness bearable to the filmmakers by granting them public support which has to be renewed every year—at great cost for the Treasury. Such failures can only be addressed by making appropriate investments. As discussed in Chapter 4, investments in film infrastructure can be funded by a mix of private and public money. If there is a need for public support, it should be done via "indirect" incentives as argued in the previous section, not via an endless addition of "direct" subsidies (tax reliefs) granted to individual filmmakers that allows them to absorb the extra costs brought on by inefficient studios.

This brief analysis deserves two final remarks. First, the duo CIC-C2I has been made even more costly by the fact that CNC has felt compelled to compete with the more generous tax reliefs granted by the UK or Germany. As these two countries have more efficient studios, there was a need to boost enormously the fiscal benefits associated with the C2I scheme—raising in turn the pressure to increase the funds to be allocated to the CIC. This "mimicking" policy has not been subjected to a careful assessment and it does not seem based on compelling arguments. Why should CNC imitate the UK film policy which has not been so successful for addressing the problems of the UK independent film industry? At the same time, why has CNC not adopted Korea's policy that has witnessed the development of a successful domestic film industry, despite the absence of tax relief schemes directed to foreign companies until 2019 (see Chapter 4)?

Second, a frequent argument for tax relief schemes attracting foreign film producers is the existence of natural landscapes and architecture in the country in question that can be featured in a blockbuster and thus helps to promote them globally. However, a recent example with Korea's use of such subsidies cast doubt on the spillover effects from attracting foreign film-making companies. In 2014, KOFIC offered substantial support to shoot two of Marvel's films in Korea, *The Avengers: The Age of Ultron* and *Black Panther*. In exchange, the first film was required to hire a Korean actor while also featuring scenes filmed in Seoul and other nearby locations. The second film was shot in Busan—the venue for the Busan International Film Festival known as BIFF—and featured the landmark Diamond Bridge. In fact, the main purpose of these tax rebates was to promote Seoul and Busan as tourist destinations, not to develop the Korean film industry. The end result though was not what was expected. First, these films were severely criticized by Korean movie-goers because they did not feature many scenes that can be recognized by an international audience as having been shot in Korea (Borowiec 2015; Iwanek 2018). The second film was criticized for having a Korean character played by a non-Korean actress who spoke Korean poorly. Indeed, it is questionable if this support has offered any benefits to the Korean film industry. Clearly, these tax rebates raised the following questions: who has promoted whom? And who has been the true beneficiary: Marvel or the Korean side—and in this case who in Korea? If an agency or a government wants to promote a country, the appropriate instrument should be then incentives directly targeting the desired tourist goal.

6 Conclusion

This chapter has extended the comparative analysis of the Korean film industry to the two last sets of potential barriers which have not yet been explored: regulations (laws and implementing acts) and institutions—the "autonomous agencies" running the film policies.

First, it has presented an as exhaustive as possible comparative review of the "restrictive" (possibly protectionist) regulations in the film industry. Korea is the country with the lowest overall level of regulations, a feature it shares with the US and Japan. However, more importantly, Korea is also the country with the most similar level of restrictions in the market access, capital, and labor "categories". This feature ensures that the overall structure of Korea's restrictive regulations has not created large distortions within its film industry—it did not favor too much some categories at a high cost for others.

Next, the chapter has compared the two agencies in charge of designing and implementing the film policies—Korea's KOFIC and France's CNC—because each of them is an archetype in terms of mandate, size, and financial autonomy. It has argued that a wide degree of regulatory and financial autonomy combined with a large budget has led to less successful film policies than those followed by a more constrained agency. This chapter has accumulated evidence explaining to a great extent this result: agencies with a large degree of autonomy have been prone to be captured by the vested interests they are supposed to regulate—a situation less likely and/or less consequential for the agencies with limited autonomy and money. For instance, KOFIC's smaller size (eight to fourteen times smaller than CNC) has forced this agency to concentrate its support on two aspects of the film policy—infrastructure and film promotion—which have a much higher chance to be beneficial to every Korean film producer than the host of direct subsidies implemented by CNC. Compared to CNC, KOFIC has also had a much more limited use of "automatic" subsidies that favor incumbents–film companies, directors, and scriptwriters—to the detriment of newcomers and creativity.

Based on these results, the last section of this chapter has argued for a systematic search of the best measures and of their appropriate level, which should be the pillar of better governance in the film industry. It has illustrated this goal by analyzing two case studies in detail. The first one has examined the ins and outs of the duo of measures composed of the seat tax and the subsidies to movie theaters. After revealing the many hidden costs that this duo generates, it has shown that a balanced cut of these two incentives can improve the welfare for moviegoers, enhance the situation for French films compared to US films, and increase the support granted to movie theaters dedicated to cultural goals. The second case has explored the duo consisting of tax-reliefs granted to foreign filmmakers and those granted to domestic filmmakers. It has revealed that not only can this policy deteriorate the situation for domestic filmmakers, but that it is also incapable of addressing the fundamental issue at stake—the lack of competitiveness among French studios. Again, a better policy would face this issue head on by providing well-designed indirect subsidies that would enhance the competitiveness of these studios.

It is important to stress that the aim of this chapter has not been to provide "one size fits all" recipes. Rather, it has been to launch and contribute to a pragmatic and substantive debate on how to support—if needed—the film industry of a country in the most efficient and effective way. The reforms suggested in this chapter go in the same direction as those in Chapter 4: they recommend looking to the Korean film regulatory and institutional framework as a source of inspirations—characterized by an agency having more limited incentives but better designed so that it favors a more effective support.

That said, this conclusion is not final. It needs to be confirmed by a careful look at a last crucial issue left aside so far: the "quality" of film production. In a nutshell, does the quality of Korean films match the quality among those of its main competitors? This is the topic for the next chapter.

References

Bredin, F. 2019. Crédit d'impôt pour le cinéma: Un tournage génère en moyenne 400 emplois directs. *Le Parisien*, February 10. https://www.leparisien.fr/culture-loisirs/cinema/credit-d-impot-pour-le-cinema-un-tournage-genere-en-moyenne-400-emplois-directs-10-02-2019-8008230.php.

Borowiec, S. 2015. Some South Koreans Say "'vengers: Age of Ultron' Shows Seoul's Ugly Side". *Los Angeles Times*, May 8. https://www.latimes.com/entertainment/movies/moviesnow/la-et-mn-south-korean-avengers-age-of-ultron-20150508-story.html.

Buchsbaume, J. 2017. *Exception Taken: How France Has Defied Hollywood's New World Order*. New York: Columbia University Press.

Centre national du cinéma et de l'image animée (CNC). 2006. 60 ans du CNC", *Centre national du cinéma et de l'image animée*. https://www.cnc.fr/series-tv/etudes-et-rapports/la-lettre-du-cnc/la-lettre-32--mars-2006_214807.

Centre national du cinéma et de l'image animée (CNC). 2013. Tout ce que vous avez toujours voulu savoir sur le CNC … sans jamais oser le demander. CNC, May. http://www.cnc.fr/c/document_library/get_file?uuid=1d6dec69-e723-435d-92c3-bb49d79d90b4&groupId=18.

Centre national du cinéma et de l'image animée (CNC). 2016. Various issues. *Bilan*. https://www.cnc.fr/cinema/etudes-et-rapports/bilans/.

Centre national du cinéma et de l'image animée (CNC). 2019. Various issues. *Bilan*. https://www.cnc.fr/cinema/etudes-et-rapports/bilans/.

Cour des Comptes. 2012. La gestion et le financement du *Centre national du cinéma et de l'image animée* (CNC): Exercices 2007 à 2011. *Cour des Comptes*, August. https://www.ccomptes.fr/fr/publications/gestion-et-financement-du-centre-national-du-cinema-et-de-limage-animee-cnc.

Cour des Comptes. 2014. Les soutiens à la production cinématographique et audiovisuelle: des changements nécessaires. Cour des Comptes. https://www.ccomptes.fr/fr/publications/les-soutiens-la-production-cinematographique-et-audiovisuelle-des-changements.

Farchy, J. 1992. *Le cinéma déchaîné, Mutation d'une industrie*. Paris: Presses du CNRS.

Feenstra, R.C. 2004. *Advanced International Trade: Theory and Evidence*. Princeton and Oxford: Princeton University Press.

Gimello-Mesplomb, F. 2003. Le prix de la qualité. L'Etat et le cinéma français (1960–1965), Politiques du cinema. *Politix* 16 (61): 95–122.

Guback, T.H. 1974. Film as International Business. *Journal of Communication* 24 (1): 90–101.

Hayward, S. 2005. *French National Cinema*. London and New York: Routledge.

Iwanek, K. 2018. How Marvel Failed to Promote Seoul and Busan. *The Diplomat*, March 26. https://thediplomat.com/2018/03/how-marvel-failed-to-promote-seoul-and-busan/.

Johnson-Yale, C. 2017. *A History of Hollywood's Outsourcing Debate: Runaway Production*. London: Lexington Book.

Laborde, F. 2018. *Projet de loi de finances pour 2018: Médias, livre et industries culturelles : Livre et industries culturelles*. http://www.senat.fr/rap/a17-112-43/a17-112-430.html.

Laborde, F. 2019. Projet de loi de finances pour 2020: Médias, livre et industries culturelles, Avis n 145 (2019–2020), Novembre 21. *Sénat de la République Française*. http://www.senat.fr/rap/a19-145-43/a19-145-43.html.

Lange, A., and T. Westcott. 2004. *Public Funding for Films and Audiovisual Works in Europe: A Comparative Approach*. European Audio Observatory, Strabgourg. https://rm.coe.int/public-funding-report-2004-en-optim-pdf/16808e46d9.

Lebelle, A., and M. Pelloli. 2018. Niches fiscales: «Les crédits d'impôt liés à la culture ont explosé». *Le Parisien*, Novembre 26. http://www.leparisien.fr/economie/niches-fiscales-les-credits-d-impot-lies-a-la-culture-ont-explose-26-11-2018-7954188.php.

Magné, M.A. 2019. Projet de rapport du règlement du budget et d'approbation des comptes de l'année 2018, Annexe 30, Médias, livres et industries culturelles : avances à l'audiovisuel public, No 1947, Assemblée Nationale.

Messerlin, P.A. 2019. Building Consistent Policies on Subsidies in the Film Industry. *Kritika Kultura* 32: 375–396.

Ministry of Culture, Sports and Tourism (MCST). 2016. *Annual Budget Expenditure Planning*. Seoul: MCST.

Newman-Baudais, S. 2011. *Public Funding for Films and Audiovisual Works in Europe*. European Audio Observatory, Strabgourg. https://rm.coe.int/public-funding-report-2011-en-optim-pdf/16808e46dc.

Organisation for Economic Co-operation and Development (OECD). 2019. Services Trade Restrictiveness Index Simulator. https://sim.oecd.org/.

Parc, J. 2017. The Effects of Protection in Cultural Industries: The Case of the Korean Film Policies. *International Journal of Cultural Policy* 23 (5): 618–633.

Parc, J., and P.A. Messerlin. 2020. Overcoming the Incoherent *'Grand Maneuver'* in the French Film and TV Markets: Lessons from the Experiences in France and Korea. *Global Policy* 11 (S2): 31–39.

Parc, J. 2020a. Between State-led and Corporation-led Co-Productions: How Has Film Co-Production Been Exploited by States in Europe. *Innovation: The European Journal of Social Science Research* 33 (4): 442–458.

Parc, J. 2020b. Understanding Film Co-Production in the Era of Globalization: A Value Chain Approach. *Global Policy* 11 (4): 458–465.

Siritzky, S. 2019. Les studios de tournage, un enjeu primordial pour la production en France. CNC, Paris. https://www.cnc.fr/documents/36995/156431/Les+studios+de+tournage%2C+un+enjeu+primordial+pour+la+production+en+France.pdf/5ec2b518-3d6e-c393-4f5a-38d97ce8d5a5.

Shapiro, C. 1983. Premiums for High Quality Products As Returns to Reputations. *Quarterly Journal of Economics* 98: 659–680.

Stiglitz. J. 1989. Principal and Agent. In *Allocation, Information and Markets*, 241–253. London: Palgrave Macmillan.

CHAPTER 6

Film Quality: The Golden Key for Sustainable Success

How can the "quality" of a film be measured? This is a critical question facing filmmakers, government officials, scholars, and above all the audience themselves. Understanding the key aspects that define quality is not only important in terms of producing successful films but is also vital for the types of policies that governments should consider designing and implementing. Like other industries, the film industry has three principal segments which consist of production, distribution, and consumption, and policies are often specifically designed to focus on each of these segments. For instance, in order to induce domestic moviegoers to watch fewer imported films, a government can implement screen quotas to limit their exhibition with the hopes that such a policy will increase the screening of domestic films. To hinder the distribution of imported films, a government can introduce import quotas to reduce the number of foreign films imported into its market.

Supporting production is complicated as it concerns two aspects, quantity and quality of films. It is then important to examine if government policies can enhance these two conditions. In particular, it is worth analyzing whether financial support or subsidies can increase the quantity and quality of films. As producing films requires financial resources to hire actors and actresses, working crews, directors, and other relevant production factors, it is easy to assume that financial abundance can be

J. Parc and P. A. Messerlin, *The Untold Story of the Korean Film Industry*, Cultural Economics & the Creative Economy,
https://doi.org/10.1007/978-3-030-80342-1_6

closely related to quantity. As stressed in Chapter 5, the public "agencies" in charge of allocating subsidies to the film industry often present the number of films that have benefitted from these subsidies as a barometer of policy effectiveness.

This is a critical point of great interest for all the countries that are seeking to build a competitive and sustainable film industry. It makes it worthwhile to explore the relations between film quality and film policy. So far, evidence in Chapter 4 has warned us that this view should not be taken for granted, especially in the long run. Building upon this, Chapter 5, has presented the economic arguments reinforcing the need for caution in the use of subsidies while offering better alternatives in this respect. This chapter takes it on further by testing the alleged existence of a positive relation between subsidies and film quality.

In providing such an evaluation, the contents for this chapter are as follows. First, it seeks out a better way to measure the quality of films. Second, in comparing the quality of Korean, French, UK, and US films over the last decade it provides a surprisingly clear-cut result: Korean films have been perceived as having on average a better quality than the movies from the three other countries. This quite unexpected conclusion holds whether one relies on the judgments of all moviegoers or on those of specialized film critics. Third, this chapter ends with a brief presentation of the tests exploring whether there is a positive relation between film quality and subsidies, revealing another aspect of the "Korean exception."

1 Measuring Film Quality

Measuring "quality" in the cultural industries is notoriously difficult, and the film industry is no exception in this regard. This section begins with the issues related to measuring quality that is common for all cultural industries. Next, it discusses the special economic feature of films from a quality standpoint, since films pertain to the category of "experience goods" meaning that their quality cannot be appreciated without "using"—watching—them. This section concludes by presenting in more detail the solutions that can address these difficulties.

1.1 Three Main Challenges

There are three main challenges when measuring quality in the film industry: subjectivity, "transitional temporality," and "regionality."

Firstly, like other art pieces or cultural products, setting up an "absolute" quality standard is extremely tricky because quality is very subjective. Each individual has a different appreciation for the same film and often for different reasons. Unsurprisingly, similar gaps in appreciation re-emerge within large groups, such as film critics or the general audience. Despite the difficulties, the challenge of subjectivity is somehow manageable by laying down side by side different evaluations—for instance the one by the general audience and the other one(s) by the critics—and then comparing both.

Secondly, in contrast with many other visual arts, films are dematerialized. Through devices such as TVs, computers, and smartphones, audiences can enjoy this new form of art at any time and any place. When compared with other artworks, the possibility to rediscover old works by today's audience is high, which reflects the transitional temporality of films. This allows films and audiences to span across time periods. A film that was well received upon its release can be criticized later and/or completely forgotten later due to a huge demand gap between times of its release and appreciation; at the same time, a film that was not well received can be rediscovered and more appreciated later. As such, the potential transitional temporality of films is often used to justify the need to support artistic films in the off-chance that they would be rediscovered later on. However, as mentioned before this is very often due to unmatched quality with a specific time period, which goes to show that these changes are relatively difficult to anticipate and make measuring the quality of a film very problematic.

Lastly, although films can be distributed widely regardless of their nationality, most are still only shown to limited local audiences except a small number of titles that have been well-distributed in the global market, such as Hollywood films and a few other blockbusters. A "shared" cultural value such as a sense of humor is rather regional or even country-specific. For instance, the *Austin Powers* series was well received in English-speaking countries but failed miserably in many Asian markets. Interestingly, such geographic or cultural limits occur also at international film festivals. Some argue that winning prizes at such festivals can be a good barometer to measure the quality of films. While this can be an interesting yardstick, each film festival has its own criteria or preference reflecting a high degree of regionality. For example, films festivals in Europe often render awards to European films while those in the Americas often grant awards to American films.

Despite these difficulties, this chapter attempts to measure the quality of films in the most rigourous possible way. As the challenges raised by transitional temporality and regionality are very high, this chapter focuses on the issue of subjectivity in a thorough manner as explained at the end of this section. In particular, this chapter compares the film quality among four major film producers—France, Korea, the UK, and the US—that the previous chapters have shown to be very different in almost every aspect of their film industries and policies. All of these differences make this comparative approach on film quality more interesting.

1.2 Films as "Experience Goods": Attractiveness vs. Quality

Measuring quality faces one more challenge in that films pertain to a special category of goods—the so-called experience goods. When customers buy such goods, it is difficult for them to judge accurately their quality: they need to consume or use them first. Regarding films, when these customers buy tickets or turn on their TV or another screen to watch a film for the first time, they all have their own expectations on the quality of the film they plan to see. Choices are therefore mostly based on the information provided by external sources or through their own experiences (this chapter does not deal with the case of people who re-watch films that they like). Sources such as the reviews by film critics, "influencers," journalists, advertisements, word of mouth, and possibly ticket prices are all important variables in this case.[1] In addition, buyers (or distributors) who know that Company A has produced attractive films that have met their audience's taste before will likely to have more incentives to purchase and distribute further films from Company A. Indeed this is why Marvel Studios is producing franchise films such as The Avengers series.

Given the limited or biased nature of this available information, it is more accurate to use the terms of "attractiveness" when people make the decision to buy tickets—as this book has done so far. By contrast, "quality" is a term that this book uses for expressing the personal evaluation of the audience—be it an individual, a film critic, or an

[1] The role of price tag as a significant indicator of the film quality per se is debatable for a host of reasons, the most important being that they do not vary much in the short run (Stephen Follows 2020).

"influencer"—once they have seen the film in question. As a result, attractiveness and quality differ every time that the audience has been satisfied or disappointed after having watched films.

Regarding subsidies, a few academic studies have examined empirically their impact on film attractiveness by looking at box office revenues. Bagella and Becchetti (1999) have been among the first to assess the effect of subsidies on the box office revenues of 977 Italian films produced over the period 1985 to 1996, which revealed no significant effect. McKenzie and Walls (2012) have looked at the case of Australian films and again found that subsidies have had no impact on box office revenues. In the same vein, Jansen (2005) analyses the impact of subsidies on the number of admissions to German films. His study suggests that subsidies tend to help producers who have consistently had above-average success with their movie performance. However, he stands negatively on providing subsidies to the film industry, arguing that subsidies favor established producers; hence distort the industry.

Meloni et al. (2015) take one step further by testing the impact of subsidies on evaluations measured by the number of awards received at international film festivals. They examined 754 Italian films produced during the period 2002–2011 and found an overall negative impact of subsidies on the number of awards (as well as on box office revenues). That said, awards do not necessarily reflect the views of the audience who have seen the same movie. Moreover, festival awards do not necessarily pass well the test of subjectivity, especially when they are granted by a small number of jury members, which is indicative of how they cannot overcome the regionality issue as explained before.

Finally, all these doubts are amplified by the fact that awards can easily turn into politically charged events (Fretts 2019). They can also mirror economic interests that should not be taken into consideration when assessing film quality. Recent examples include the controversial treatment of Netflix's *Okja* and *The Meyerowitz Stories* at the 2017 Cannes Film Festival (Terrazas 2017). Rather than making assessments based upon their quality, these decisions reflected the conflict between traditional and new media companies as mirrored by the debate regarding the French regulations on *chronologie des médias,* that gives exclusive priority to movie theaters over streaming platforms for premier screenings (see Chapter 7).

To sum up, the literature reviewed in this section is not well suited for measuring the quality of experience goods such as films nor for assessing the relations between the quality level and subsidies. One needs a new approach based on more appropriate indicators of quality.

1.3 A New Approach to Measure the Quality of Films

As film ratings on dedicated websites reflect the evaluations of the audience once they have seen the film, they seem the most appropriate sources of information for assessing their "quality." This approach has an additional interest, especially in the case of other media outlets besides movie theaters as it does not depend on whether the films are newly released or not. This then helps to address to some extent the challenge of transitional temporality.

This chapter uses the ratings provided by three websites: Internet Movie Database (IMDb), Metacritic (MC), and Rotten Tomatoes (RT). These three sources offer the additional advantage to take into consideration the differences among audiences—critics vs. general audience. They respect thus the subjectivity—an essential feature of "quality": a multifaceted concept which depends not only on films per se, but also on the "evaluators" themselves.

More information on these three websites highlights their suitability for this study. IMDb uses a rating scale from one to ten in which users can score films. There are roughly 200 million evaluations for the films surveyed in this chapter. By contrast, the ratings by RT and MC are based upon film "critics" writing articles for the press including general newspapers, film magazines, and websites. It is though a much smaller source of votes, roughly 400,000 for the films covered in this chapter. Finally, it is noteworthy that each of these websites has their own methodology for aggregating the information collected on individual ratings. IMDb ratings summarize the audience evaluations by calculating scores ranging from 0 to 10. RT ratings break down complex opinions into "certified fresh," "fresh," or "rotten," while MC ratings aggregate scores into "meta-scores" from 0 to 100.

The dataset used in this chapter covers films released during the period 2009–2018. The choice of this period has a specific purpose: it allows for a lag of three years between the observation period for film quality (2009–2018) and the observation period for public support (2006–2015) which has been used in Chapter 4. The purpose for such a lag is the need to take into consideration the time necessary for the physical production of a film—from the first draft of its script to its final release in movie theaters.

Table 1 Number of films (2009–2018)

Year	*France*	*Korea*	*UK*	*US*	*Total*
2009	53	45	73	175	346
2010	50	30	72	184	336
2011	59	29	78	189	355
2012	57	41	125	192	415
2013	50	67	98	193	408
2014	50	56	114	179	399
2015	47	50	107	175	379
2016	160	34	133	182	509
2017	142	54	117	176	489
2018	97	32	62	169	360
Total	765	438	979	1,814	3,996

Data Source OMDb

A recent study of 782 US films released between 2006 and 2016 suggests that the production of a typical film requires roughly 870 days, almost 2.5 years (Stephen Follows 2018). Six months have been added to this period in order to take into consideration the time needed for securing funding—especially the time needed for getting public support and the need for adjustment to comply with the provisions—shooting locations and nationality of the actors, among other factors—which are required by the public support schemes.

Table 1 presents this database which consists of almost 4,000 films, all extracted from the Open Movie Database that gathers data from IMDb, MC, and RT. As a number of these films are co-productions between the US, the UK, or France, they raise the issue of the nationality to assign to these films. The solution adopted has been to use the nationality assigned to every coproduced film by the Lumiere database of the European Audiovisual Observatory. It is important to note that an interesting feature of the Korean film industry is that it has had few co-productions with one of these three countries according to UNESCO Institute for Statistics.

2 Comparing the Evolution of the Film Quality

A comparison of film quality by country can be very meaningful, particularly with Korean films vis-à-vis their three counterparts as Korea has shown sharp differences from the other selected industries in almost every dimension examined: it adopted and maintained an open domestic market (Chapters 1 and 2); it has outperformed all its direct competitors in terms of box office revenues or admissions for the last twenty years (Chapters 2 and 3); its public support has been significantly lower (Chapter 4); and it has benefited from better governance over the last twenty years (Chapter 5).

2.1 *Breaking Prejudices*

Table 2 presents the average ratings of film quality in the selected countries for the overall decade 2009–2018—hence displayed from a long-term perspective. To make this comparison easier to read, ratings are presented in a "relative" way: we set the ratings of Korea at 100, then calculate the relative ratings of the others. It suggests several—all unexpected—results. First, the average quality of Korean films is the highest among all the selected countries for the three ratings. This result is very important from a film policy perspective: it means that the characteristics mentioned above regarding the Korean film industry have not been an obstacle toward gaining higher quality scores in the IMDb ratings and those of the RT and MC ratings.

That said, there are several interesting nuances to be added to this overall result. IMDb ratings suggest that Korean films hold a slight degree of quality over UK and US films, a surprising result since these two types of films are generally perceived as the best commercial films in the world.

Table 2 Average ratings of the films over the whole decade (2009–2018)

		France	*Korea*	*UK*	*US*
Ratings					
	IMDb	6.09	6.48	6.41	6.36
	RT	69.3	75.2	64.2	54.9
	MC	63.3	67.0	60.3	54.5
Relative ratings[a]					
	IMDb	93.9	100.0	98.9	98.1
	RT	92.2	100.0	85.3	73.0
	MC	94.5	100.0	90.1	81.3

Note [a]Ratings for Korean films are set at 100
Data Source OMDb

Indeed, the fact that the IMDb evaluations of the films produced in the UK and the US are close to each other is likely to reflect the fact that these films are produced by the same set of US studios or through co-production, a good example of such co-production is the film *Gravity* (2013). The quality premium of Korean films with respect to French films is notably larger than the one with the UK or US films. This wider gap is consistent with the frequent observation that the French film industry has been facing recurrent difficulties to produce attractive blockbusters. Turning to the MC and RT ratings, they show a substantial quality premium for Korean films compared to UK and US films whereas the premium quality for Korean films compared to French films is as large as the one in the IMDb ratings.

These results raise many interesting questions. Why is the quality of Korean films not as widely recognized as it should be according to these ratings? For example, the remarkable achievement of Bong Joon-ho's *Parasite* (2020) at so many international film awards is commonly perceived as a one-off moment rather than as part of a long successful process. The full answer to these questions is beyond the scope of this book. It requires a study on its own because it is such a complex outcome of many factors, such as the unjustified premium enjoyed by incumbents, language barrier, distributors' focus on Korean films from fringe genres such as dark and violent themes, and broad cultural differences.

2.2 Short-Term Comparisons

Does this higher quality among Korean films prevail also in the short run—for instance on an annual basis? Naturally, one should not interpret too narrowly the results below given the volatile film industry—nor probably in the case of any cultural industry for that matter. However, this exercise can shed some interesting light on a better understanding of the above long-term results. Figures 1, 2, and 3 show the evolution of the annual quality ratings for each year between 2009 and 2018. As expected for the highly volatile film industry, quality ratings vary a lot from year to year in each of the four countries.

Still, Fig. 1 on the IMDb ratings shows that, despite this volatility, film quality on a yearly basis presents the same pattern of differences as the results from the overall decade 2009–2018. There are small differences between the quality of the Korean, UK, and US films, while there is a much larger one with French films. Interestingly, the annual quality

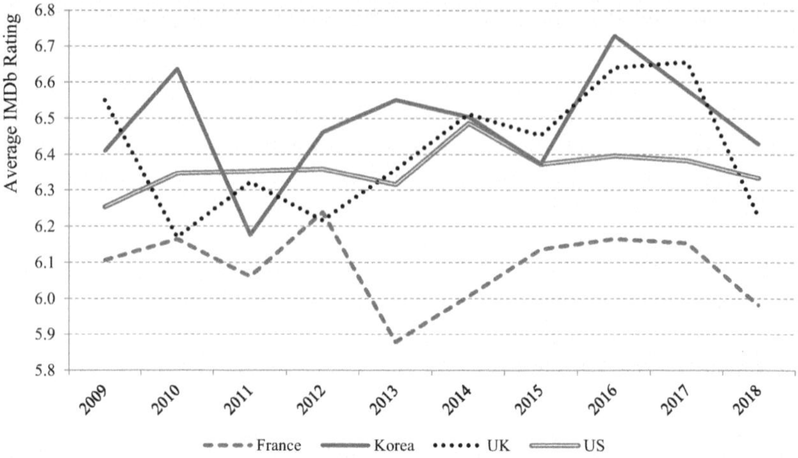

Fig. 1 Evolution of the IMDb ratings (2009–2018) (*Data Source* OMDb)

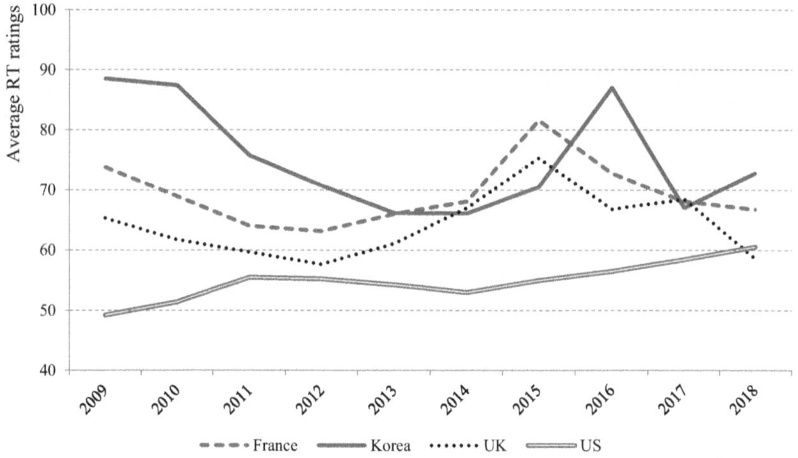

Fig. 2 Evolution of Rotten Tomatoes ratings (2009–2018) (*Data Source* OMDb)

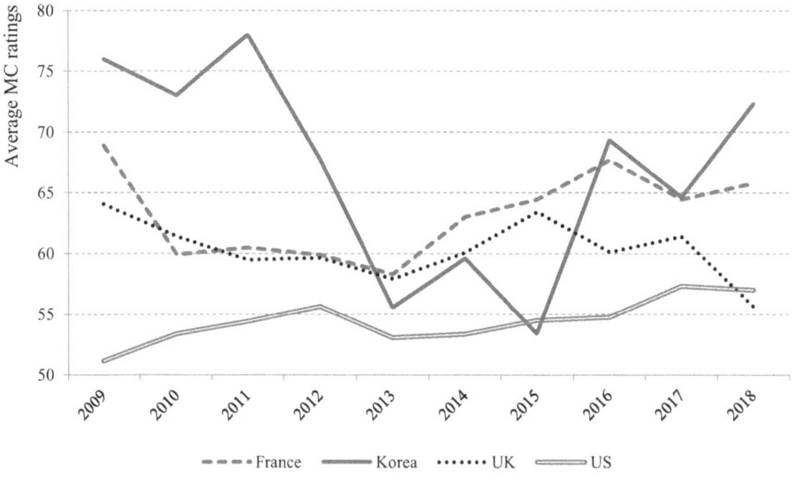

Fig. 3 Evolution of Metacritic ratings (2009–2018) (*Data Source* OMDb)

of French films never exceeds the lowest quality level reached by the other three film industries. That said, there are notable differences. There are good and bad "vintage" years for Korean films—for instance 2010 and 2016 (good vintage) and 2011 (bad vintage). The same prevails for the UK and French films. By contrast, US films do not show markedly different vintages—a feature that may be due to the higher number of US films in the database or to a better mastering by US studios of the quality that moviegoers expect.

Figures 2 and 3 focus on the evaluations among critics on film quality. First, the quality of US films is the lowest for both RT and MC ratings, but it shows a slightly but continuously improving trend during the period 2009–2018. Second, the evaluations for the French, Korean, and UK films show notable volatility, as what could be expected for such films. This feature may mirror the higher intrinsic volatility of these kinds of films; but it may well also reflect a higher volatility in the assessments of the film critics, again as one could expect—artworks have often unleashed strong opinions. Lastly, the RT ratings suggest a roughly similar time pattern among the French, Korean, and UK films, with a lower vintage for the years 2011–2015. By contrast, the MC ratings show bad vintage years for Korean films (2013–2015), which are more marked than those exhibited by French and UK films.

3 Public Support and Quality

The above evaluations have raised serious doubts on the widespread belief that subsidies enhance film quality. There is thus a need to go deeper by using a rigorous approach based on econometric tests for assessing this alleged positive relationship. It goes beyond the scope of this book to present these tests in detail (Parc et al. [2021]).[2] What follows summarizes briefly the methodology used, the results obtained and, more importantly, their consequences in terms of film policy.

In a nutshell, one tests whether there are significant correlations between public support and the quality of films in four countries, France, Korea, the UK, and the US. Total public support data are derived from Table 1 in Chapter 4. The quality of films as evaluated by audiences (IMDb) and critics (Metacritics and Rotten Tomatoes) is based on the data used in the previous section. In order to ensure that the results are not blurred by variables not included in the model, such as the quality of film schools or studios of a country, these regressions include "fixed" effects.

The tests presented in Parc et al. (2021) deliver two main results. First, they do not support a significant positive correlation between the amount of subsidies and film quality for the four countries that is generally assumed in the public debate. Second, this result is clearly driven by the presence of Korea which has a singular position in this context: it is the country that exhibits the highest quality of films among the four countries and it has the lowest level of subsidies. In other words, the Korean "exception" in terms of level of subsidies revealed in Chapter 4 has a "twin,"—the Korean "singularity" in terms of quality.

These results are crucial for policymakers as well as for film producers. They stress that if public support can be a component of a film policy's "tool kit," its impact has limits. Hence it is crucial to verify the efficiency of every dollar of public support spent for improving film quality. This conclusion reinforces the lessons identified in the previous chapters. First, a better subsidy policy for the film industry should shift away from the current obsession of endlessly increasing the overall level of public support

[2] Parc, J., Umana-Dajud, C., and Messerlin, P.A. 2021. Subsidies and Film Quality: Empirical Evidence from France, Korea, The United Kingdom, and the United States. Mimeo.

(Chapter 4). Second, it should pay the highest attention to make a sound assessment of the goals to be achieved by the subsidy policy and of the best types of subsidies available for reaching each of them (Chapter 5).

4 Conclusion

The quality of films is a feature far more important for the prosperity and sustainability of a film industry than other criteria such as the number of films produced. The notion of quality raises important challenges: its subjectivity, its "transitional temporality" (quality varies over time), and its "regionality" (quality varies over location). Having an "absolute standard" for quality is thus out of reach. Moreover, films pertain to a special category of goods—the so-called experience goods. When customers buy such goods, it is difficult for them to judge accurately their quality: they need to use them first—meaning to watch the films.

All these challenges mark a clear difference between "attractiveness" when people decide to buy tickets on the one hand and "quality" on the other which requires the rating of a film by an individual, a film critic, or an "influencer"—once these individuals have seen the film in question. As such, this chapter has measured quality by relying on the film ratings available on dedicated websites (IMDb, Metacritics, and Rotten Tomatoes) which collect and process these individual ratings.

The comparison of the ratings from a large number of Korean, French, UK, and US films expressed by a huge number of evaluators has provided surprising results. The most remarkable one is that, looking at a long period (2009–2018), the average quality of Korean films is higher than that for the films from the three other countries—much better than the French one from the perspective of audiences' evaluations and much better than the UK and US ones from the perspective of critics' evaluations.

Finally, regarding the relationship between the level of public subsidies and that of film quality, the available evidence does not support the notion that public support is correlated with film quality, in particular with the case of Korea. It reveals the fact that Korea is the country which exhibits the highest quality of films and has the lowest level of subsidies among the four countries. All of these findings suggest that a film industry can produce quality films without being reliant upon a large amount of subsidies.

References

Bagella, M., and L. Becchetti. 1999. The Determinants of Motion Picture Box-Office Performance: Evidence from Motion Pictures Produced in Italy. *Journal of Cultural Economics* 23: 237–256.

Fretts, B. 2019. Oscars Rewind: The Most Political Ceremony in Academy History. *The New York Times*, January 11. https://www.nytimes.com/2019/01/11/movies/oscars-1978-politics-vanessa-redgrave.html.

Jansen, C. 2005. The Performance of German Motion Pictures, Profits and Subsidies: Some Empirical Evidence. *Journal of Cultural Economics* 29 (3): 191–212.

McKenzie, J., and W.D. Walls. 2012. Australian Films at the Australian Box-Office: Performance, Distribution, and Subsidies. *Journal of Cultural Economics* 37 (2): 247–269.

Meloni, G., D. Paolini, and M. Pulina. 2015. The Great Beauty: Public Subsidies in the Italian Movie Industry. *Italian Economic Journal* 1 (3): 445–455.

Open Movie Database (OMDb). http://www.omdbapi.com/.

Stephen Follows. 2018. How Long Does the Average Hollywood Movie Take to Make? *Stephen Follows*, May 7. https://stephenfollows.com/how-long-the-average-hollywood-movie-take-to-make/.

Stephen Follows. 2020. Do Bad Movies Cost Less than Good Ones? *Stephen Follows*, July 13. https://stephenfollows.com/do-bad-movies-cost-less-to-buy/.

Terrazas, L. 2017. Cannes 2017: Pour Netflix, «un film peut recevoir la palme sans sortir en salle», *LeFigaro*, May 20. http://www.lefigaro.fr/festival-de-cannes/2017/05/20/03011-20170520ARTFIG00085-cannes-2017-pour-netflix-un-film-peut-recevoir-la-palme-sans-sortir-en-salle.php.

CHAPTER 7

Distribution and Exhibition: Clouds on the Horizon?

The previous chapters have sought to show the extent to which the Korean film industry has developed since the mid-1970s. Overall, the size of the Korean box office market has increased twelve times from 1975 to 2018. As of 2019, Korea has the fourth largest box office market in the world following the US, China, and Japan (MPA 2020). The Korean film industry is now able to produce films that are as attractive as those from Hollywood within its domestic market. Moreover, Korean films have won prestigious awards at internationally well-known film festivals. This is not limited to such success, the Korean film industry is also a constituent part of *Hallyu* or the Korean Wave, which has helped to increase its international audience.

Despite these milestones, the Korean film industry has not become complacent about its success. There are a diverse range of voices who have criticized sharply the industry—arguing that there are factors hindering its further development. Among them, the so-called screen monopoly has been the main contentious issue that has drawn attention from not only the public, but also the Korean government. Yet, there is a fundamental confusion to eliminate here. A monopoly, in the basic sense, is

This chapter is a revised version of Parc and Messerlin (2021).

J. Parc and P. A. Messerlin, *The Untold Story of the Korean Film Industry*, Cultural Economics & the Creative Economy,
https://doi.org/10.1007/978-3-030-80342-1_7

a situation in which a specific firm is the only supplier of a particular good. As such, there is then a lack of competition, limited supply of the good, and a higher price imposed on the consumers. Although screen monopoly sounds to be similar to the general definition of a monopoly, it is actually quite different. In fact, screen monopoly means that a specific film is exhibited on a large number of screens and is seen as taking over the exhibition chances for other films. Many scholars, media outlets, and even voices from film audiences themselves in Korea as well as elsewhere consider screen monopoly as a critical problem for various reasons which are described in the following sections.

One of the first cases to highlight this issue in Korea was the film *The Host* (2006) directed by Bong Joon-ho, which was shown on 38% of all screens (620 out of 1,648 available) at that time. This issue has persisted and in 2019, the Korean comedy *Extreme Job* created another hot stir over the screen monopoly as it attracted the highest ever number of admissions (more than 16.2 million) after an initial release on 1,978 screens (KOFIC 2020a, p. 13). But these grievances have not been limited to domestic films. In February 2020, the Korean NGO Public Welfare Committee filed a complaint requesting an investigation into Walt Disney over its suspected screen monopoly of the Korean film market. This was due to the success of *Frozen 2* that was released on 88% (2,648 out of 3,079) of screens in Korea on its opening day (KOFIC 2020a, p. 23). PWC argued that this feature was an infringement of a provision from the Korean anti-trust law that defines any individual or company with over 50% of market share as a "market-dominant enterprise."

In response to this criticism, the Korean government has begun to consider tightening screen quotas as a way to solve the issue. A large number of scholars and practitioners in Korea argue that they should adopt the French "anti-screen monopoly" regulations. In fact, similar complaints have also been raised in other countries including France—despite the fact that this country has already adopted such regulations almost forty years ago. Hence, it is important to scrutinize the true issues related to screen monopoly and to analyze its effective (or expected) impact in France and Korea. Once we understand them more clearly, we can present a more detailed and effective solution—if there is such a need.

This chapter deals with this thorny issue in five steps. Section 1 examines the meaning of the "screen monopoly" in the context of the Korean debate. Section 2 presents and analyzes in detail the Paramount case and the French anti-screen monopoly regulations given that they are regularly cited as key examples in the Korean debate. Sections 3 and 4 aim to analyze the effectiveness of the screen monopoly argument: markets with a large number of distributors and exhibitors would be more diverse than a concentrated market with only a few players. For this, Sect. 3 examines the overall context of the exhibition markets in Korea and France whereas Sect. 4 takes a step forward by analyzing separately the two segments of films—"hit" and "non-hit." Finally, Sect. 5 presents evidence on the "turnover" of newly released films—how long films last in the movie theaters—as diversity related to screen monopoly issues should also be considered over a longer period, such as one year for instance. Interestingly, this crucial feature is little mentioned in the debate on screen monopoly although it modifies considerably the assessment which can be made on this issue. Based on the analysis done, we conclude that introducing the French anti-screen monopoly regulations in Korea does not seem a beneficial option.

1 The Current Debate and Its Critical Assessment

Regarding the negative effects that screen monopoly can bring about, there are a number of existing studies that have covered this issue. Broadly they emphasize three points. First, a screen monopoly favors films produced by large companies. Second, it limits the films that an audience can select due to unavailability (or slim availability) of films produced by small and medium-sized enterprises (SMEs). Last, such an outcome makes achieving cultural diversity significantly difficult. As one can see, the first point is crucial as it is the origin of the other two points.

For this, Kim (2019) argues that screen monopoly is derived from corporate behavior to maximize profits. In general, it is easily assumed that large and powerful companies have better resources to produce attractive films and secure an effective distribution channel. Therefore, films produced by SMEs cannot have a fair chance to be exhibited at movie theaters. For instance, she states that 19.23% of films have been exhibited less than seven days per year and most of these films are produced and/or distributed by SMEs.

Furthermore, Kim links the screen monopoly issue to the oligopoly in the distribution sector by insisting the fact that three companies share almost 98% of the Korean film exhibition segment. In order to provide a level of this “anomality” in Korea’s film distribution and exhibition, Kim et al. (2018) calculate the Herfindahl–Hirschman Indices (HHI) for France, Germany, Japan, and the United States.[1] They tend to show that these countries have lower HHI when compared with Korea; However, France is the only country that has a lower HHI than Korea, but only in the distribution sector. Nam (2017) and Song (2016) are also in line with these arguments and highlight the danger of screen monopoly and oligopoly in distribution and exhibition by citing the Paramount Case of 1948. This legal action was widely believed to be needed in order to improve the situation in the US film industry and their alleged distorted practices at the time.

Based on these findings, many argue that screen monopoly and oligopolistic distribution and exhibition reduce the number of films available at movie theaters and they limit, therefore, the choice among audiences. Furthermore, many believe that the continuous use of these “unfair” practices will severely hurt SMEs in the Korean film industry, which then has a negative impact upon cultural diversity.

In brief, these scholars argue that screen monopoly favors large (production and distribution) companies, limits audiences to choose films, and hinders cultural diversity. In this regard, several scholars such as Bae (2015), Kim et al. (2018), and Roh (2016, 2019) consider France’s regulations against screen monopoly as a good example to follow. However, all of these factors and arguments should be carefully examined before adopting such a policy.

In particular, Kim (2019) argues that 19.23% of films are distributed by SMEs and they have been exhibited less than seven days per year. In this regard, it is important to mention that since 2016, KOFIC (2020b,

[1] The Herfindahl–Hirschman Index (HHI) is a commonly accepted measure for market concentration. The HHI takes into account the relative distribution size of the firms in a market. It is calculated by squaring the market share for each firm competing in the market and then summing up the resulting numbers. For example, for a market consisting of four firms with shares of 30, 30, 20, and 20 percent, the HHI is 2,600 ($30^2 + 30^2 + 20^2 + 20^2 = 2{,}600$). It approaches zero when a market is occupied by a large number of firms of relatively equal size and reaches its maximum of 10,000 points when a market is controlled by a single firm. In other words, the HHI increases both as the number of firms in the market decreases and as the disparity in size between those firms increases. Competition or regulatory authorities generally consider markets in which the HHI is between 1,500 and 2,500 points to be moderately concentrated and consider markets in which the HHI is in excess of 2,500 points to be highly concentrated (The US Department of Justice [2018], https://www.justice.gov/atr/herfindahl-hirschman-index).

p. 23) has published two types of data for film releases: "actual release" and "nominal release."[2] Films for actual release should be exhibited more than forty times a year—a number that can be reached when a film is exhibited seven days consecutively at movie theaters. By contrast, films that are nominal release are exhibited less than forty times a year[3]; films through nominal release actually seek to be diffused (and gain revenues) more through video-on-demand (VoD) service providers than through movie theaters. It is important to mention that many of these films are R-rated, in other words, for adults who are more than 19 years old.[4]

In this context, it is important to stress that the films with nominal release are mostly produced or imported by SMEs in Korea. Surprisingly, the percentage of them among the total number of Korean films reaches 44.7% in 2016, 56.4% in 2017, 56.9% in 2018, and 60.3% in 2019. For foreign films for this type of release, they reach 66.3% in 2016, 63.4% in 2017, 55.2% in 2018, and 63.8% in 2019. Overall, the percentages are between 55.7 and 62.8%.[5] In this regard, Kim's (2019) figure of 19.23% is unconvincing when criticizing the screen monopoly as this number corresponds only to the subset of films with nominal release.

The argument with HHI has its own problems. Kim et al. (2018) show the average HHI of the top three distributors from Japan, US, UK, and France during the period of 2013–2016 is 61.9, 54.3, 51.4, and 35.9, respectively. According to KOFIC (2017, p. 38), the same figure for Korea is 49.2. In other words, Korea does not have any serious problem with its distribution segment when compared with others; thus, if there are any monopoly issues, then it is in the exhibition segment. Yet, this specific issue also needs further in-depth analysis.

First, as shown before, a large number of films are produced and distributed by SMEs but their exhibition days at movie theaters are very much limited as their commercial activities are more focused on VoD

[2] The terms that KOFIC utilizes are "actual" release in order to distinguish films that are exhibited at movie theaters more than forty times a year. To make this distinction clearer, this chapter employs "actual" release and "nominal" release, respectively.

[3] According to KOFIC (2020), screening a film forty times can be achieved in seven consecutive days; thus, a week.

[4] Under Korean law, if an audio-visual content is exhibited at a movie theater, it is classified as a "movie." Once it is recognized as a "movie," it can then receive a premium from VoD service providers when it is in service.

[5] Data is based on KOFIC (2020, p. 23); all the percentages are calculated by authors.

service providers rather than on movie theaters. Second, the unit of analysis for the screen monopoly issue should remain at the film-level, not the company-level as screen monopoly is about a specific film dominating a large number of screens at the expense of other films. To put it in a different way, if Company A produces (and/or releases) Films X, Y, and Z during the same period and Film X turns out to be a big hit, then the "victims" of screen monopoly will be Films Y and Z which are produced (and/or released) by the same company. Third, this concept can now be extended to the company-level. This means when the market is concentrated in the hands of a few large companies, the main "victims" of screen monopoly of a film will also be the other larger companies, not merely SMEs. Fourth, the fact that Korea has the highest HHI for the exhibition segment cannot satisfactorily explain the screen monopoly of foreign films, if there is one, in Korea as many of them are not produced or distributed by Korean companies. Here, it is important to mention that the Korean exhibitors carefully choose attractive films in order to increase the possibility for revenue (or profit) maximization. In other words, the most important fact for exhibition is the attractiveness of films, not the size of production or distribution companies.

One of the main characteristics of the Korean film industry is that its major producers, distributors, and exhibitors are vertically integrated (Parc 2021). This fact leads many to highlight the Paramount Case as a way to warn about the dangers associated with the vertical integration of the film industry. However, Kim et al. (2018) note that the original decision against the vertical integration of Hollywood studios was subsequently re-examined and several studios have been again able to operate their own movie theaters since the 1980s. It is also important to be remind the fact that the Paramount Case is about the vertical integration and monopoly in the film industry, not directly about the screen monopoly.

To sum up, much of the criticism aimed at the screen monopoly in Korea is not based upon solid evidence. This is mainly down to the fact that many observers seem to confuse screen monopoly with the broader concept of monopoly, which reveals the extent that this issue does not have any solid practical and theoretical basis. There is then little support for arguments that believe screen monopoly limits audiences' right to choose films and cultural diversity. Despite this fact, many describe France as an exemplary country that has "strict" rules against such screen monopoly. These calls though are based upon the mere description of the regulations without proper analysis of how they actually function in France. In this regard, it is meaningful to compare more rigorously Korea and France.

2 The True Impact of the Remedies: Lessons from the Past

Many scholars involved in the debate on screen monopoly argue that there is a better way to enhance diversity. They mention two historical precedents as a source for reference: the recourse to US anti-trust law in the late 1930s with the so-called the Paramount case, and the ad hoc French regulations put in place in the early 1980s that sought to limit the "monopolization" of the screens in movie theaters by a few films using the private commitments of the large distributors and exhibitors. What follows presents a brief description of these precedents and then discusses their relevance in the Korean context.

2.1 The "Paramount Case"

In 1938, the US Department of Justice (DOJ) brought action against eight major US studios—one of them being Paramount, hence the case came to be known by its name. The objective of this action was to examine whether these studios "conspired to control the motion picture industry through their ownership of film distribution and exhibition." The initial investigations by the US District Court focused on the major illegal pricing practices in the US film industry during the 1930s: bundling multiple films into one theater license (block booking), setting minimum movie ticket prices (resale price maintenance), granting exclusive film licenses for overly broad geographic areas (unreasonable clearances), and circuit dealing (a studio plays its films only at a certain "circuit" of movie theaters, excluding other circuits or movie theaters).

In 1948, the US Supreme Court ruled that the ownership of movie theaters by Hollywood studios was a violation of the Sherman Act—the basic US anti-trust law—and that the remedy needed was for the movie studios to divest themselves from the movie theaters. The individual consent decrees—the so-called Paramount Decrees—that the studios signed one by one between 1940 and 1949 spell out the detailed remedies to be implemented by each company for addressing these specific infringements in addition to the divestment provisions putting an end to the "vertical integration" between Hollywood major studios and exhibitors in the US.

At this point, it is important to highlight the fact that the previously mentioned illegal pricing practices can exist without vertical integration between studios and distributors or exhibitors. Indeed, three of the eight US studios involved in the Paramount Decrees did not own movie theaters. In fact, the first two decisions (June and December 1946) of the District Court did not find any evidence of monopoly (or attempt to monopolize) of the exhibition activities; in these conditions, banning these pricing practices could have been a sufficient set of remedies. To sum up, all the remedies taken in the Paramount case have little in common with screen monopoly, contrary to what people believed.

In the two decades following the ruling of the Supreme Court, the US exhibition segment has faced three unexpected events. The methods for allocating films to exhibitors which were devised in the Paramount decrees generated costly legal disputes between distributors and exhibitors (Cassady and Cassady 1974). Next, the rental rates that exhibitors had to pay for the films increased as the whole divestment process exacerbated the competition among the exhibitors when seeking out films (De Vany 2004). Finally, TV began to emerge as a strong competitor to movie theaters. Ironically, these turns of events pushed the movie theaters to request the DOJ to allow the studios to re-enter the exhibition market.

Lastly, the very recent evolution of the case undercuts severely the advocacy in Korea to introduce anti-screen monopoly regulation based on the Paramount case. In 2018, the US anti-trust authorities found that the seventy-year-old Paramount case was deserving of a thorough review. In August 2020, they concluded that there was no reason to maintain the initial decision and thus they "terminated the remedies, effective immediately."[6]

The District Court justified the reversal of its decision by the fact that the exhibition market of the 1940s has nothing in common with that of the 2020s. Most of the US metropolitan areas of the 1930s had only a few best "first run" theaters (those being the first to screen a movie in a region), which all operated one screen and showed one movie at a time. These conditions facilitated the collusion among the studios. By contrast,

[6] Except for a two-year sunset period on the provisions banning block booking (bundling multiple films into one theater license) and circuit dealing (obtaining mass licenses for entire theater chains, instead of for individual theaters and films).

most films today are released at the same time in all the movie theaters—a marketing technique known as a "single theatrical run." Furthermore, there are other competitive means to distribute and exhibit films such as TV, DVDs, streaming services which can be much faster, more effective, and reach a wider range of audiences.

All these circumstances minimize the risks of a possible collusion among studios and exhibitors. The District Court noted that "changes in the motion picture industry over the last seventy years have made it unlikely that the remaining studios could or would reinstate their cartel to monopolize the motion picture distribution and theater markets" (US District Court, Southern District of New York 2020). With its technological advancement, Korea is similar to the current US market with many outlets available for films. Therefore, Korea has no incentive to adopt similar regulations to the Paramount decree as a remedy to solve the alleged screen monopoly.

2.2 *The French "Anti-Screen Monopoly" Regulations*

In the early 1980s, French policymakers began to express concerns about the fact that a notable proportion of the films screened at movie theaters were chosen by a handful of large distributors (sometimes integrated with producers) or exhibitors—the long-established French or US film companies, but also those related to a few large French TV stations which were increasingly involved in film production at the instigation of the government (see Chapters 3 and 5 on TV quotas). They claimed that this situation was a threat to "free competition and the wide dissemination of the films desirable for the general interest."—to quote the mantra always used when referring to the intent of these regulations. In order to address these two concerns—concentration and diversity—lawmakers introduced general provisions in the 1982 law on the audiovisual sector sketching broad guidelines for *engagements de programmation et de diffusion* or programming and dissemination commitments. Moreover, every three years, exhibitors have to specify the detailed commitments that they will implement in accordance with the law broad guidelines. Over time, the broad guidelines have been extended and made ever more complex. Box 1 presents a succinct description of those in force in 2020.

Box 1 The French Anti-screen Monopoly Regulations

There are four kinds of "*engagements*" (CNC 2017; Gessati and Chapron 2017). For being subjected to these regulations, exhibitors should meet a complex set of criteria in terms of size: for instance, being multiplexes with more than six screens or being theaters with a number of admissions larger than a national or regional threshold.

(1) Programming commitments aim to limit the capacity of an exhibitor to show the same film on more than a certain share (for instance 33%) of his/her screens or daily sessions ("multi-diffusion"). These commitments should be agreed by the distributors concerned.

(2) Disseminating commitments seek to promote the exhibition of European and French films as well as "rarely screened works" (*films peu diffusés*). They specify the minimum share in percentage of the total number of sessions—generally 40 to 50%—that is to be devoted to these films (or a category of these films). In addition to these specifications, these films will be exhibited for a minimum of two weeks in accordance with written contracts.

(3) Commitments to support certain distributors focus on distributors qualified as "independent" (not affiliated to the large French cinema chains or US distribution networks operating in France) and "fragile" (such as those having less than two million admissions per year). In this case, exhibitors agree to show a fixed number of films from these "smaller" distributors.

(4) Commitments to exhibit "recommended artistic" (*art et essai*) films qualified as "leading" (*porteurs*, defined as those exhibited on 175 to 250 screens) consist of reserving a minimum quota (17%) for these films in cinemas located in towns with less than 50,000 inhabitants. This quota is increased to 25% if these films are shown on more than 250 screens.

Every three years, these commitments are revised by the film companies concerned, then registered and monitored by the CNC. Conflicts on the implementation of the commitments are sent to a special private arbitrator (*Médiateur*). Those exhibitors who do not comply with the commitments are subjected to penalties, including potentially the cancellation of "selective" subsidies (for the definition of these subsidies, see Chapter 5).

Besides these regulations, creating new multiplexes or expanding existing ones is subject to legal authorization granted by ad hoc committees established at the local level (*département*) hence often dominated by vested interests. Such a regulation has no close equivalent in the rest of the world.

In 2019, 77 exhibitors—all large movie theaters, multiplexes, and their chains accounting for roughly 60% of admissions—were required to adopt their own commitments. It is critical to stress that commitments are private decisions undertaken by the exhibitors. Too often, they are seen as public decisions because of the broad framework of guidelines specified in the 1982 law and its successors. The following analysis shows that the private nature of these commitments is a crucial feature with far-reaching consequences.

With such a large number of exhibitors and admissions involved, there can be the impression that these regulations have had a wide impact. Yet the limited amount of available evidence does not support this view. The first study on the commitments implemented between 2000 and 2007 shows that the films chosen by the exhibitors as part of their programming commitments have had a limited audience. Only a small number of these films (27 on average for the whole period) have attracted more than 100,000 admissions, with only two having exceeded one million admissions (Maistre 2009, p. 11). In other words, the segment of those that can be considered "hits" (films with more than one million of admissions, see the next section) was not really concerned by the commitments. A second more recent study based on a survey of the six largest exhibitors (CGR, Les Cinémas Gaumont-Pathé, Kinépolis, Mégaram, MK2, and UGC) reports that programming commitments undertaken in 2018 involve an average of 108 films (CNC 2018). However, this represents only 22% of the total annual number of the European films released. More importantly, these films have had only a total of 100,000 weekly admissions during their screening, an average of 25 admissions per session.

How can then one explain the contradiction between these modest numbers and the high importance attached to these regulations by the French film industry—their negotiations are a critical moment in the life of the industry? Two main reasons—one related to the film producers and the other related to exhibitors—deserve to be examined.

The first reason requires decoding the mantra "the wide dissemination of the films desirable for the general interest" which is always presented as emphasizing cultural diversity. It can be argued that this is the case as the exhibitors limit the number of their sessions showing the same films. However, it is impossible to assess to what extent these limits impose tight or soft constraints on the effective programming of the exhibitors. Only the exhibitors themselves can tell.

This mantra can be interpreted in a very different way. In reality, it has a clear protectionist intent as reflected by the fact that the exhibitors decide with their disseminating commitments to "reserve a share of their annual sessions"—generally 40 to 50%—for certain groups of films. When doing so, exhibitors establish a de facto screen quota on European films since the mantra is interpreted as defining the films "desirable for the general interest" by their nationality—"European films, including French films, and rarely screened works" (see Box 1)—not by the criteria of cultural quality. Such a screen quota has been a constant goal for French film policies since the late 1980s. The disseminating commitments are thus a major success for all the various interests of French film production—producers, directors, artistic agents, and film editors—involved in the negotiations of the official guidelines.

This "private" definition of the commitments has a couple of decisive advantages over the alternative of a screen quota imposed by a government. One is that it is much more difficult for foreign countries to legally challenge private screen quotas in the case of conflicts since they are business decisions taken by private enterprises, not a public measure to be enforced. Another advantage is that individual commitments offer to every exhibitor the possibility to design their own tailor-made screen quota based upon the range of films that fits best with the demand among its audience. This is crucial because the screen quota on US films should be the least costly for French movie theaters as in reality they need US blockbusters to be profitable. The best way to achieve this goal is to leave the decision on the exact coverage and content of the screen quota to each exhibitor.

This reliance of French exhibitors on US blockbusters has never been more glaring than during the COVID pandemic throughout 2020. Richard Patry, the president of the Fédération Nationale des Cinémas Français (FNCF), has stated during an interviewed for Radio France (Franceinfo 2020) that the small number of admissions to the French movie theaters in summer of 2020 was due to a "supply" problem that he describes as "there are French films, but no US films whereas 70% of the admissions in the summer relies upon US films [in France]." And Patry adds that the European movie theaters "fight for telling Hollywood" that it must release US films in Europe.

The other reason that explains the importance of the commitments for the French film industry involves the exhibition segment. A prime *raison d'être* among the multiplexes is to exhibit diverse films—an objective especially important amidst the current boom of films released. In this context, the programming commitments have artificially "intensified the competition between the artistic movie theaters and the multiplexes" (Benhamou 2017). This is because multiplexes screen attractive—both commercial and artistic—films whereas artistic movie theaters tend to only screen artistic films—successful or not. In addition, annual memberships (and bundle tickets) for multiplexes provide them a favorable condition with their audiences who can enjoy discounts for both kinds of films at any multiplex of a relevant cinema chain (Maistre 2009).[7]

The unintended and unexpected negative consequences of the anti-screen regulations on diversity can be illustrated by the following typical example. Interviewed by the newspaper *La Nouvelle Republique* (Rimbaux 2017), Pierre-Alexandre Moreau, the president of a well-known artistic movie theater "Studio" based in Tours (a town in Central France with a long history of artistic films), argues that exhibiting the "40 or so most attractive artistic films" is vital for the survival of his movie theater because "they represent half of the box office revenues [of his theater] and allow to show the 360 other films which are not profitable."

This frontier between the films shown in multiplexes and in artistic theaters is in constant flux. One reason is common to France and Korea: the number of first-released films has significantly increased over the last decade, leading to widespread complaints in the film industry that there are "too many" films. This criticism seems strange, especially in a country obsessed by cultural diversity like France. An interview a few years ago from Vincent Maraval, a well-known French film producer, helps to clarify this apparent inconsistency: "I hear this leitmotiv: there are too many films produced. No. There are too many films produced for being exhibited in the same way. One should be able to choose where to release of a film as a function of its potential – to screen it in a movie theater or on a VoD platform. Case by case" (Libiot 2016). This statement has to be put into the French context which is quite different from the Korean one. This context is dominated by the so-called *chronologie des médias*

[7] In France, cinema chains sell annual memberships or bundle tickets. They offer a discounted price when compared with individual tickets of the same number of movie tickets. Regarding annual memberships, once an audience purchase it, (s)he can enjoy films as many as (s)he wants during that period.

that splits all the outlets showing movies into roughly a dozen "windows"—from the movie theaters to free streaming platforms—to which films can accede only in a sequential manner according to a rigid mandatory timetable. Such a requirement imposes self-inflicted damage because it inevitably exacerbates the tensions between a stable number of movie theaters and an ever-increasing number of films fueled by ever-growing production subsidies.

In this context, only two options are left for solving this impasse: building more cinemas or cutting production subsidies (Collectif des cinéastes 2013). The first option sheds new light on the rationale of the French subsidies to the private exhibition segment. As documented in Chapter 5, French subsidies to this segment are generous enough to keep alive many movie theaters—probably "too many" if one looks at the global average (see the following section). This is amplified by two other factors. A substantial number of public movie theaters—at least 15% of French theaters—are owned by municipalities or associations, raising the usual issue of fair competition between public and private endeavors (Perrot, Leclerc, and Verot 2008). Moreover, the decisions to create or expand multiplexes are taken by ad hoc administrative committees dominated by local vested interests—a powerful force that tends to slow down and/or distort the needed restructuration, investments, and closures of movie theaters.

The whole context is quite different in Korea. Film producers can release their films in movie theaters but it is not an obligation. And if the expected success is not there, they can shift as quickly as possible to any other outlet—the exact opposite of what is possible under the *chronology des médias*.

All these considerations deserve one final remark. The above analysis of the implementation of the French regulations shows the dominance of issues far from the cultural diversity stressed by the mantra "the wide dissemination of the films desirable for the general interest." This result is not surprising when one considers the decision process that generates these regulations. First, there are the negotiations on the broad guidelines that will be used as a basis for individual commitments. No less than sixteen major business associations from the French film industry negotiate these guidelines—a negotiating structure propitious to multiple and complicated compromises, not to strong and decisive decisions. Second, when writing its own set of commitments, each exhibitor is likely to try to minimize the costs of its commitments. Combined, these two conditions are formidable obstacles to the adoption of commitments which would seriously challenge the usual business plans of all the exhibitors subject to commitments.[8]

2.3 *Summary*

Many believe that there is a serious screen monopoly issue in Korea and they argue that it should benchmark the US or French cases to address and overcome this problem. However, this section suggests that these US or French precedents do not address the core issue as perceived by the on-going debate in Korea—the overwhelming domination of the screens by a few films. The competitive environment of Korea's film exhibition market has nothing in common with the one prevailing in the US during the 1940s when the Paramount ruling was adopted by the Supreme Court. In fact, this environment should rather induce Korea to follow the recent decision of the US authorities to overturn this ruling. The French anti-screen monopoly regulations established a screen quota that Korea already has (see Chapter 3). And they have not clearly addressed the overwhelming domination of the screens by a few films. Rather they have intensified the competition between the multiplexes and the artistic movie theaters at the risk of generating unexpected and negative consequences for the latter.

3 Overall Comparison of the French and Korean Exhibition Markets

The French film industry has implemented its anti-screen monopoly regulation since 1982 while the Korean film industry has had no such provision. The French and Korean exhibition markets differ significantly in terms of the level of concentration in distribution and exhibition, as documented later in this chapter. Is there then any empirical evidence suggesting that the less concentrated and allegedly better regulated

[8] This complex decision process allows to understand why the "general" guidelines adopted seem so arcane for outsiders. For instance, these guidelines impose a threshold of 17 percent for the leading artistic films shown in towns of less than 50,000 inhabitants: why 17 percent rather than 16 or 18 percent is likely to reflect specific market conditions that only the parties involved in the negotiations understand.

French exhibition market has offered more choices to moviegoers in terms of the number of released films—has it shown greater diversity?

3.1 Concentration of the French and Korean Exhibition Segment

To gauge a sense of the market concentration in France and Korea, it is worthy to look at the share of revenues and/or admissions among the main companies in each country's distribution and exhibition segments. As annual data can be significantly influenced by a few particularly successful films, Table 1 presents the average shares for the four-year period 2016–2019. It shows that the level of concentration in the distribution segment is relatively similar in the two countries, but that the exhibition segment is significantly more concentrated in Korea than in France.

A few additional points need to be emphasized here. First, if the overall level of concentration in the French and Korean distribution segments are not much different, then why have the Hollywood distributors been able to dominate the market in France while the situation is more balanced in Korea? In other words, the anti-screen monopoly regulations in France have not prevented US companies from keeping a strong share of its distribution segment.

Regarding the concentration of exhibitors, as previously mentioned, Korea's HHI for the exhibition segment is much higher than that for France as shown in Table 1. In other words, the level of HHIs presented here suggests that the only policy for lowering them would be to create more cinema chains and/or to increase the number of independent movie theaters in Korea. This seems hardly a feasible option in a market-driven sector.

Lastly, despite the fact that French companies constitute most of the exhibitors in their domestic market, more than half of their revenues are generated from US films while the situation in Korea is very different (see Chapter 2). It hints that the anti-screen monopoly in the exhibition segment is not effective enough to achieve diversity while it brings about other unexpected problems.

Table 1 The main distributors and exhibitors in France and Korea (2016–2019)

Distributors: share of revenues				*Exhibitors: share of admissions or revenues*			
France		*Korea*		*France (admissions)*		*Korea (revenues)*	
Walt Disney	16.3	CJENM	17.0	Gaumont-Pathé	22.2	CGV	49.3
Warner Bros	9.3	Walt Disney	15.8	UGC	12.2	Lotte	29.5
Universal	9.1	Lotte	10.9	CGR	10.4	Mega box	18.2
20th Fox	8.8	Show Box	8.7	Kinépolis	3.3		
Pathé Films	6.7	Fox	8.1	SAS Cineville	2.5		
Sony Pictures	5.6	Universal	8.0	Megarama	2.3		
Studio Canal[a]	5.4	NEW	7.9	MK2	2.0		
UGC Distri[a]	4.9	Warner Bros	5.8				
Gaumont	4.9	Sony	5.3				
SND (M6)	4.9	Megabox	4.8				
Concentration indexes							
C4 share	43.5	C4 share	52.4	C3 share	44.8	C3 share	97.0
HHI	0.07	HHI	0.09	HHI	0.09	HHI	0.36
Sum of the above firms							
French firms	21.7	Korean firms	49.3	French firms	54.8	Korean firms	97.0
US companies	49.0	US companies	43.0	US companies	0.0	US companies	0.0

Notes Data for Korean exhibitors are based on movie theaters that are under direct control of these exhibitors; some movie theaters have sub-contracted their choices of films to exhibitors that do not own them; C4 (C3): aggregate share of the four (three) largest companies. [a]Average calculated on the years with available data

Sources CNC (various issues), KOFIC (2020b, p. 43)

3.2 Numbers of Films Admissions, Screens, and Seats in Korea and France

The argument that the screen monopoly limits the audience's selection of films can be assessed by looking at a few key variables which reveal the level of diversity in the exhibition segment: the numbers of released (foreign and domestic) films, admissions, screens, and seats.[9] In what follows, only newly released films are taken into consideration. Re-releases are left aside because most of these re-released films are available on other outlets such as streaming services and online service providers. In addition, they reflect the diversity of past years and can result in double-counting when the data covers several years. For the same reason as in the previous chapters, comparisons cover an extended period—the last decade 2010–2019.

Another important preliminary remark concerns the number of released films in Korea. Since 2016, there are two kinds of data for the number of released films: "actual releases" and "nominal releases"—the latter aims to be diffused through channels outside of movie theaters. The number of actual releases for this category is available only for the years 2016–2019 in Table 2, which is significantly smaller than the total number of films—roughly 40%.

There is a striking difference between the number of films released in France and Korea. By focusing first on the number of actual releases, it would appear that this figure is smaller in Korea than in France. However, a fairer comparison requires adjusting for the size of the population—a significantly larger population is likely to absorb a higher number of films than a smaller one—hence to calculate the number of actual releases per capita. Over the four years 2016–2019, there has been an average 12.4 films per million of inhabitants released in the Korean movie theaters, compared to an average 10.5 in France. This substantial difference of 18% sends the message that the Korean exhibition segment offers more choice to moviegoers than French ones; thus, more diversity.

As the Korean population is three quarters of the French population, one may expect under the *ceteris paribus* condition, more admissions in France than in Korea, yet this is far from the case. Moreover, one can compare the growth rates of the admissions in the two countries over the

[9] All the growth rates presented in this section are "compound average growth rates" calculated between the average two first years and the average two last years.

Table 2 Annual number of films released and screens in Korea and France (2010–2019)

	2010	*2011*	*2012*	*2013*	*2014*	*2015*	*2016*	*2017*	*2018*	*2019*	*Growth rate*	*Average*
KOREA												
No. films	426	439	631	905	1,095	1,176	1,520	1,620	1,647	1,739	16.4	1,120
No. actual released	–	–	–	–	–	–	578	619	730	647	3.6	644
Admissions (million)	149	160	195	213	215	217	217	220	216	227	4.1	203
No. screens	2,003	1,974	2,081	2,184	2,281	2,424	2,575	2,766	2,937	3,079	4.7	2,430
No. seats	349	342	359	350	372	399	421	438	450	463	3.1	394
No. actual released film/cap.	–	–	–	–	–	–	11.2	12.0	14.1	12.4	3.5	12.4
Admission/screen[a]	74	81	94	98	94	90	84	79	74	74	−0.6	84
Screen/capita	40	39	41	43	44	47	50	53	57	59	4.4	47
Seat/screen	174	173	173	160	163	165	163	158	153	150	−1.5	162
FRANCE												
No. films	579	588	614	654	663	652	716	693	683	746	2.3	659
Admissions	184	201	181	175	189	182	192	190	176	191	−0.5	186
No. screens	5,465	5,464	5,508	5,580	5,647	5,741	5,842	5,913	5,981	6,114	1.1	5,726
No. seats	1,048	1,047	1,053	1,065	1,071	1,094	1,099	1,119	1,126	1,141	0.9	1,086
No. film/cap.[b]	8.9	9.0	9.4	9.9	10.0	9.8	10.7	10.3	10.1	11.0	0.2	10.5
Admission/screen[a]	34	37	33	31	34	32	33	32	29	31	−1.6	33
Screen/capita	84	84	84	85	85	86	87	88	89	90	0.7	86
Seats/screen	192	192	191	191	190	191	188	189	188	187	−0.2	190

Notes Data since 2016 for Korea are based on actual films, hence the large decline between 2015 and 2016 in terms of number of released films; Growth rate-compound annual growth rate between the average two first years and the average two last years; [a]Number of released films per million of inhabitants; [b]Thousands of admissions per screen. [c]All growth rate and average are calculated over the years 2016–2019 in order to be comparable to the Korean figures; Regarding the data for the number of films in Korea, it may not match the figures when the numbers for hits (Table 3) and non-hits (Table 4) are integrated. This is due to discrepancies between processed data and raw data both produced by KOFIC. The number of films in Table 2 is based on processed data, while the numbers of hits and non-hits are based on raw data

Sources Korea Box-Office Information System (KOBIS), CNC (2021a)

Table 3 The exhibition markets for hits: selected indicators (2010–2019)

	2010	*2011*	*2012*	*2013*	*2014*	*2015*	*2016*	*2017*	*2018*	*2019*	*Growth rate*	*Total or average*
KOREA												
No. of 'hits'												**Total**
Total[a]	43	42	52	53	47	45	51	54	53	49	2.0	489
US	19	19	17	22	24	20	26	25	24	19	1.4	215
Korean	23	23	32	30	23	23	24	28	29	30	2.8	265
Non-US	1	0	3	1	0	2	1	1	0	0	–	9
No. of admissions												**Total**
Total[a]	96.5	115.2	151.5	168.6	164.1	165.6	170.0	173.0	167.6	186.1	5.9	1558
US	41.4	49.7	45.8	53.0	78.4	74.5	70.0	69.9	83.2	85.7	7.1	652
Korean	52.8	65.5	100.2	112.7	85.7	87.6	98.7	99.5	84.3	100.4	5.1	888
Non-US	2.3	0.0	5.5	2.9	0.0	3.6	1.3	3.6	0.0	0.0	–	19
Admissions per hit												**Average**
US	2.18	2.62	2.70	2.41	3.27	3.72	2.69	2.79	3.47	4.51	5.8	3.04
Korean	2.30	2.85	3.13	3.76	3.73	3.81	4.11	3.55	2.91	3.35	2.2	3.35
Non-US	2.29	–	1.83	2.86	–	1.78	1.28	3.64	–	–	–	1.37
FRANCE												
No. of 'hits'												**Total**
Total[a]	51	52	54	55	55	44	53	56	42	51	−1.1	513
US	31	30	31	35	33	29	34	35	31	32	0.4	321
French	19	20	22	17	20	14	18	18	11	17	−3.6	176
Non-US	1	2	1	3	2	1	1	3	0	2	–	16
No. of admissions												**Total**
Total[a]	126.5	126.7	121.3	109.1	123.6	116.1	120.7	124.4	105.2	124.5	−1.1	1198
US	84.3	71.9	71.3	76.5	63.2	80.6	84.7	82.4	72.9	89.8	0.5	778
French	41.0	52.1	46.8	27.6	55.0	33.1	34.1	35.3	32.3	31.3	−4.1	389
Non-US	1.2	2.7	3.2	5	5.4	2.4	1.9	6.7	0	3.4	–	32
Admissions per hit												**Average**
US	2.72	2.40	2.30	2.19	1.92	2.78	2.49	2.35	2.35	2.81	0.1	2.43
French	2.16	2.61	2.13	1.62	2.75	2.36	1.89	1.96	2.94	1.84	0.0	2.23
Non-US	1.20	1.35	3.20	1.67	2.70	2.40	1.90	2.23	–	1.70	–	1.84

Note Growth rate-compound annual growth rate between the average two first years and the average two last years
Source KOBIS, CNC (various issues)

Table 4 The exhibition markets for the "non-hits": selected indicators (2010–2019)

	2010	*2011*	*2012*	*2013*	*2014*	*2015*	*2016*	*2017*	*2018*	*2019*	*Growth rate (%)*	*Average*
KOREA												
No. non-hits	383	397	579	852	1,048	1,157	1,519	1,710	1,810	1,894	18.9	1135
Admissions for non-hits	38.4	37.8	36.0	35.8	38.9	36.8	38.1	40.0	34.3	34.9	−1.1	37
Total admission	149	160	195	213	215	217	217	220	216	227	4.1	203
No. domestic films	117	127	144	153	194	234	313	467	631	667	20.4	305
No. imported films	266	270	435	699	854	923	1,206	1,243	1,179	1,227	18.2	830
FRANCE												
No. non-hits	528	536	560	599	608	608	663	637	641	695	2.6	608
Admissions for non-hits	57.5	74.3	59.9	66.1	65.4	65.9	71.3	65.3	71.0	66.9	0.5	66
Total admission	184	201	181	175	189	182	192	190	176	191	−0.5	186
No. domestic films[a]	200	203	220	253	261	242	271	294	277	310	4.3	253
No. imported films[b]	328	333	340	346	347	366	392	343	364	385	1.4	354

Notes The distinction between actual and nominal releases of Korean films began in 2016; Growth rate-compound annual growth rate between the average first two years and the average last two years. The sum of the numbers between domestic and imported films shows a tiny difference with the total number of non-hits. This difference, which is due to number of imported films, is small enough (one to three units) to be neglected all the more because all the sources used are from CNC; [a]Films which are classified by CNC as "100% French" and those which are classified as "Majority French" of co-produced films are reported as domestic films. [b]Films classified by CNC as "Minority French" of co-produced films are included in the category "imported films"

Sources KOBIS, CNC (2021c), and Table 3

decade. As Table 2 shows, there is a positive growth rate in the number of admissions in Korea compared to a slightly negative one in France (4.1% compared to −0.5%)—suggesting a much higher dynamism in terms of choices among films in Korea than in France over the whole period.

When looking at screening equipment in Table 2, France is in an enviable position since it is endowed with twice more screens than in Korea. Adjusting for the size of the French and Korean populations does not change this result: the number of screens per capita is still 1.5 times larger in France than in Korea in 2019—with 86 screens per one million of inhabitants in France compared to 47 in Korea. However, this situation has not prevented Korea to outperform France since 2012 in terms of number of admissions: in other words, the more limited number of screens in Korea has been better utilized than its larger French equivalent from the perspective of diversity.

The growth rate in the number of screens is a last critical variable to consider. It is three times larger in Korea than in France. This huge gap reveals the existence of much larger investments in Korea than in France over the last decade, hence it strongly suggests that Korean movie theaters are furnished with more advanced equipment and facilities. Korean cinema chains have realized their growth potential in terms of the number of admissions and for that they have utilized their private investment to upgrade facilities and equipment. By contrast, French cinema chains have faced the anemic potential growth of admissions in France by increasingly relying upon public subsidies to upgrade their facilities.

Indeed, one additional factor has played a significant role in shaping the strategies of the French cinema chains. The *chronologie des médias* mandates movie theaters as the only outlet for the first four months of newly released films in France. In other words, it grants de facto a transitory monopoly to movie theaters for the fate of films. This may seem an enviable condition, but it has a strong negative side effect: it reduces the incentives among movie theaters to upgrade their facilities and equipment—the main remaining incentive for doing so being access to public subsidies. By contrast, with a market not subjected to such constraints, Korean movie theaters have to compete with alternative outlets as well as online pirated films. Thus, they have strong incentives to upgrade their facilities as well as their equipment in order to be an attractive option when compared to watching movies at home or elsewhere. A good example is ScreenX which is a panoramic format that projects films on a 270 degree screen. Korean movie theaters adopted this early in 2012 whereas French movie theaters adopted this only in 2018.

3.3 The "Utilization" of Screens in Korea and France

Combining screens and seats is an essential aspect to consider when assessing the capacity of an exhibition market to cope with the diversity of films: a lower number of seats per screen tends to be more propitious to the diversity of the films released because it introduces flexibility when programming the sessions. In Table 2, the number of seats and their growth rate show the same differences between the two countries as the number of screens: a much smaller number in absolute value in Korea and significantly higher growth in Korea than in France. However, there is an important nuance to note here: the growth of seats is smaller than the growth of screens in the two countries, but this feature is more marked in Korea than in France. Hence, the average number of seats per screen has declined more in Korea than in France over the past decade, a sign of potential increased flexibility in programming in Korea.

This decline of the average number of seats per screen in Korea occurs at such a regular pace that it is likely to reflect a conscious strategy among the owners of Korean movie theaters who operate in a market dominated by multiplexes since the mid-1990s—in 2019, 79.3% of Korean movie theaters are multiplexes compared to 43.6% in France (CNC 2019, p. 80, KOFIC 2020b, p. 21).[10] A smaller seat/screen ratio offers thus a strategic advantage during times when there is an increasingly abundant supply of films—as during the last decade or so. By contrast, the significantly higher seat/screen ratio in France combined with a much larger number of movie theaters generates an intrinsic underlying risk of "over-capacity" of seats when owners try to exhibit a diversified portfolio of films.[11]

One can synthetize these results by calculating the "utilization" of the screens defined as the number of admissions divided by the number of

[10] Multiplexes are defined as movie theaters with more than seven screens in Korea, and more than eight screens in France. However, the French anti-screen monopoly regulations cover multiplexes that have six screens or more.

[11] CNC publishes data on the "occupancy rate"—the ratio of the number of admissions per the number of seats available. This is calculated as the number of sessions times the number of seats for each screen (CNC 2019). The French rate is remarkably low—15 percent on average for the last decade—and it is steadily decreasing, supporting the hypothesis of a massive overall overcapacity of the French exhibition sector.

existing screens. If one uses the sums for the years 2016–2019 (for relying on comparable data in terms of released films), the Korean exhibition market has released 2,574 films on 2,839 screens, roughly 0.91 films per screen. In France, the number of films released is 2,838 for these four years. Calculating the number of screens devoted to the first releases in France requires some preliminary adjustments. Using the large number of screens in France shown in Table 2 would be inaccurate because French movie theaters exhibit a large number of films from the previous years (roughly 6,500 every year). However, if the number of these films is huge, the number of sessions devoted to them is small—roughly 7% of all the sessions throughout the year (CNC 2021b). In other words, the number of screens effectively devoted to new releases in France is 93% of the total number of screens, that is, 5,500 screens. The French movie theaters exhibit thus 2,838 films on 5,500 screens or 0.51 films per screen. In short, the Korean exhibition market shows a higher utilization of its screens—almost twice more—than the French one.

All these comparisons do not support the criticism of a screen monopoly prevailing in the Korean exhibition market. In fact, if they have had such an intent, the economic analysis would expect local exhibitors to restrict their supply of films while increasing their seat prices in order to boost profits. To sum up, not only the evidence accumulated on the Korean exhibition market does not support such a strategy among Korean exhibitors, but it also raises serious doubts on whether introducing in Korea the French programming and disseminating commitments could be beneficial to the Korean film industry and—more importantly—to Korean moviegoers.

4 Screen Monopoly and Diversity: Unexpected Results

The screen monopoly argument perceives large distributors and exhibitors as powerful enough to significantly restrict the diversity of films that are released in movie theaters. This view induces the need to focus on a notion of diversity based on a "balance" between successful films (the "hits") and other films (the "non-hits"). In this respect, the greater number of available films for moviegoers to watch is seen as more important for cultural diversity than the nationality of the films. As it is often assumed that large firms invest mostly in big-budget films in order to draw in a large number of moviegoers, their influence is expected to be particularly strong with the hits, which thus deserves a separate examination.

4.1 *The Performance of "Hits"*

The definition of "hits" used in this chapter is based on CNC (various issues) which are films that have attracted more than one million admissions during the first year of release. At this stage, it is important to stress that what follows relies on "hits"—not "mega hits" since there is no agreed standard to define the latter. The supporters of the anti-screen monopoly regulations believe that such provisions would allow a greater number of films available (or screened) at movie theaters. In this regard, it is interesting to examine whether France with its regulations leads to the release of a greater number of films and exhibits more hits than Korea.

Table 3 does not provide evidence supporting such a hypothesis when one looks at the total number of US, domestic, and non-US hits: they are almost the same in Korea and France, with 489 and 513 films respectively, over the whole decade (again, the data for Korea is based on the actual release films). However, if one takes into consideration the total populations, as one should, Korea has a larger number of hits per year than France contrary to this hypothesis: roughly 9.6 hits per million of inhabitants (489 hits for a population of 51 million of inhabitants), compared to roughly 7.6 hits per million of inhabitants (513 hits for a French population of 68 million of inhabitants).

Turning to the number of admissions for hits, it is 30% larger in Korea than in France over the whole decade. Although Korea and France have a similar total number of hits, Korea has a greater number of domestic hits compared with France. This significant gap has been interpreted so far as a sign of the fact that Korean films are more attractive than French films at least domestically. Indeed, the previous chapters have accumulated a considerable amount of independent and converging evidence that supports this result. Table 3 confirms once more this result: during the 2010s, 176 domestic hits have attracted 389 million admissions in France, whereas 265 Korean domestic hits have attracted 888 million admissions during the whole decade.

The advocates of the anti-screen monopoly though would still argue that this result is a sign of the market power among a few large firms in the Korean film industry. This interpretation needs thus to be scrutinized with a detailed analysis splitting the hits into US hits and domestic hits since these two categories may face different levels of concentration. We can then compare more accurately the alleged inter-actions among diversity, concentration, and anti-screen monopoly regulations in each of these categories.

In order to undertake this properly, one needs to stress the different meanings of "diversity" in France and Korea. In France, this expression is associated with an increase (in relative terms) in the audience for domestic films. This view reflects the fact that French films have a relatively low market share, hence more French films are seen as ensuring higher diversity—a "better" balance between French and US films. By contrast, as already mentioned, the Korean debate on the screen monopoly defines diversity as the possibility for moviegoers to watch a larger number of—domestic or foreign—films at movie theaters. This view mirrors the fact that the share of domestic film admissions is larger than that of US films in Korea since many years, hence is not seen as a primary concern. Ignoring this critical difference between these two views would lead to a serious misinterpretation of the evolutions that have occurred over the last decade.

According to the Korean definition of diversity, one would expect higher growth in the number of hits exhibited—with more evenly dispersed admissions for a greater number of films—in France (which is a less concentrated market under the anti-screen monopoly regulations) than in Korea (a more concentrated market with few regulations). Table 3 reflects a different story. The growth rates for the number of hits are higher in Korea than in France. Furthermore, if one focuses on domestic films one would expect even stronger differences in the growth rates among these films since they are under the particularly strong influence of the large domestic distributors and exhibitors. Again, this is not what Table 3 shows.

Adopting the French definition of diversity shifts the criterion to be used from the number of films exhibited to the number of admissions among domestic and foreign films in each country. There are striking differences in Table 3 which shows the growth rates of admissions in Korea and France, but they are not those expected by the supporters of the screen monopoly argument. The French market is characterized by a substantial fall in the admissions for French hits and a modest increase in admissions for US hits—in other words, a decline in diversity.[12]

Finally, one needs to consider the number of hits from third countries if one wants to have a complete overview on the level of diversity in terms of a film's nationality. Table 3 indicates that France has a greater number of hits from third countries than Korea—nine in Korea and sixteen in France over the whole period. One might consider this gap big enough to be a sign that the Korean exhibition market is less diverse than the French one with respect to films from third countries. This interpretation misses a key point: seven out the total of sixteen non-US foreign hits in France are European films. As the French exhibition market is part of the overall European film market—even if this integration is far to be perfect—European films have some preferential access to the French exhibition market which is strengthened by their legal status in the programming commitments (see Sect. 2). Taking into consideration this factor suggests that the level of diversity within the Korean and French exhibition market in terms of hits from "strictly" (non-European and non-US) third countries is similar—or higher if one uses per capita estimates.

Lastly, and crucially from a cultural diversity perspective—again the core issue in the debate on the screen monopoly—a better balance between domestic and foreign films in Korea compared to France is presented in Table 3: the share of the number of domestic hits among the total number of hits is 54% (265/489) in Korea, compared to 34% (176/513) in France despite the various efforts by the French government to revive its film industry, including the anti-screen monopoly regulations.

4.2 *The Performance of "Non-Hits" Films*

When looking at the number of films and admissions for the non-hit films in Korea, it is largely based on those with nominal release because, by definition, all the nominal releases are non-hits in terms of audiences in movie theaters. The number of non-hits has grown much more sharply in Korea than in France, as can be seen in Table 4, suggesting more diversity in Korea than in France. However, the increase of the non-hit

[12] This result is influenced by the exceptional success of one French film, *Intouchables*, which was released in 2011. However, if one sets aside this exception, the decade still witnesses an even more negative growth rate for the admission of the French hits.

films in Korea is due to the import of a large number of foreign films. Many companies produce and import films for an increasing number of streaming services and IPTVs in Korea. By contrast in France, the number of domestic films grows significantly more than the number of foreign films in non-hit categories.

Turning the focus to admissions, their number for non-hits has slightly declined in Korea and slightly increased in France. Two explanations are possible here. First, Korean moviegoers are—on average—not much interested in the non-hits, which are an amorphous aggregate of films of widely different quality. Second, as they are aware that such films will end up on other—cheaper—outlets like streaming platforms in a short period of time, they will not pay regular ticket prices to watch such titles in movie theaters.

Still, comparing the annual number of domestic films and the admission for non-hits of Korea and France shows interactions among the two results. First, as documented in Chapters 4 and 5, the Korean and French subsidies have a key difference beyond their sheer overall amount: the French subsidies are granted to all French films produced. The downside of this feature is that it increases the number of films, not necessarily their quality: this quality effect is particularly important in the case of French films as shown by the evidence gathered in Chapter 6. Second, the *chronologie des médias* artificially inflates the number of non-hit films in French movie theaters. All the films should be exhibited at movie theaters even if the producers of these films want to diffuse their films through other outlets such as DVDs, cable TVs, and streaming services. And as argued before, this provision has a stronger impact on French films than on foreign ones.

5 The Film "Turnover": An International Comparison

The previous sections have not revealed the presence of a screen monopoly in Korea nor is there evidence to suggest that there would be any gain from enforcing anti-screen monopoly regulations like those in France. However, the results presented so far are based upon annual data, whereas some scholars argue convincingly that the impact of a screen monopoly should be assessed on the basis of weekly data.

Based upon such a view, this approach compares Korea and other countries by using the weekly "turnover" from the exhibition of films in a country: in a nutshell, how many weeks on average a film is on the screens of a movie theater before being replaced by another film. The

Table 5 Weekly share of total box office revenues for top 5 US hits (2019)

	Week 1	*Week 2*	*Week 3*	*Week 4*	*Week 5*	*Rest (after week 5)*
Korea	47.7	76.6	88.8	95.1	97.4	2.6
France	28.6	54.1	70.8	78.7	86.8	13.2
UK	30.5	56.7	72.0	80.1	84.9	15.1
Japan	16.9	46.2	64.2	74.5	81.4	18.6
US	33.3	64.9	78.6	85.3	89.7	10.3

Note The top five films are *Avengers Endgame*, *The Lion King*, *Star Wars: The Rise of Skywalker*, *Frozen II*, and *Toy Story 4*
Source Box Office Mojo (2019)

turnover reflects the optimal strategy of distributors and exhibitors in terms of duration and revenues simply generating the highest revenues possible in the shortest possible number of weeks. It has also an important meaning from the perspective of moviegoers: a faster turnover means the possibility of more choice for the audience among the newly released films. In this sense, a faster turnover can be interpreted as a critical contribution by the exhibitors to address the screen monopoly issue.

An interesting point on this question is presented in Table 5 by calculating the shares of the box office revenues earned on a weekly basis by films since their first day of release. It focuses on hits since these are the films that are the ones most in demand at movie theaters. The films selected for Table 5 are US hits because those are the only ones shown across many countries and for which the information necessary—weekly box office revenues—is available on a consistent basis in the database compiled by Box Office Mojo. Table 5 reports the weekly box office revenues of five most successful US hits in 2019 around the world.[13]

The main result of Table 5 is that, after five weeks, a paltry 2.6% of the total revenue remains to be generated by these films in Korea. By contrast, the "rest" in the other countries range from 10 to 18%—four to seven times higher than in Korea. The fact that Korea has a significantly higher turnover than any of its four competitors in 2019 supports the argument regarding the relatively better utilization of Korean movie theaters as underlined in the previous section.

[13] China's turnover is similar to the Korean one but it has been left aside because its exhibition market is highly regulated in an unpredictable manner (Parc, Messerlin, and Kim [2020 mimeo]).

Clearly, focusing on the relatively high concentration of Korean audiences during weeks 1 and 2—as generally done—gives the impression that a few films monopolize the Korean screens more than is the case in other countries. However, this does not take into consideration week 3 and the following weeks—where the Korean movie theaters begin to exhibit other films while the movie theaters in other countries are still showing the same movies.

By considering that the box office revenues of France, Korea, and UK are very similar despite the fact that Korea has a significantly smaller number of screens, it can be argued that the fast turnover in Korea is not a sign of screen monopoly, but rather an effective utilization of screen time. The US can be considered as an exceptional case given that its domestic market is fully occupied by domestic films. Furthermore, it is a hybrid and open exhibition market ranging from traditional movie theaters in remote areas to various new platforms including streaming services. The turnover trend in the UK is similar to that of France. Japan has a large market but it is known to have a strong preference toward domestic films. A more in-depth analysis of these differences is beyond the scope of this study.

When Korea is compared with France, some would see Korea's rapid turnover in Table 5 as clear evidence that it has a screen monopoly problem. However, this is without taking into consideration constraints imposed in France that slow down the French turnover—the best illustration being the *chronologie des médias*. This regulation requires that French movie theaters cannot adopt a quick turnover strategy: all the films should be available in movie theaters for four months regardless of their popularity.[14] Again, by considering the larger population, France has more screens but with roughly a similar annual number of released films that Korea exhibits. In short, the fast turnover of Korea cannot be seen as an evidence of screen monopoly.

Unfortunately, the information focusing on the performances over the two first weeks is the one that the supporters for the anti-screen monopoly regulations tend to put forward. Clearer and more accurate information should be provided: when based on a yearly basis, it will show that Korean movie theaters exhibit relatively more films per year, hence attract a higher

[14] According to the regulations of the *chronologie des médias*, films should be exhibited at movie theater at least four months, but there are a few exceptional cases. But even for this case, these films should be exhibited three months before diffusion through other outlets.

total number of admissions than other countries. Such a rapid "turnover" in Korea emerges thus as an essential driving force behind the better utilization of the country's theaters shown in the previous section.

6 Conclusion

This chapter has examined the concentration of a few large companies in the distribution and exhibition segments of the film industry, which have attracted a lot of criticism in Korea. This is largely due to the widely prevailing belief that this practice has brought about a distortive effect on the film industry, notably the exhibition market. It is interesting to note that across all industries including the film business, there is a significant distrust toward large and powerful distribution and exhibition firms. Film producers and the public are convinced that large distributors or exhibitors can "monopolize screens" in their favor—in particular, impede access of some films to the screens in favor of their own film production.

This chapter has scrutinized the screen monopoly argument from different perspectives. First, it has presented the screen monopoly argument as put forward by Korean scholars (and largely shared in other countries) and has stressed its many theoretical and empirical shortcomings. Second, it has examined the two solutions proposed by the screen monopoly literature to address this behavior—assuming that it exists on a notable scale: an antitrust policy as illustrated by the Paramount antitrust case in the US and anti-screen monopoly regulations as adopted in France.

Next, this chapter has shifted the focus to an empirical question: Is there any evidence of a screen monopoly? And if applied, can anti-screen monopoly regulations be effective? To answer these questions, this chapter has used the common approach of this book: it has compared countries with differences sharp enough over a period long enough to offer robust results. The French film industry illustrates the case of a moderate concentration in the exhibition segment subjected to anti-screen regulations whereas the Korean film industry illustrates the opposite case of a highly concentrated film industry with no anti-screen monopoly regulations. These comparisons have been made at two levels: the overall exhibition segment and that of the hits and non-hits categories since these two categories face very distinct levels in terms of concentration. These detailed analyses do not suggest the existence of noticeable screen monopoly behavior nor the existence of notable gains from anti-screen monopoly regulations.

Lastly, an interesting concept has been introduced in this chapter—the film "turnover"—which puts the screen monopoly in a longer time frame. The choice is between either reserving many screens for showing a film over a short period of time or exhibiting the film in question on a smaller number of screens for a longer period of time. Korea emerges as the leading country in terms of fast turnover, which counters the impression that its screens are taken over by a few films. At the opposite end of the spectrum, France, the UK, and above all Japan are the champions of a slower turnover.

This chapter has left aside the key role of distributors and exhibitors of the Korean films at the international level, such as CJ or Lotte who are major owners of multinational cinema chains. This aspect goes beyond this book. It raises though two inter-acting sets of issues. The economic ones are dominated by the fact that this international function can act as a buffer to face unexpected events in the global film markets—a hedging process of a well-developed and mature film industry—and as a source for capturing new opportunities among the high growth markets in the rest of the world. But, as so often in this book, this economic dimension has a twin cultural aspect. Distributing and exhibiting films in foreign countries is an invaluable source of information on the cultural trends of film production that goes beyond Korea—hence a precious input to a more sustainable film industry.

References

Bae, J.S. 2015. "Yŏnghwa ŭi dayangsŏng gwa hankukyŏnghwa ŭi hyun-juso" [The Current situation of Diversity in Film Industry in Korea]. *Yŏngsanbŏpryulyunch'ong* 12 (1): 125–154.

Benhamou, F. 2017. Le cinéma d'art et d'essai piégé par la politique des multiplexes. *Le Nouvel Observateur*, January 24. https://www.nouvelobs.com/rue89/rue89-en-pleine-culture/20091104.RUE8642/le-cinema-d-art-et-essai-piege-par-la-politique-des-multiplexes.html.

Box Office Mojo. 2019. *Worldwide Box Office*. https://www.boxofficemojo.com/year/world/2019/.

Cassady, R., Jr., and R. Cassady. 1974. *The Private Antitrust Suit in American Business Competition*. Bureau of Business and Economic Research: University of California, Los Angeles.

Centre national du cinéma et de l'image animée (CNC). 2017. Modèle d'engagement de programmation pour une entreprise-propriétaire. https://www.cnc.fr/professionnels/etudes-et-rapports/modele-dengagement-de-programmation-pour-une-entreprisepropriétaire_234960.
Centre national du cinéma et de l'image animée (CNC). 2018. Synthèse du bilan 2017–2018 de l'accord du 13 mai 2016 sur les engagements de programmation et de diffusion. https://lemediateurducinema.fr/wp-content/uploads/2020/04/Synthe%CC%80se-du-bilan-1718-des-EPD.pdf.
Centre national du cinéma et de l'image animée (CNC). 2019. *Bilan*, p. 80. https://www.cnc.fr/documents/36995/1118512/Bilan+2019+du+CNC.pdf/406786cb-2610-8134-1c85-c17424116365.
Centre national du cinéma et de l'image animée (CNC). 2021a. Exploitation, Fréquentation et films en salles, Fréquentation des salles de cinéma, Excel file entrées-sortie. https://www.cnc.fr/professionnels/etudes-et-rapports/statistiques/statistiques-par-secteur.
Centre national du cinéma et de l'image animée (CNC). 2021b. Exploitation, Fréquentation et films en salles, Excel file Fréquentation des films selon leur âge. https://www.cnc.fr/professionnels/etudes-et-rapports/statistiques/statistiques-par-secteur.
Centre national du cinéma et de l'image animée (CNC). 2021c. Exploitation, Fréquentation et films en salles, Fréquentation des salles de cinéma, Films en première exclusivité. Excel file Films en première exclusivité selon leur nationalité. https://www.cnc.fr/professionnels/etudes-et-rapports/statistiques/statistiques-par-secteur.
Centre national du cinéma et de l'image animée (CNC). various issues, *Bilan*. https://www.cnc.fr/cinema/etudes-et-rapports/bilans/.
Collectif des cinéastes. 2013. Ne laissons pas la loi du plus fort priver d'écrans le cinéma indépendant. *Le Monde*, May 6. http://www.lemonde.fr/idees/article/2013/05/06/ne-laissons-pas-la-loi-du-plus-fort-priver-d-ecrans-le-cinema-francais_3171993_3232.html.
De Vany, A. 2004. *Hollywood Economics: How Extreme Uncertainty Shapes the Film Industry*. New York: Routledge.
Franceinfo. 2020. Cinémas: il y a un problème d'offre. *Radio France*, July 27. https://www.francetvinfo.fr/sante/maladie/coronavirus/deconfinement/cinemas-il-y-a-un-probleme-d-offre-aucun-film-americain-alors-que-l-ete-hollywood-represente-70-des-entrees-alerte-la-federation-nationale_4053881.html.
Gessati, P., and J. Chapron. 2017. *L'exploitation cinématographique en France*. Paris: Editions Dixit.
Kim, Y. 2019. Sŭkŭrin dokkwajŏm haeso rŭl uihan yŏnghwasanŏp gyujech'ekye ŭi mosaek: Pŭrangsŭ model ŭl jungsim ŭro [A Study on Regulation System of Film Industry to solve the Screen Monopoly: Focusing on the French Model]. *Gyŏngjaengbŏpyŏngu* 39: 369–406.

Kim, M., K.E. Kim, and C. Ko. 2018. Haewae juyo kukga ŭi yŏnghwasanŏp gujo was jedo robutŏŭi jŏngch'aekjŏm sisajŏom: Sujikgyeyŏlhwa wa baegŭp mit sangyŏngsijang ŭi jipjungdo rŭl jungsim ŭro [Policy Implications from Film Industry Structure and System in Overseas Countries: Focusing on the Vertical Integration Structure and the Concentration of Distribution and Screening]. *Yŏnghwayŏngu* 76: 317–344.

Korea Box-Office Information System (KOBIS). http://www.kobis.or.kr.

Korean Film Council (KOFIC). 2017. *2016nyŏn hankuk yŏnghwa gyŏlsan* [The Korea Cinema Annual Report 2016]. KOFIC: Busan.

Korean Film Council (KOFIC). 2020a. *2019nyŏn hankuk yŏnghwa gyŏlsan* [The Korea Cinema Annual Report 2019]. KOFIC: Busan.

Korean Film Council (KOFIC). 2020b., *Korean Cinema Yearbook 2019*. Busan: KOFIC (in Korean).

Libiot, E. 2016. Vincent Maraval : Il faut désacraliser le grand écran. *L'Express*, June 26. http://www.lexpress.fr/culture/cinema/vincent-maraval-il-faut-desacraliser-le-grand-ecran_1804924.html.

Maistre, R.-O. 2009. *Les engagements de programmation*. Le Médiateur du cinéma. https://www.cnc.fr/documents/36995/156431/rapport+de+Roch-Olivier+Maistre+sur+les+engagements+de+programmation.pdf/d6d2c110-d416-1a6b-f454-6efb557543c0.

Motion Picture Association (MPA). 2020. THEME Report 2019. https://www.motionpictures.org/wp-content/uploads/2020/03/MPA-THEME-2019.pdf.

Nam, K.Y. 2017. Yŏnghwasanyŏp ŭi dokgwajŏm siltae wa haeso bangan [Research on the Actual Monopoly of the Movie Industry and the Resolution Methods]. *Sports Entertainmentwa Bŏp* 20 (4): 125–146.

Parc, J. 2021. Business Integration and its Impact on Film Industry: The Case of Korean Film Policies from the 1960s until the Present. *Business History* 63 (5): 850–867.

Parc J., and P. A. Messerlin. 2021. *Screen Monopoly and Diversity: A Comparative Study between the Korean and French Film Industries*. Mimeo.

Perrot, A., J.P. Leclerc, and C. Verot. 2008. Cinéma et concurrence, Ministère de la Culture. https://www.culture.gouv.fr/Espace-documentation/Missions/Cinema-et-concurrence-PERROT-Anne-LECLERC-Jean-Pierre-VEROT-Celia.

Rimbaux, N. 2017. Une remise en cause de notre modèle économique. *La Nouvelle République*, July 8. https://www.lanouvellerepublique.fr/actu/un-risque-de-remise-en-cause-de-notre-modele-economique.

Roh, C.H. 2016. Munhwajŏk dayangsŏng gwa gyŏngjejŏk gongjŏngsŏng Ganghwa rŭl uihan kŭkjang jŏngch'aek yŏngu: Pŭrangsŭ ŭi gyuje mit jiwon jŏngch'aek ŭl jungsim ŭro [A Film Policy Study on Multiplex Chains to

Enhance Cultural Diversity and Economic Fairness: Focused on French Restriction and Support Policies]. *Yŏngsanggisuly Ŏngu* 32: 87–111.

Roh, C.H. 2019. Hankukyŏnghwasijang ŭi daehyŏngyŏnghwa baegŭp sangyŏng bangsik yŏngu: 2010nyŏndae ch'ŏngmangwangaek hankukyŏnghwa ŭi hŭnghaeng ŭl jungsim ŭro [A Study on the Distribution and Screening of Big Budget Movies in Korean Film Industry: Focus on the Ten Million Audiences' Movies in 2010s]. *Asiayŏnghwayŏngu* 12 (2): 49–76.

Song, S.E. 2016. Hankuk yŏnghwa ŭi sujiktonghap mit dokgwajŏmhwa e daehan gongbŏpjŏk daeŭng [The public legal measures to the vertical cartel and monopolization in Korean Film Industry]. *Hongikbŏphak* 14 (4): 119–146.

US District Court Southern District of New York. 2020. Order: U.S. v. Paramount Pictures, Inc. and Loew's Incorporated et al. https://www.justice.gov/atr/page/file/1302816/download.

Epilogue: Korea as a "Game Changer"

Over the last forty years, the majority of governments have followed the same approach of "protect, subsidize, and regulate" in order to support and promote their film industries when confronting Hollywood's dominance. The success of these measures though has been limited, to say the least. Its ineffectiveness has been cruelly revealed with the impact of the COVID-19 pandemic on movie theater audiences. When Hollywood froze its distribution of new films in July 2020, French exhibitors lobbied hard for them to resume the supply of these blockbusters, recognizing openly that screening French and European films by themselves without the presence of US films lacked attractiveness.

Until recently criticism of the "protect, subsidize, and regulate" approach has not been widely welcomed because much of it is based upon economic and business arguments, and was not supported by real-world examples until the Korean case emerged. It was easy thus to dismiss such approaches given that economic and business considerations are generally seen as hostile to culture. In contrast to such prevailing beliefs, this book argues that these economic and business approaches can make a valuable contribution toward developing more effective and culture-friendly film policies. In fact, there are a few policymakers who have recognized these positive interactions but have not been ready to risk their political career by opposing the powerful and vocal vested interests within the film industry.

J. Parc and P. A. Messerlin, *The Untold Story of the Korean Film Industry*, Cultural Economics & the Creative Economy,
https://doi.org/10.1007/978-3-030-80342-1

In this regard, a "game changer" is needed that presents a real-world example of a film industry's successful emergence through well-designed film policies. Such a case exists in the form of the Korean film industry, which has been the subject of this book. This example is all the more important because it has taken off despite considerable handicaps in its early days: exploitive occupation by Japan, widespread destruction from the Korean War, strict censorship, and extreme poverty up to the 1960s as well as an unfavorable location nestled between two powerful countries, China and Japan.

The emergence of the Korean film industry is even more meaningful when considering the fact that most of the other global players have not been successful in their competition with Hollywood in the domestic market despite more favorable conditions. This case, thus, deserves to be studied carefully. This is the task that this book has pursued as it has gathered facts and data from the past forty years to ensure robust evidence and placed them in an economic and business analytical framework. Throughout the seven chapters, it has presented the Korean film industry as a "game changer" based on three "anchors" that are credible alternatives to the current limited approaches.

The first anchor is the progressive opening of its domestic film market. Korea decided to eliminate its import quota in the late 1980s, which was not an easy political decision. At first it did not bring many rapid benefits that could be instantly identified: rather it took a decade for the Korean film industry to witness its positive outcome in the early 1990s. This made it hard for the Korean government to resist calls to close up its market again, yet it maintained the course it was set on. In doing so, successive Korean governments provided the new Korean film companies, such as CJ and Lotte, a stable environment that has allowed them to master the new strategies they needed in every segment of the film industry. The result is dynamic competition between Korean companies and Hollywood in its domestic market.

The second anchor is the "wise" use of subsidization. Subsidies can be a positive instrument when they are used for collective objectives such as education or infrastructure, which can then be beneficial to all filmmakers in a country. But subsidies can also be toxic when they target meaningless goals such as simply increasing the number of films produced. Furthermore, when they are badly designed—such as the "automatic" subsidies granted on the basis of past performances that favor incumbents—film companies, directors, and scriptwriters can abuse this system to the detriment of newcomers and future creativity. As a result, subsidies run the permanent risk of spiraling out of control as they are abused by vested interests, even when ultimately they harm the film industry they were supposed to help—a result rarely evoked in the industry although this book gives plenty of illustrations of these unintended negative consequences.

Given this context, the duration of financial support schemes only amplifies their costs: the longer the duration of a scheme, the bigger its size, the larger its likely negative effects on the film industry it is supposed to help. Korea's subsidy policy has escaped the most dangerous traps described above largely for two reasons: precedent Korean governments could not afford to subsidize the film industry due to lack of capital and a relative decline of subsides has occurred in recent years unlike what has been prevailing in other countries.

The third anchor is efficient regulations. Most studies of the film industry talk about "government's policies" as if they were decided in detail by the country's policymakers and implemented by them without any bureaucratic interference or deviation. Such an oversight is a great mistake. "Autonomous agencies," such as Korea's KOFIC or France's CNC, are the real caretakers of their respective domestic film industry: they inspire and draft the regulations to be adopted, they monitor their implementation and are often deeply involved in granting the accompanying subsidies. Comparing KOFIC and CNC suggests that agencies with a high degree of autonomy and large funds are more prone to be captured by vested interests, curbing their capacities to regulate efficiently on behalf of the general interest. By comparison, agencies with a smaller size are, paradoxically at first glance, forced to concentrate their support to the key objectives of public action—infrastructure and film promotion—which have a much higher chance to be beneficial to every domestic film producer than a host of direct subsidies funding every film.

Finally, two remarks need to be stressed here. First, based on these anchors, Korea's film policy has contributed to the fact that, over the last decade, its films have enjoyed better evaluations in terms of quality than their French, UK, and US competitors—reflecting the positive relationship between a good film policy and cultural diversity. Second, the anchors may require difficult reforms for other countries that are eager to follow the Korean track. However, other than the initial elimination of the import quota, Korea's film policy has been progressive. This is encouraging news for countries starting from scratch in designing their film policies and for those that need to streamline some aspects of their existing policies.

That said, a well-designed film policy is no substitute to creative film producers, actors, technicians, entrepreneurs, and last but not least the moviegoers themselves. As films have been considered a form of art, many critics have emphasized the production side and highlighted that the materiality of (directors' and/or actors') artistry is more "significant." This unfortunately has led many to often ignore and disregard the importance of the audience. Some may even be disparaging when addressing "commercial" films in a pejorative way thereby dismissing what a large number of audiences want to enjoy. They often dichotomize films into either commercial or artistic (or cultural) productions. Yet if a film production company only has limited budget to make films but wants to keep producing further projects in the future, what would be the most effective and sustainable strategy? Surely, it should be to produce attractive films that can generate enough profits by drawing in a large number of audiences, which then helps to fund future productions. Critically, such a sustainable business-like model does not have to come at the expense of cultural diversity as seen with the example of Korea. This is the crucial point stressed by Miky Lee in her acceptance speech at the 2020 Oscar Award Ceremony for *Parasite* when she thanked Korean moviegoers: "without our Korean film audience – we are not here." How did such an educated audience emerge? Simply, the Korean audiences have been exposed to various films regardless of their origin and the producers of films should thus satisfy their demands. This is the only true way to breathe life into a work of art that people can understand and enjoy.

Index

J. Parc and P. A. Messerlin, *The Untold Story of the Korean Film Industry*, Cultural Economics & the Creative Economy,
https://doi.org/10.1007/978-3-030-80342-1

J

K

L

M

N

O

P

V

W

The manufacturer's authorised representative in the EU is Springer
Nature Customer Service Centre GmbH, Europaplatz 3, 69115 Heidelberg,
Germany. If you have any concerns regarding our products, please
contact ProductSafety@springernature.com

Printed and bound by CPI Group (UK) Ltd, Croydon, CR0 4YY
30/09/2026
02225698-0008